Foreign Direct Investment

Foreign Direct Investment

The Indian Experience

Leena Ajit Kaushal

Management Development Institute (MDI) Gurgaon
Gurugram, India

BEP BUSINESS EXPERT PRESS

Foreign Direct Investment: The Indian Experience

First published in 2019 by
Business Expert Press, LLC
222 East 46th Street, New York, NY 10017
www.businessexpertpress.com

ISBN-13: 978-1-94944-349-3 (paperback)
ISBN-13: 978-1-94944-350-9 (e-book)

Business Expert Press Economics and Public Policy Collection

Collection ISSN: 2163-761X (print)
Collection ISSN: 2163-7628 (electronic)

Cover and interior design by Exeter Premedia Services Private Ltd., Chennai, India

First edition: 2019

10 9 8 7 6 5 4 3 2 1

Printed in the United States of America.

To my daughter, Ayushi Kaushal

Abstract

The book will offer students, researchers, policymakers, and industry bodies an insight about the changing perspectives regarding FDI from traditional theory to new theory, from local to global link, and from opportunity to responsibility. The readers of the book can understand the various factors, determinants, and theories that underpin the presence of firms in the global economy. The book illustrates by way of case studies specific implications of FDI policy and practice on issues like ecology and environment, technology transfer, labor market, and relevance of further liberalization policies in FDI in the context of Indian economy. Though many cases give positive and negative implications of foreign investment, however, the book compiles specific cases that are well debated by Indian lawmakers and public institutions. The coverage for such an important theme is so vast to cover in a single volume therefore, this volume restricts its analysis to select few themes and hope that this endeavor will trigger an ongoing debate on myriad aspects and concerns of FDI in countries like India.

Keywords

foreign direct investment; sustainability; India; international trade; multinational corporations (MNCs); multinational enterprises (MNEs); public policy; regulation; development; growth

Contents

Epilogue

This book has presented certain perspectives and viewpoints on select themes and subthemes of FDI—The Indian experience. It is indeed, a very daunting task for any developing economy to formulate coherent FDI policy even when they liberalize and undertake macroeconomic reforms. Substantial time is required to formulate laws and regulations and put appropriate institutions in place for implementing FDI policy as an integral part of public policy. India did launch economic reforms in 1991 which followed a series of measures for re-ordering and creating newer institutions for public policy implementation. Over the years modern regulations and rules have evolved, though, some are yet to evolve for it's a cumbersome process. Political executive, judiciary, and the existing institutions all are under pressure to respond to the dynamics of international trade and business. Globalization has prompted large Indian firms to internationalize and promote significant OFDI from India.

If a nation wants to benefit from FDI, it has to rearrange its institutional order and ensure that the eventual costs do not outweigh the actual intended benefits. Not only the institutional reforms have to match the pace of global economic development and changes in geopolitical relations across the world; the attitudes and aptitudes of those in charge of implementing FDI policy also need proper fine-tuning. In a developing country like India, there is a need for all to comprehend the objectives of FDI policy otherwise the sheer political economy considerations may mold public opinion against FDI investments in strategic sectors. In some cases, on account of asymmetric information, the public often overemphasize their apprehensions; however, there is some awareness in respect of damage to the environment and pollution. The FDI projects, like POSCO and Vedanta, were opposed based on adverse environmental impact, quite justifiable, and besides it, there is also ongoing trouble with Vedanta Resources—Copper plant in Tuticorin in South India.

Since the declaration of the 17 Sustainable Development Goals for the period 2015–2030 by the UN, some debate has ensued worldwide on how FDI projects can promote some of the SDGs; this is crucial for developing economies where the resource curse phenomenon is very clearly evident. No large project either promoted by an Indian firm or FDI can succeed without meeting some of the basic SDGs; the existing FDI projects in the developing nations have to reorient their corporate strategies to address some of the basic SDGs.

The inherent justification for adopting FDI policy reflects the intrinsic limits to managerial, financial, and physical resources a nation has for globalization. In the core areas of investment FDI supplements government resources. Most countries including India have adopted a gradual and incremental FDI policy; however, new corresponding legal rules, regulations and institutional order need to be initiated and sustained as and when required. Also, political consensus and presently even social consensus on select FDI policies is hard to achieve; this, in turn, slows down the whole FDI process. A fragmented policy and weak institutional regime in a country like India has resulted in a tardy process of public policy formation and implementation, especially for FDI like policies which are in the proper domain of international business and globalization.

FDI policies in most developing countries are under the scrutiny of activists and NGOs who take up the cause of the mixed stakeholders. For instance, in the last two decades, many international human and environmental rights organizations have raised several objections to FDI policy in India and elsewhere. Further, the policy formation process for FDI is also dependent on the nature of bilateral and multilateral trade agreements that the government of India (GoI) decides to finalize.

There are two schools of thought; one supports FDI while the other rejects the concept and practice of FDI. Some oppose FDI on ideological, environmental, and societal grounds whereas the support comes from the ruling elites, the MNEs, and the multilateral bodies backed by other prominent groups of stakeholders. The opposite and hostile viewpoint emanates from labor unions and unorganized markets. Also, there are arguments against FDI focusing on the negative implications such as trade colonization and even what is often termed by critiques as "digital colonization" of the West, for instance, WalMart's takeover of Flipkart. The indigenous entrepreneurs perceive these tendencies of globalization in some cases as a threat. Critiques often argue that the subordination of economic, social and environmental interests and brand it as a "sell out" to the Western imperialist regimes.

There are apprehensions that FDI would result in employment loss, ownership transfer to foreign agents, and imperfect markets becoming further imperfect giving rise to supernormal rents to the global corporations. The dark side of FDI is debated in India mostly without deliberating on the sector view which permits FDI. This opposition delays the process of FDI implementation, and often there is protracted litigation offsetting. However India has showcased nominal up-gradation through its ease of doing business rankings. Usually, the main opposition to the FDI projects are on the grounds of land alienation of the tribal and indigenous people in a given location. In the case of resistance from the environmental angle the Courts in India, in the past have allowed FDI projects to come up on the grounds of economic benefits. Thus, there are issues of conservation of the environment in India.

It is ironical that in 1986 and 2006 the matter concerning environmental apprehensions went to the Courts for intervention, despite the existing Environment Policy of GoI. This shows the feeble enforcement of regulations and rules—market imperfections are thus compounded by human-made policies rather than the supernatural forces. But even in the cases where the justice system has acted in favor of the stakeholders the irreversible damage is done as all these matters are time-consuming.

What are then the lessons learned from the past FDI policy?

The GOI needs to evolve a transparent and accountable public policy framework of durable nature. The state needs to ensure that the conflicts between the core stakeholders and FDI project management are not perpetual. Evolution of suitable institutions is the need of an hour for FDI policy implementation. Further, lots of overlaps and ambiguities in multiple regulations need correction else large firms would exploit them in their favor. The process and content of stakeholder engagement need to strengthen further. The GoI should ensure a certain degree of consistency of FDI policy with other macroeconomic policies. Active and ongoing research is obligatory on various aspects of FDI policy formulation and implementation; this is rather infrequent and limited in Indian academic institutions. To evolve a suitable public policy framework the failures of FDI and OFDI projects also need to be studied.

GoI also needs to ensure that large companies adhere to corporate governance practices and treat their stakeholders equitably. The GoI should be cautious in treating and responding to the "winners curse" that is managing the riskier implications post FDI approval for the economy and society. The competition authorities need to assess whether a given FDI project alarms the process and content of competition—the Flipkart-Walmart approval is under scrutiny presently by the competition commissioner of India (CCI). An assessment should also be carried out on the likely intended or unintended effects of FDI projects on the Bottom of the Pyramid markets especially in emerging countries like India.

Another matter of study that is required is the role of the public sector in OFDI and inward FDI collaboration and strategic alliances. Similarly, the role of family firms in OFDI also deserves evaluation. Last but not least, the Indian Chambers of Commerce, NGOs, and academic institutions should also have joint research focus on FDI issues.

Leena Ajit Kaushal

Management Development Institute (MDI) Gurgaon

Gurugram, India

Preface

Foreign direct investment has become a keystone both for the governments and firms. It plays a crucial role in the growth of developing and emerging markets. Firms in these economies need multinationals' funding and expertise to expand not only international but also their national footprints. Emerging economies need private investment in infrastructure, energy, and other manufacturing sectors to increase jobs and wages. At the same time, firms investing abroad also benefit by creating opportunities for themselves both concerning higher growth and income. Diversification always increases returns within a reasonable framework of risk management. The controlling interest in foreign assets enables a firm to efficiently acquire new products and technologies besides seeking a new market for their existing products.

The host country's businesses benefit from the best global practices in management, accounting and the legal guidance from their investors. It also enables incorporation and assimilation of the latest technology, operational practices, and financing tools. These practices not only enhance employees' lifestyles but also raise the standard of living of more and more people in the recipient country. In 2017, developing countries received 37 percent of the total global FDI. Investments in Asia, the largest recipient of FDI also rose by two percent.

The narrative on FDI—past and the present—is not without its share of claims and counterclaims on the expected or actual costs and benefits to the host countries because FDI is an outcome of increasing trade liberalization subsequent to an ever-growing number of economies in the world becoming democratic. Like most economic policy decisions, the decisions on allowing or banning FDI in select segments is as much a product of political economy as popular populism by the lawmakers. The perceived benefits like—employment—high wages for the skilled labor and technology transfer are often not weighed in terms of the relative capability of the host economies; whether it is capable in terms of its resources, institutional and regulatory framework to benefit from FDI; for the benefits are not automatic.

The developed economies like the European Union and the United States also need FDI; however, for different reasons such as restructuring or refocusing their core businesses. In developed countries investments mostly take place via mergers and acquisitions between mature companies. Besides being a critical driver of economic growth, FDI is also a significant source of non-debt financial resource for the economic development of India. Multinational enterprises (MNEs) investing in India take advantage of relatively lower wages, special investment privileges such as tax exemptions, and so on, whereas the host country on the other hand benefits from technical know-how and employment generation.

With the growing global concern to meet the sustainable development goals (SDGs) and climate change commitments, the emphasis is now on promoting the right kind of FDI which is known as "sustainable FDI." The governments all over the world, especially developing economies are in the process of redefining their policy instruments toward achieving SDGs by 2030.

Most nations are integrating sustainability goals in their domestic and international macroeconomic policies; however, it is also important to ensure that MNEs take on greater responsibility toward supporting sustainable development through their investments. MNEs should contribute to sustainable development by transferring environmentally sound technologies, using environmental management schemes in all the countries in which they operate and by generally committing themselves to international codes of conduct such as the OECD, ILO, and the UN Guidelines for MNEs.

The Indian government with its favorable policy regime and robust business environment expects foreign capital inflow to strengthen further in the years to come. The government has taken many initiatives in recent past such as relaxing FDI norms across sectors such as defense, public sector oil refineries, telecom, power sector, and stock exchanges, among others.

India has become the most attractive emerging market for global investment partners as per a recent market attractiveness survey conducted by Emerging Market Private Equity Association (EMPEA). Indian economy has shown drastic improvement in its ease of doing business ranking by climbing to 77th position in 2018 compared to 142 in 2014. As per the Union Bank of Switzerland (UBS) report, annual FDI inflow in the country is expected to rise to US$ 75 billion over the next five years. According to the World Bank's estimates, private investments in India are expected to grow by 8.8 percent in FY 2018–2019 to overtake private consumption growth of 7.4 percent, and thereby drive India's gross domestic product (GDP) growth in FY 2018–2019.

Free trade proponents argue in favor of FDI citing multiple benefits, but eventually, a public policy choice is as good as the local institutions; because it is the institutions that implement FDI. On the cost side, there are arguments on FDI crowding out private investments from the domestic sector and therefore driving out private entrepreneurship. Besides damaging the ecosystem of developing nations these, in turn, get compounded by the mixed evidence of spillover effects of FDI on an economy-knowledge-productivity, and so on. Further, there is not much we can say on an optimal policy benchmark for FDI in particular segments; for instance, we cannot put a safe number for the automobile sector in India—whether 26 passenger car projects by way of FDI were required?

In the long run, the Indian government is likely to promote sustainable investment through favorable and enabling investment environment and provide appropriate levels of access in goals-related sectors to private and foreign investors. Infrastructure projects in power and renewable energy, transport, and water, for instance, have a higher potential for foreign investment. In some sectors that are not yet open to foreign investment, a gradual opening seems likable through various means like public-private partnerships or contracts; however, the actual modes will only be known in times to come. Notwithstanding the aforementioned-mixed evidence, this volume deals selectively on strategic aspects of FDI from the stakeholder perspectives.

The book will offer students, researchers, policymakers, and industry bodies an insight about the changing perspectives regarding FDI from traditional theory to new theory, from local to global link and from opportunity to responsibility. The readers of the book can understand the various factors, determinants, and theories that underpin the presence of firms in the global economy. The book illustrates by way of case studies specific implications of FDI policy and practice on issues like ecology and environment, technology transfer, labor market and relevance of further liberalization policies in FDI in the context of the Indian economy. Though many cases give positive and negative implications of foreign investment, however, the book compiles specific cases that are well debated by Indian lawmakers and public institutions. While preparing the text for such an important theme and sub-themes, I realize that the coverage is too vast to capture in a single volume. Therefore, this volume restricts its analysis to select few themes and hope that this endeavor will trigger an ongoing debate on myriad aspects and concerns (explicit and not-so-explicit) on the cumulative impact of FDI on countries like India. It also suggests the direction for an informed debate on the future stream of costs and benefits of FDI. There is a need for more research-based books on strategic aspects of FDI management which will be beneficial to students and practicing managers.

CHAPTER 1

Theories of International Trade and Foreign Direct Investment

Cross-national business activities are best explained with the help of international economics, international finance, and global business literature. However, over the last couple of decades, there have been significant advances in international trade, foreign direct investment (FDI) theories exploring rampant globalization and cross-border investment activities. International trade theories generally concentrate on reasons for trade flow between at least two nations. They also refer to the nature and extent of gains or losses to an economy besides addressing the effects of trade policies on an economy. Most theories of international trade like classical, neo-classical and product life cycle theory discuss the reasons for trade flow between nations (Morgan and Katsikeas 1997).

FDI theory, on the contrary, attempts to address the limitations of international trade theories. FDI attained a critical position in the global economy after the Second World War. Theoretical studies on FDI facilitates a better understanding of economic mechanism and behavior of economic agents, both at the micro and macro level encouraging cross border investments. FDI theories could be broadly classified under macroeconomic and microeconomic perspectives (Gray 1981; Petrohilos 1983; Denisia 2010; Lipsey 2004). Macroeconomic FDI theories highlight country-specific factors and align well with trade and international economics. Macro-level factors that impact the host country's ability to attract FDI include market size, GDP, growth rate, infrastructure, natural resources, institutional factors such as political stability, socio-economic factors, and so on, of the country, amongst others.

Microeconomic FDI theories being firm-specific relate to ownership and internalization benefits and incline toward industrial economics and market imperfections. These theories examine FDI motivations from the investor's viewpoint and connect with firm-level or industry-level perspective in decision making. FDI theories are reasonably complex to explain and apply. The chapter attempts to summaries different FDI theories, however; there is no generally accepted theory, and every new approach is adding certain new elements with criticism or improvement on the earlier one.

Definitions of Foreign Direct Investment

IMF defines FDI as a category of international investment where the resident entity in one economy being the direct investor obtains a lasting interest in an enterprise resident in another economy known as direct investment enterprise.[1] The term "lasting interest" highlights the existence of a long-term relationship between the direct investor and the enterprise apart from the significant degree of influence in the management of the enterprise.

India Definition

FDI is characterized by a lasting interest which signifies the existence of a long term relationship and a significant degree of influence. In general, more than 10 percent ownership of the ordinary shares or voting power signifies this relationship. It includes both initial and subsequent transactions. According to the definition, FDI entails any foreign investment exceeding 10 percent limit through eligible instruments in an Indian listed company. However, all the existing foreign investments made under the FDI Route will be treated as FDI even if they are below the threshold limit.[2] FDI also entails initial investments below 10 percent threshold

---

[1] IMF Balance of Payments Manual, Fifth Edition, para. 359; OECD Benchmark definition of Foreign Direct Investment, Third Edition.

[2] http://finmin.nic.in/the_ministry/dept_eco_affairs/investment_division/Reportpercentage20ofpercentage20Drpercentage20Arvindpercentage20Mayarampercentage20committeepercentage20onpercentage20FDI_FII.pdf (accessed June 2014).

which are later raised to 10 percent or beyond within one year from the date of the first purchase. The onus of rising to this level lies solely on the company, and if it does not touch 10 percent mark, then the investment shall be treated as portfolio investment. Nevertheless, if an existing FDI falls to a level below 10 percent, it will still be treated as FDI without an obligation to restore it to 10 percentage or more, as the original investment was an FDI. Foreign Investment in an unlisted company, irrespective of the threshold limit is considered as FDI. However, an investor can either hold the investments under the FPI route or the FDI route, but not both.[3]

International Finance Corporation (IFC)

According to the IMF and OECD definitions, direct investment reflects the aim of obtaining a lasting interest by the direct investor of one economy through direct investment in an enterprise located in another economy. The "lasting interest" entails the existence of a long-term relationship between the two and a significant degree of influence on the management of the enterprise. Direct investment involves both the initial and subsequent capital transactions between investor and enterprise which could either be incorporated or unincorporated. Capital transactions which do not account for any settlement, like an interchange of shares among affiliated companies, are also recorded in the Balance of Payments and the IIP.

Direct investor and direct investment enterprise, as defined by the IMF and the OECD may be an individual, an incorporated or unincorporated private or public enterprise, a government, a group of related individuals, or a group of related incorporated and/or unincorporated enterprises which have a direct investment enterprise, operating in a country other than the state of residence of the direct investor. A direct investment enterprise is an incorporated or unincorporated enterprise in which a foreign investor owns 10 percent or more of the ordinary shares or voting power of an incorporated enterprise or the equivalent of an unincorporated enterprise. Direct investment enterprises may be subsidiaries, associates or branches. A subsidiary is an incorporated enterprise in

---

[3] Report of the Dr. Arvind Mayaram Committee on rationalizing FDI/FII.

which the foreign investor controls directly or indirectly (through another subsidiary) more than 50 percentage of the shareholders' voting power. An associate is an enterprise where the direct investor and its subsidiaries control between 10 and 50 percent of the voting shares. A branch is a wholly or jointly owned unincorporated enterprise.[4]

Organization for Economic Cooperation and Development (OECD) 2008

The Benchmark Definition of FDI sets the world standard for direct investment statistics. It mainly focuses on the FDI statistics around direct investment positions and related direct investment financial and income transactions (flows).

The OECD Benchmark definition of FDI serves several objectives. It provides a single point of reference for compilers and users of FDI statistics. Apart from this it also gives clear guidance to individual nations in a compilation of direct investment statistics to develop or change their statistical systems. It provides international standards for FDI considering the effects of globalization. The international standard also provides the basis for economic analysis, especially for international comparisons and for identifying national deviations from the norm that impact on the comparison. The definition also guides practical users of direct investment statistics in studying the relationship of FDI to other measures of globalization. It governs in methodologically measuring differences between national statistics that are required for both cross-country and industry analysis of FDI.[5]

Several economic studies have recognized inter-dependence and complementary relationship between trade and FDI. Approximately 50 percent of world intra-firm trade takes place between affiliates of multinational enterprises. According to WTO members, FDI being a vital generator of business also need formal rules like the one developed for trade.[6]

---

[4] Duce, M. July 31, 2003. Definitions of Foreign Direct Investment (FDI): A methodological note. Banco de España. https://bis.org/publ/cgfs22bde3.pdf

[5] https://oecd.org/daf/inv/investmentstatisticsandanalysis/40193734.pdf

[6] http://trade.ec.europa.eu/doclib/docs/2004/july/tradoc_111123.pdf

A significant proportion of world FDI operations are already addressed in the WTO system of rules, for instance, the provision of services through commercial presence, as provided for in mode 3 of the GATS, is a form of FDI.[7] According to UNCTAD, FDI in services sectors accounts for approximately half of world FDI stocks. Most of the existing Bilateral Investment Treaties (BITs) aiming to protect existing and future investment between the parties have "asset-based" definition and broad coverage of both FDI and portfolio. The OECD Code of liberalization of capital movements, on the other hand, adopts a "transaction-based" definition of capital movements. It lists all forms of transactions covered by the code to liberalize the capital movements instead of protection of the assets. FDI is the form of investment that establishes lasting economic relations by effectively influencing the management. According to the Canada-US Free Trade Agreement of 1988, the "enterprise-based" definition of investment deals with the acquisition of a business enterprise where the investor gets the controlling rights over the business.

International Trade Theories

International trade theories aim to explain international trade. Trade is the notion of exchanging goods and services between two people or entities however International trade is a step further where the trade occurs between entities located in different countries. Trade takes place on the pretext of profit making. Prima facie this may appear quite simple; nonetheless, there is a great deal of theory, policy, and business strategy involved in international trade. There is a brief description of a few significant international trade theories that form the very basis of trade relations between different nations.

Theory of Absolute Advantage

Scottish economist Adam Smith in his 1776 work, "An Inquiry into the Nature and Causes of the Wealth of Nations" illustrated absolute advantage as a certain country's inherent capability to produce more of

---

[7] UNCTAD World Investment Report. 2001.

a commodity than its global competitors. Absolute advantage refers to the capacity of any economic agent to produce a larger quantity of a product than its competitors. Smith also used the concept of absolute advantage to explain gains from free trade in the international market. He argued that the absolute advantages enjoyed by countries in different commodities would facilitate free international trade through exports and imports. Adam Smith did not develop long-run growth theory but referred to the importance and effects of increasing labor productivity as well as saving which helps in deducing the conclusions on growth. Smith referred to technical progress as a means to raises aggregate output but profoundly emphasized on the potential of the division of labor for improving labor productivity.

Classical Theory of International Trade

English political economist David Ricardo in his book "Principles of Political Economy and Taxation" developed a Classical theory of comparative advantage is also known as the classical theory of international trade. It explains why countries engage in international trade even when one country's workers are more efficient at producing every single good than workers in other countries. The theory adequately describes the scenario where a country produces goods and services in which it has advantages. However, after fulfilling domestic consumption, it may export the surplus. On the other end, it deemed rational for countries to import those goods and services in which they have economic disadvantages. These disadvantages may arise from the differences in factors such as resource endowments, labor, capital, technology or entrepreneurship.

Classical trade theory identified differences in production characteristics and resource endowments as the prime basis for international trade but was silent about the causes of such differences. The factor proportion theory, on the contrary, explained differences in advantages between the trading countries. According to this theory, countries tend to use their abundant resources to produce and export goods and services whereas, import those goods and services that require large amounts of production factors which may be relatively scarce (Hecksher and Ohlin 1933).

David Ricardo initially emphasized that machinery-led productivity augmentation would benefit the social classes but eventually concluded that technological progress might postpone, but not prevent the incidence of a stationary state. The stationary state is a condition where capital accumulation and population size reach their ceilings, which hampers the economy from progressing further.

Joseph A. Schumpeter (1926) looked at the issue of growth from the lenses of innovations, technical and technological progress apart from capital accumulation. He distinguished between economic growth and development. According to Schumpeter, economic development relates to endogenous factors contributing to groundbreaking innovation which changes the technique and productive organization. An entrepreneur with the ground-breaking new technology is the driving force behind economic development making it a cyclical process. The endogenous growth theorists in 1990s widely used the term coined by Schumpeter "creative destruction" to describe the process of transformation that goes along with innovations. The 1960s witnessed significant technological progress and the rise of cross border trade. The era witnessed the emergence of new international trade theories to reflect changing business realities because Adam's and Ricardian theories were not able to explain the latest evolving trade patterns.

Neo Classical Theories

Several empirical studies point out a significant link between trade liberalization and growth. The traditional neoclassical growth model, with appropriate open-economy modifications, emphasizes that an endogenous growth process is significantly affected by the extent of trade openness. The open economy modifications facilitate a multi-country analysis that is relevant in the current scenario and goes beyond the two-country, two-region study. The trade-growth relationship is the result of knowledge spillovers which are also significantly contributed by FDI.

Solow model is the neo-classical framework for the long run growth comprising of production and capital accumulation functions.

The equation is given as : $Y=F(K,L)=K^\alpha L^{1-\alpha}$

According to the model technological progress facilitates long-run sustained economic growth barring which; capital accumulation will encounter diminishing returns. The model solely relied on technological progress to account for differences in growth rates across countries, which showed a clear association between the periods of high techno-logical progress and high output growth but could not address the issue of inequality in per capita income level across countries. Lucas (1988) extended the Solow model by revising the simple assumption of labor to include human capital, which includes workers with skills and education, to drive growth and suggested equation as $Y=K^{\alpha} (hL)^{1-\alpha}$

The technology was assumed to grow exogenously, but the economy could accumulate human capital by spending time learning new skills, which sheds some light on income inequality among different countries. Mankiw, Romer, and Weil (1992) extended the Solow model by includ-ing the accumulation of human capital in addition to physical capital. The extended model focused on economies that converge to their steady states as long as the levels of both physical and human capital per worker rise. Human capital embodied the skills and education of workers.

New Growth Theory

The new growth theory also provides linkage between international trade and growth. The endogenous growth theory was developed in the mid-1980s by economists, including Paul Romer and Robert Lucas. The approach attempted to explain the avenues of technological changes as the neo-classical growth models did not disclose the origination of tech-nological changes in the economy. Endogenous growth theory states that economic growth is generated internally and not by external forces as suggested by the neo-classical model. The driver of growth in this model was an exogenous factor, being the constant rate of innovation and invention. The endogenous growth theory argues that technological change is a response to economic incentives in the market that can be influenced by the government or the private sector. The model seeks to explain the cause of persistent growth and differences in the growth rate across nations. Romer (1986) developed a model wherein the creation of new knowledge by one firm assumed to have a positive external effect on the production possibilities of other firms. This non-rivalry of knowl-edge was further developed by Lucas (1988), considering that the human capital releases spillovers hence the average level of human capital in an economy benefits other producers in an economy. Endogenous growth theory was further developed by Romer (1990), Grossman and Helpman (1991), and Aghion and Howitt (1992), to model the interdependence and feedback effects of various producers and sectors of the economy. These models were useful in explaining the interdependence and developments of factors within one economy, but become highly complex when used for collective study of many economies. The new literature also lacks numerous relevant factors affecting growth like institutions, social capital, infrastructure, political instability, health among others.

In the neoclassical growth model, technological progress and labor growth are exogenous, inward FDI merely increases the investment rate, leading to a transitional increase in per capita income growth without long-run growth prospects (Hsiao and Hsiao 2006). The new growth theory in the 1980s indigenizes technological progress, and FDI has been considered to have permanent growth effect in the host country through technology transfer and spillovers. The theories established by Adams Smith and David Ricardo mainly emphasized the absolute and comparative advantages that led to international trade between nations. However, the neoclassical and new growth theories re-looked at the international trade with a different lens. They aimed mainly at establishing the link between trade and growth. These theories postulate that technological progress facilitates long-run sustained economic growth. Neo classist emphasized the growth process with the technological progress as exogenous variable however the new growth theorist, Paul Romer, and Robert Lucas proposed indigenous innovation and invention the main drivers of growth. Nevertheless, collectively the international trade theories emphasized certain country-specific advantages that initiated international trade; however, trade liberalization and growth relationship gave it further momentum. It was evident through several studies that trading nations mutually benefitted by the technological and knowledge spill over's.

Macroeconomic Foreign Direct Investment Theories

The international trade theories discussed earlier draws attention to the nation's potential for international trade relationships with other countries. However, the macroeconomic FDI theories emphasize macro factors that facilitate or initiate the trade relationship between countries. For instance, a country is competitive on the global level, but certain macro factors are crucial in establishing and strengthening this relationship. The following discussion will emphasize certain theories which highlight the factors guiding this movement.

Gravity Model

The Gravity model was first used by Jan Tinbergen in 1962 to study trade between two countries. This model of international trade predicts bilateral trade flows between economies based on the economic sizes often measured in terms of GDP and distance between two units. The basic theory behind the gravity model of international trade is quite simple and predicts that geographically close located economies tend to have higher volumes of trade with one another. This model is analogous to Newton's Law of Gravity, which states that the gravity between two objects is directly related to their masses and inversely related to the distance between them. The model is used to study trade between two countries, indicated as i and j and is written as follows:

$$F_{ij} = G * Y_i * Y_j / D_{ij}$$

Where F_{ij} denotes the flow from country i to country j. Y_i and Y_j are the economic sizes of the two countries, usually measured as the gross domestic product (GDP), or per-capita GDP. D_{ij} is the distance between countries. G is a gravitational constant.

According to this equation, other things constant, a high total product of the GDPs of countries I and J and a low total distance should result in a high volume of trade. As the distance between the two countries rises, it may lead to lower trade volume whereas the increasing product of the two GDPs leads to higher total trade volume. The model is used by economists to analyze the determinants of bilateral trade flows such as shared borders, common languages, common legal systems, common currencies, common colonial legacies, and it has been used to test the effectiveness of trade agreements and organizations such as the North American Free Trade Agreement (NAFTA) and the World Trade Organization (WTO). It is also helpful in evaluating the impact of treaties and alliances on trade between international counterparts.

Proximity Concentration Theory

There are primarily two ways through which firms serve foreign buyers or international market. They can either export domestically produced goods or can supply the destination market with products manufactured by foreign affiliates, which are a form of FDI. Firms prefer international locations for production to avoid transportation costs and trade barriers against the diseconomies of scale that result from splitting output across multiple affiliates. This choice is known as the proximity-concentration trade-off, which is a leading framework to study horizontal FDI. In the horizontal FDI, a firm gives up the concentration of production by setting up a duplicate plant in a foreign destination to achieve proximity to the overseas market via international production facility. However, while opting for export; the firm prefers to concentrate production in its domestic plant, over setting up producing plant in the foreign market.

Transportation costs and trade barriers escalate the exporting cost however, investment barriers adversely impact the FDI cost. Studies argue that scale economy at the plant level support concentration of production indicating exporting more convenient than FDI yet the scale economies at the corporate level favor more than one production plant at multiple locations. Nevertheless, multinational production-location decisions can be explained by a trade-off between maximizing proximity to customers and concentrating production to achieve scale economies. Models of proximity-concentration trade-off are typically static, though creating a foreign affiliate or an export network essentially requires significant upfront costs. In a stochastic environment, firm decision to serve the international market either through overseas production or exports depends on the evaluation of initial costs against the expected future profits. While forming expectations about future profit flows, the firm must take into account the stochastic properties of production costs and demand, both within and across countries. The proximity-concentration theory emphasizes that firms should expand horizontally across borders provided the advantages to access the destination market outweigh the benefits from production scale economies.

The gravity model and proximity-concentration theory emphasize the trade relationships between countries that are close to each other and are of same size and strength based on the economic dimensions often measured in terms of GDP. It has been proved empirically at several instances, though there is also evidence that partially nullifies this hypothesis. The trade relation between India and the UK is not weighed down by the distance between them, primarily because the UK is mostly the importer of Indian services, which in turn does not contribute to substantial transportation costs. However, the trade relationship between the same economic-size nations could be proved as India is on its way to number 5 country in terms of GDP by overtaking the UK, possibly next year.

Institutional FDI Fitness Theory

Wilhems and Witter (1998) developed the term 'FDI Fitness' which focuses on the country's ability to attract, absorb and retain FDI. The four fundamental pillars or institutions of FDI fitness theory entail government, market, educational and socio-cultural fitness. The theory proposes that it is institutions, their policies, and implementation rather than their generic variables that enable a country to compete in the global FDI market. Generic variables are the fundamental conditions that are inflexible or inherent to a country (Karau and Mburu 2016). Socio-cultural factors form the base of the pillar and are the oldest and most complex of all institutions. According to Wilhelm's, the higher open and integrated country's socio-culture attracts greater FDI due to the perceived cultural proximity by foreign investors. Educational fitness creates FDI through information, research, development, and technology. Open competitive markets with protective regulation more conducive to FDI compared to markets with authoritative regulation. Government fitness is responsible for the overall supervision and coordination of the other three institutions through policies and their implementation hence determining FDI inflows. The institutional FDI fitness theory commonly known as "FDI fitness" developed by Wilhems and Witter proves to hold several instances. The theory emphasizes fitness on various parameters such as education, skill, policies, and so on. Ever since 2014, the present Indian government is promoting "FDI fitness" through several FDI reforms and measures. India welcomes 100 percent FDI (mostly through automatic route except in a few cases government approval is required) in almost every possible sector, such as telecom, defense, civil aviation, mining, petroleum and natural gas, to name a few. The government knows that mere allowing 100 percent foreign investment will not lead to actual inflow, unless and until the nations are capable of providing a smooth business operation to these foreign investors on various parameters. The World Bank's ease of doing business index rightly reflects India's FDI fitness or preparedness. India has jumped from the 137th spot in 2014 to 77th spot in 2018. The most notable "Skill India" and "Start-up" initiatives besides many others are also catering toward the FDI fitness of the country by raising youth's confidence, improving productivity and giving direction through proper skill development. Several other reforms such as GST also signal India's improved business environment. In 2016, Developing Asia remained the second largest FDI recipient in the world, with China, Hong Kong (China), Singapore and India ranks among the top 10 FDI host economies (WIR 2017).

Microeconomic Foreign Direct Investment Theories

As discussed earlier, the macroeconomic FDI theory underpins the macro factors that enable selection of international trade partners. However, these factors alone cannot drive successful international trade without duly screening the microeconomic factors which are primarily indicated by the established firms or the market structure in the host nation.

The Theory of Industrial Organization

Stephen Hymer in his 1960 doctoral dissertation developed the FDI theory approach of industrial organization which was a systematic approach to study FDI. He was the pioneer in explaining international production in an imperfect market framework, which was later supported by Kindleberger (1969) in his imperfect markets model, Knickerbocker's (1973) in his oligopolistic reaction theory, Buckley and Casson (1974) in the internalization theory and Dunning (1974) in its eclectic paradigm, among others. Imperfect markets form the base for various microeconomic FDI theories.

According to Grazia (2012), Hymer's FDI theory went beyond the existing neo-classical theories, emphasizing the reason behind firms' decision to go abroad. Neoclassical trade theories were primarily based on macro-economic principles. The classical theory of trade relied on absolute cost advantages, product differentiation advantages, economies of scale and existence of perfect competition. Hymer's hypothesized that the MNEs compete with host country firms that are in an advantageous position concerning culture, language, the legal system, consumer's preference and also subjected to foreign exchange risk. The theory argues that foreign investors must possess some market power, that is, "firm-specific" advantage such as superior technology, differentiated product, popular brand name or lower costs due to economies of scale, cheaper sources of finance, and so on, if they want to operate overseas. In a world of perfectly competitive markets, local firms have an intrinsic advantage of knowing local tastes, business customs, legal and institutional framework however FDI assumes imperfections in the markets related to knowledge and technology to operate. Due to the presence of market imperfections or defects, firms' market power helps them reap good returns by investing abroad. However, the critics argue that possessing firm-specific advantages is not the only criteria for overseas investment as firms might also exploit their advantages through exporting or licensing. Though, there are various other factors such as local government policy, local market conditions and size, rival firms reaction and the risk profile of investment that might also influence the choice between FDI and licensing or exports. Though Hymer's work shed a lot of light on FDI but failed to explain the situation that gives rise to FDI which has been attempted by the eclectic approach of Dunning (1977) and the internalization theory by Buckley and Casson (1976).

FDI Based on Monopolistic Power

Kindleberger (1969) extended the work of Hymer and proposed an FDI theory based on monopolistic power. Kindleberger argued that MNEs came into existence due to structural market imperfections. MNEs enjoy monopolistic advantages in the foreign country on account of superior technology, managerial expertise, patents, privileged access to inputs, scale economies, and so on. To completely exploit these advantages, MNEs prefer foreign investment over sharing knowledge with potential competitors in the international market. The higher probability of earn-ing monopoly profits further encourages firms to invest directly overseas. Kindleberger exemplified various forms of advantages that were generally enjoyed by MNEs in the host country; however, he failed to describe any specific advantage to be focused on by the firm. Besides this, the exploitation of monopolistic advantage by the MNE was subject to the host country's government policy, which was subject to denial on the grounds of national interest.

Oligopolistic Theory of FDI

Knickerbocker (1973) formulated the oligopolistic theory of FDI based on market imperfections. The accessibility to the host country's market and the need to utilize relatively abundant factors present there are two crucial determinants that the economic literature emphasizes choosing a specific host country for foreign investments. Knickerbocker postulated that a firm might also invest in a country to match rival's move, which was coined as a third motivation. Firms often demonstrate imitative behavior by following the internationalization of competitors to retain their strategic advantage. Knickerbocker argued that oligopolistic firms within an industry tend to imitate rival's location for investment to over-come the possibility of being underpriced. Firms are generally indecisive about the production costs in the country to which they are currently exporting and always wary about of risk of being undercut by a rival's move. To overcome this risk they set up manufacturing subsidiary instead of exporting goods. Knickerbocker's proposition of firm following rival's move generally holds for a sufficiently risk averse oligopolistic firm who is uncertain about the costs in the host country though, in the case of certainty, the chances of the firm following rival diminishes. However, the theory remains silent on the factor motivating overseas investment in the first place.

Internalization Theory of Firms

Buckley and Casson (1976) provided another explanation of FDI by emphasizing intermediate inputs and technology. They shifted the focus of the international investment theory from country-specific toward industry-level and firm-level determinants of FDI (Henisz 2003). Buckley and Casson analyzed MNEs within a broad-based framework developed by Coase (1937) and proposed the internalization theory that justifies the creation of MNEs. They articulated their theory based on three postulates: firstly, the firms maximize profits in an imperfect market; secondly, when markets in intermediate products are imperfect, there is an incentive to bypass them by creating internal markets and thirdly, the internalization of markets across the world leads to MNEs. Hence they concluded that MNEs capability to commence international production depends on internalizing information and knowledge and utilizing it on a global level.

The theory of internalization of firms, first discussed by Coase (1937) is closely related to the organization theory. According to him, under certain circumstances, it is more efficient to serve internal market rather than to incur the prohibitive transaction costs of an outside market. Buckley and Casson (1976) and Rugman (1980) extended this argument to MNEs and argued that MNEs should possess some firm-specific advantage to internalize its operations to serve foreign markets through FDI rather than through exporting or licensing. Firms internalize their activities to exploit market opportunities by minimizing transaction cost and increasing production efficiency.

If we collectively look at the argument and theories proposed by Hymer, Kindleberger, Knickerbocker, Coase, Buckley, and Casson, it is evident that they mostly focused on the market structure of the host economy, the imperfect market structure, which was the driving force behind FDI. The MNEs aimed at utilizing "firm-specific" advantages to capture the host economy and maximize profit rather than exporting or licensing. The internalization theory by Buckley and Casson attempted to overcome specific criticisms of Hymer's theory by trying to explain the situation that gives rise to FDI.

Knowledge-Capital Model

The knowledge-capital model presented by Markusen et al. (1996) is a technical device that embeds both vertical and horizontal FDI to exploit both multi-plant scale economies and factor-price differences. Before proceeding to the model, let us understand the term vertical and horizontal FDI. The formal theories of the multinational firm are divided into three rough categories: the horizontal model, the vertical model, and the knowledge-capital model. The horizontal model describes a firm similar business operations at multiple locations. According to this model, FDI is the result of interaction between firm-level economies of scale and trade costs. According to Markusen and Venables (2000) horizontal model reduces the activity of MNEs due to dissimilarity in relative endowments and predicts that there exist negative relation between absolute skill differences and FDI activity. The vertical model, proposed by Elhanan Heipman (1984) suggests that the factor cost difference is the main incentive for firms to locate different operations in different countries. However it also indicates that FDI should only flow from the skill abundant country to the unskilled country since a firm's nationality is identified with the location of its skill-intensive headquarters; moreover, there is no reason to engage in FDI between identical countries with no cost differences. The intangible assets such as human capital refer to knowledge capital, and this has led to the origination of the term "knowledge-capital." One of the main characteristics of this model is to explain the investment decisions of multinationals based on the differences in skilled labor present between the source and the host country, as a measure of relative endowments. The approach enables understanding of the strategic actions undertaken by MNEs, either to exploit larger markets through horizontal FDI or to reduce production costs by vertical FDI.

The knowledge-capital model predicts that skill differences can have positive and negative effects. As predicted by the vertical model, the variation in the abundance of skilled labor between countries raises the flow of FDI from the skilled country to the host country provided the host country is big in size. This argument holds for many countries like China and India, the top two populated countries in the world with abundant low-cost labor that attract huge FDI inflows. However, a skill abundant large parent country generally has more outbound FDI than a skill scarce or a small parent country and to corroborate, the United States, Japan, the UK among many other developed countries has been one of the largest overseas investors over the years. This model also restates microeconomics factors a driver of FDI.

The Eclectic Theory of FDI

The eclectic theory of FDI proposed by Dunning in 1970s is widely known as the Ownership, Location, and Internalization (OLI) framework. Its attraction lies in the fact that it brings together various explanations of FDI such as the oligopolistic and internalization theories. Dunning added a third dimension in the form of location theory that explains why a firm opens a foreign subsidiary. According to this theory the propensity of a firm to engage in international production depends on the existence of three advantages:

1. Ownership advantage or firm-specific advantages that include some form of intangible assets like knowledge and know-how;
2. Location advantage, or the advantage of operating in foreign countries that possess suitable environment in terms of resource endowments, market size, and structure, institutional environment, and so on; and
3. Internalization advantage or the advantage that motivates investing firms to internalize their firm-specific assets and utilize it themselves rather than sell or lease them.

Several theories explain the drivers of OFDI. Other than the traditional ones, Dunning's OLI (Ownership, location, and internalization) framework provides a widely accepted rationale for overseas investment by MNEs both in developed and developing economies. OLI framework immensely contributes to the OFDI decisions by focusing on ownership to exploit monopoly powers over advantages, choice of location and the approach to safeguard monopolistic advantages from predators. The firm faces several disadvantages in the international market on account of transaction cost, lack of local knowledge, cultural barriers, lack of distribution networks, and so on, but still prefer to operate to leverage ownership advantages in terms of accessing natural resources, acceptance to the brand, intellectual property, and certain other core competencies. Locational advantages arise on account of political, economic and social parameters. Political parameters include the country's judicial mechanism, political risk, labor laws and ease of doing business, and so on. On the economic front size of the market, growth rate, infrastructure, competitive cost structures, and so on, are essential considerations whereas the firms benefit from the similarities in culture, conduction of business, social structure, and so on, on the social front. The firms operate in a foreign country either through marketing alliances, acquisitions or greenfield endeavor. The firms internalize to avoid the high cost of external transactions provided the markets offer favorable regulatory power. Dunning further explains different motives for the firms to internationalize, that is, market seeking, resource seeking, efficiency seeking and asset seeking. He suggested that market seeking and resource seeking motives are the most sought-after by novice firms in the foreign market whereas veteran MNEs aligns more to efficiency-seeking and asset seeking motives. He also suggests that firms seek opportunity rather than a threat to internationalize by acquiring strategic assets like the latest technology, distribution network, brands, and raw materials.

Investment Development Paradigm

The investment development paradigm (IDP) proposes that countries undergo five stages of economic development based on the inward and outward investment pattern which is sequentially based on Dunning OLI paradigm. Stage 1 and 2 draws resource seeking inward FDI whereas stage 3 witnesses decline in inward FDI but rise in OFDI due to a certain level of acquired technological capabilities by the domestic firms to compete globally. The OFDI further accelerates in stage 4, and while catching up the pace with inward FDI, the net FDI almost nullifies in stage 5. The rapid economic development of the newly industrialized economies seems to have altered the unique IDP theory, for instance, Korea that did not experience stage 1 and 2 instead directly ventured overseas by accumulating its technological capabilities through preferential industrial policies by the country. The economic literature suggests various theories and models attempt to explain the underlying reason or motive of a firm to move overseas and Dunning eclectic theory of FDI is the most renowned theory in this filed. The firms FDI motive cannot be justified by any one generalized theory; however, there seems to be a unanimous consensus among many approaches that firms move overseas to reap the benefit of advantages enjoyed by them in the form of ownership, location, and so on. Stephen Hymer's FDI theory went beyond the existing neo-classical theories, emphasizing on why the firms go abroad. However, Hymer's thesis was deficient in providing a complete explanation for FDI because it fails to explain where and when FDI takes place which was further attempted by the internalization theory by Buckley and Casson (1976) and eclectic approach by Dunning (1977). As stated earlier, new theories will see the daylight to incorporate the ever-changing economic and global scenario refuting the earlier ones, but every approach is unique in itself as it provides ample ground to select the most appropriate theoretical framework to study and evaluate the ever-changing business scenario.

This chapter attempts at elucidate dominant theories of FDI. Though we have explained many FDI theories, there is no single stand-alone theory which comprehensively explains FDI. However, these theories are an integral part of research and form a specific theoretical background. These theories provide adequate ground for selecting the most appropriate conceptual framework for future scholarly work in the areas of international economics, international finance, international trade and business, FDI and firm internationalization.

References

Anderson, J.E. 2011. "The Gravity Model." *American Economic Review* 3, no. 1, pp. 133–60. Available at http://nber.org/papers/w16576.pdf

Asiedu, E. 2006. "Foreign Direct Investment in Africa: The Role of Natural Resources, Market Size, Government Policy, Institutions and Political Instability." *World economy* 29, no. 1, pp. 63–77.

Athreye, S., and S. Kapur. 2009. "Introduction: The Internationalization of Chinese and Indian Firms—Trends, Motivations, and Strategy." *Industrial and Corporate Change* 18, no. 2, pp. 201–21.

"Chapter 2 Neoclassical Growth Theory and Standard Models." Available at www.springer.com/cda/content/document/cda.../9783790826364-c1.pdf?SGWID

Blonigen, B.A., R.B. Davies, and K. Head. 2003. "Estimating the Knowledge-Capital Model of the Multinational Enterprise: Comment." *American Economic Review* 93, no. 3, pp. 980–94.

Buckley, P., and M. Casson. 1976. *The Future of the Multinational Corporation.*

Buckley, P.J., and M. Casson. 1976. *The Future of the Multinational Enterprise.* London: Macmillan.

Caves, R.E. 1974. *Economic Analysis and Multinational Enterprise*. London: George Allen and Unwin.

Caves, R.E. 1974. "Multinational Firms, Competition, and Productivity in Host-Country Markets." *Economica* 41, no. 162, pp. 176–93.

Chaney, T. 2013. *The Gravity Equation in International Trade: An Explanation* (No. w19285). National Bureau of Economic Research.

Coase, R.H. 1937. "The Nature of the Firm." *Economica* 4, no. 16, pp. 386–405.

Denisia, V. 2010. "Foreign Direct Investment Theories: An Overview of the Main FDI Theories." *European Journal of Interdisciplinary Studies* 3.

Dresner, S. 2008. *The Principles of Sustainability*. Earthscan. Business & Economics.

Dunning, J.H. 1974. *The Distinctive Nature of Multinational Enterprise*. London: George Allen and Unwin.

Dunning, J.H. 2000. "The Eclectic Paradigm as an Envelope for Economic and Business Theories of MNE Activity." *International Business Review* 9, no. 2, pp. 163–90.

Dunning, J.H. 2006. "Comment on Dragon Multinationals: New Players in 21st Century Globalization." *Asia Pacific Journal of Management* 23, no. 2, pp. 139–41.

Dunning, J.H., and R. Narula. 1998. "The Investment Development Path Revisited: Some Emerging Issues." In *Foreign Direct Investment and Governments*, eds. J.H. Dunning and R. Narula. London: Routledge.

Enders, J.C., and M. Remig. 2014. *Theories of Sustainable Development*. Routledge.

Foss, N.J. 1997. "The Classical Theory of Production and the Capabilities View of the Firm." *Journal of Economic Studies* 24, no. 5, pp. 307–23.

Gray, H.P. 1981. *Macroeconomic Theories of Foreign Direct Investment: An Assessment*. University of Reading, Department of Economics.

Hecksher, E., and B. Ohlin. 1933. *Interregional and International Trade*. Cambridge, MA: Harvard University Press.

Helpman, E. 1984. "A Simple Theory of International Trade with Multinational Corporations." *Journal of Political Economy* 92, no. 3, pp. 451–71.

Henisz, W.J. 2003. "The Power of the Buckley and Casson Thesis: The Ability to Manage Institutional Idiosyncrasies." *Journal of International Business Studies* 34, no. 2, pp. 173–84.

Hofmann, P. 2013. *The Impact of International Trade and FDI on Economic Growth and Technological Change*. Springer Science & Business Media.

Ietto-Gillies, G. 2012. *Transnational Corporations and International Production: Concepts, Theories, and Effects*. Edward Elgar Publishing.

Karau, J.N., and T.K. Mburu. 2016. "Institutional, Governance and Economic Factors Influencing Foreign Direct Investment Inflows on East Africa." *Journal of Economics and Development Studies* 4, no. 3, pp. 87–98.

Kindleberger, C.P. 1969. *American Business Abroad*. New Haven, CT: Yale University Press.

Kindleberger, C.P., ed. 1970. *The International Corporation: A Symposium.* Cambridge, Mass.: MIT Press.

Kristjánsdóttir, H. 2010. "Foreign Direct Investment: The Knowledge Capital Model and a Small Country Case." *Scottish Journal of Political Economy* 57, no. 5, pp. 591–614. Available at http://pages.uoregon.edu/bruceb/ Estimating_the_Knowledge_Capital_Model_Comment.pdf

Lipsey, R.E. 2004. "Home-and Host-country Effects of Foreign Direct Investment." In *Challenges to Globalization: Analyzing the Economics,* 333–82. University of Chicago Press.

Markusen, J.R. 1984. "Multinationals, Multi-Plant Economies, and the Gains from Trade." *Journal of International Economics* 16, nos. 3–4, pp. 205–26.

Markusen, J.R. 1995. "The Boundaries of Multinational Enterprises and the Theory of International Trade." *The Journal of Economic Perspectives* 9, no. 2, pp. 169–89.

Markusen, J.R. May 1984. "Multinationals, Multiplant Economies, and the Gains from Trade." *Journal of International Economics* 16, nos. 3–4, pp. 205–26.

Markusen, J.R., A.J. Venables, D.E. Konan, and K.H. Zhang. 1996. *A Unified Treatment of Horizontal Direct Investment, Vertical Direct Investment, and the Pattern of Trade in Goods and Services* (No. w5696). National Bureau of Economic Research.

Markusen, J.R., A.J. Venables, D.E. Konan, and K.H. Zhang. 1996. *A Unified Treatment of Horizontal Direct Investment, Vertical Direct Investment, and the Pattern of Trade in Goods and Services* (No. w5696). National Bureau of Economic Research.

Markusen, J.R., and A.J. Venables. 2000. "The Theory of Endowment, Intra-Industry and Multi-National Trade." *Journal of International Economics* 52, no. 2, pp. 209–34.

Moran, T.H. 1998. *Foreign Direct Investment and Development: The New Policy Agenda for Developing Countries and Economies in Transition.* Peterson Institute.

Morgan, R.E., and C.S. Katsikeas. 1997. "Theories of International Trade, Foreign Direct Investment and Firm Internationalization: A Critique." *Management Decision* 35, no. 1, pp. 68–78.

National Bureau of Economic Research. October 1997 "Trade Versus Investment Liberalization." Working Paper No. 6231, Cambridge, MA.

Nayak, D., and R.N. Choudhury. 2014. "A Selective Review of Foreign Direct Investment Theories (No. 143)." ARTNeT Working Paper Series.

Nelson, R.R., and S.G. Winter. 1974. "Neoclassical vs Evolutionary Theories of Economic Growth: Critique and Prospectus." *The Economic Journal* 84, no. 336, pp. 886–905.

OECD Global Forum on International Investment. 2017. "Global Forum on International Investment-Identifying and Measuring the Sustainability Characteristics of FDI." *Paris*, available at http://oecd.org/investment/globalforum/2017-GFII-Background-Note-Identifying-and-measuring-the-sustainability-characteristics-of-FDI.pdf (accessed March 6, 2017)

Petrochilos, G.A. 1983. *Foreign Direct Investment and the Development Process: The Case of Greece*. Gower Publishing Company.

Ramondo, N., V. Rappoport, and K.J. Ruhl. 2013. "The Proximity-Concentration Tradeoff Under Uncertainty." *Review of Economic Studies* 80, no. 4, pp. 1582–621.

Rugman, A.M. 1980. "A New Theory of the Multinational-Enterprise-Internationalization Versus Internalization." *Columbia Journal of World Business* 15, no. 1, pp. 23–29.

Subramanian, R., C. Sachdeva, and S. Morris. 2010. "FDI Outflows from India: An Examination of the Underlying Economics, Policies, and their Impacts." Working paper no.2010-03-01, IIM Ahmadabad.

World Investment Report 2017. Available at https://unctad.org/en/Publication Chapters/wir2017ch2_en.pdf

CHAPTER 2

Emerging Perspectives of Foreign Direct Investment

The analysis in this book joins the worldwide debate on the type of political systems that suit to FDI as there are different regime types with differing effects on FDI and therefore, economic development. The earlier debate was cast in terms of either or options that aimed at analyzing two regime frameworks, that are, democracy and authoritarianism; but contemporary literature extends this debate to various shades of political ideology and outlines potential problems and issues. Based on the rapidly changing geopolitics of the world and economic progress the multilateral institutions have classified the world economy into several categories. This classification has changed with mega-events in the regime types, that is, the end of the cold war, the formation of the European Union, the fall of the Berlin Wall, China's entry into WTO and the rise of emerging competitive markets and newly found democracies in South Asia and South East Asia.

As we prepare this backgrounder BREXIT fall out effects, loom large on England and other economies dealing with EU and England. There have been serious developments in the conflict zone of West Asia which have fought bitter wars within themselves resulting in political instability of the region and associated irreversible effects for the world economy. The main contention of this note is that political regime types and political environments are one of the most crucial determinants of FDI flows (both inward and outward).

The primary drivers of FDI in the last three decades or so have been the increasing degree of democratization of many economies, gradual retreat of the state and privatization programs of the United States and UK and later EU, and the process and content of globalization among others. We also, develop an understanding of how the political regimes of the day impact different types of FDI. The OLI model of Dunning emphasize that there may be different effects for each of the three types of FDI: resource seeking, market seeking and strategic asset seeking. We also briefly note the theories that explain the links between regime types and FDI. Studies indicate that since the 1990s, when most countries adopted economic liberalization and market-friendly policies, the relative ability of the MNEs to influence the developing economies has weakened. This is the result of the growth of national level regulatory and other institutions, the rise of civil society and voluntary organizations like the NGOs. The active and fairly independent judiciary like in India, improvements in organizational and competitive capabilities of domestic investors and the presence of several "veto players" in these countries are also significant contributors.

While the overall quality of the institutional system may aim at improving the environmental and taxation policies, the political executive in many democracies like India has yet to resolve the issues of enforcing contracts. This is so, as a five-year term of a popularly elected legislative executive is no guarantee to the strengthening of public institutions and delivery system in a large democracy. Legislative reforms and public policy formulation in countries like India take a very long time because of a fragmented polity; this may offer some temporary advantage to the MNEs to renegotiate the terms of investment better. Also, it is one of the many reasons why comprehensive democratic frameworks may find it difficult to abruptly reverse public policies regarding FDI (to that extent the political risks of nationalization and expropriation are much less or a rarity). Further, if concurrent measures by way of government policy are not in place for improving the absorptive capability of domestic investors, developing countries like India may not be able to realize in full measures the advantages of FDI.

Democracy and FDI

Busse (2003) recognized a positive relationship between democracy and FDI flows. However, this was not the case in the 1950s and 1970s when foreign investors from the United States and UK usually invested in countries rich in natural resources. In the developing economies national policies are influenced by foreign investors, as development proceeds and countries globalize, foreign investors tend to exert higher levels of pressures on domestic policies. The institutional environments of the host countries are affected in terms of the contract enforcement mechanisms. Lower to moderate contracting and contract dispute settlement costs are assumed to attract higher FDI inflows (Ahlquist and Prakash 2010). Horizontal FDI is "market seeking" in nature whereas vertical FDI is "cost saving" in nature. In a democratic country, there arises the risk of expropriations, that is, action by the state government for foreign investors. Democratic countries mostly attract Horizontal FDI whereas autocratic regimes relatively attract more vertical FDI. The MNEs fragment their production and invest in low-income countries on account of saving labor costs (vertical FDI). Horizontal FDI flows could move toward countries showing similar average income and demand preferences (Manzocchi et al. 2006).

The lower-middle income countries require a minimum threshold of human capital to benefit from FDI. Therefore, the absorptive capacity of domestic human capital cannot be undermined for extracting maximum FDI gains (Elkomy et al. 2016). While most of the past studies concentrate on the economic determinants of FDI, nevertheless the recent literature focuses on political risks and institutions. The study by (Li and Resnick 2003) emphasized that democratic rights lead to improved property rights protection which consequently increases FDI inflows. The survey by Busse and Hefeker (2007) examined the influence of government stability, socio-economic conditions and internal conflicts, democratic accountability and quality of bureaucracy, among others. Amongst them, government stability, religious tensions, and democratic accountability emerged as the most critical factors impacting FDI inflows. In a democratic country, the foreign investor is likely to face expropriation when the political leaders face constraints or due to frequent leadership turnover. Autocracies are less likely to expropriate foreign investors when they face high political constraints and have stayed in power for a long time. Both types of regimes may expropriate, but democracies may do so less frequently (Li 2009). The recent debate also explores the effects of international trade agreements on developing countries. Political variables are the cause for significant amounts of variations in FDI flows. The international institutions can increase the credibility of the government's commitments and promote transnational cooperation, henceforth, Bilateral Investment Treaties (BITs) have attracted sustained attention and only recently.

Trends in World Stability and Peace

The latest Freedom House Survey Reports (2016) reveal that democracies were undermined in countries dependent on the sale of natural resources which in turn led the authoritarian governments to contain local dissent. These developments according to the Survey contributed to the 10th consecutive year of decline in global freedom. Democracies in the EU and the United States were struggling with the unresolved conflicts of West Asia and other regions as also are confronted with refugee crises and well-being of repressive petro-states from Angola to Azerbaijan. According to Gilpin (1975; 2016) and Jacobsen and Jacobsen (2011), economic nationalism is viewed as a theory of state-building and economic independence. The supporters of economic nationalism contest against FDI and demand protectionist policies for domestic investors. Dependency theory entails the worldview of the 1960s and 1970s. Dependency theory emphasizes the economic development of a state in terms of external influences such as political, economic, and cultural on national development policies (Sunkel 1969). Dependency school believes mass expropriation in the 1960s and 1970s generated a political reaction to foreign capital and external dependency (Wallerstien 1976). However, liberalization wave toward the end of the previous century changed the discernment toward trade openness and FDI.

In the aftermath of "Washington Consensus" during the 1980s, the select Latin American countries liberalization led to a wave of protests but later increasing democratization in many countries opened up opportunities for public participation in policymaking. To the extent FDI benefits local labor markets (higher wages, labor standards, and employment, and so on), the "left majority" would welcome FDI (Milner and Kubota 2005) though the proponents of political right-defensive nationalism took the contrary view. According to a study by Guerin and Manzocchi (2007) democracy does have positive effects on FDI flows between developed and developing countries, arising through the total factor productivity channels. According to Mansfield et al. (2000) democratic countries overcome trade barriers and thereby encourage more open trade relations. Studies argue that government stability, institutional quality, non-existence of internal conflict and fundamental democratic rights significantly determine FDI inflows. Emerging democratic countries subject foreign investors to low expropriation risk (Jensen 2006) though parliamentary democracies are more likely to attract FDI than presidential ones. Rodrik (1996) links democracy with FDI and suggests that countries with weaker democratic rights attract less capital from the United States.

Sun (2014) examined the dual political effects of foreign direct investment in 124 developing countries over the period 1970–2005. Since the late 1980s, 70 percent of developing countries have made substantial efforts to promote political freedoms (Rudra 2005; Freedom House 2010). But the evidence on the impact on FDI is somewhat mixed: some suggest positive effects while the others suggest adverse effects. The findings of (UNCTAD,2006) are threefold: first, although the overall political impact of FDI is significantly negative in the developing world, FDI from advanced democracies presents a consistently positive effect on freedom. Second, FDI in the primary sector exerts a negative political impact. And third, the political impacts of FDI vary across regions. FDI directed toward the primary sector such as mining are most likely to hurt growth, while investment in the manufacturing sector has a positive effect (Schulz 2009). Time and again, resource-seeking FDI is linked with authoritarian regimes. The recent literature on the political resource curse suggests that authoritarian regimes take advantage of the substantial revenues generated by foreign investors "to consolidate state power" (Johnson and Li 2017). It is rational to compare the diverse effects of political risks in developed and developing economies. The most popular policies to attract FDI are subsidies and incentives, although they are politically and economically expensive and divisive. Li (2006) argues that the quality of institutions, political stability, and the rule of law attract FDI to developing economies and will have long-lasting effects as compared to an extensive range of subsidies and incentives to the multinationals and discrimination against domestic small and medium-sized firms. The three most important political risks being nationalization or expropriation of foreign assets, policy instability and arbitrary regulation in FDI-related policies, war and political violence, including terrorist activities, are capable of damaging foreign assets and adversely impacting the productivity of a host economy (Jensen 2008; MIGA 2010).

Dutta and Roy (2011) argued that even with a higher level of political risk; financial development is capable of absorbing the benefits of FDI inflows in more efficient ways, and therefore lays the importance of financial stability. Kucera (2014) evaluates US FDI outflows to 15 industries across 54 countries and suggest that BITs with the United States correlate positively with investments in fixed capital however it indicates varying effects of the BITs in inducing FDI-from moderate to nix relationship.

Asiedu and Lien (2011) in their study analyzed that the impact of democracy on FDI depends upon the importance of natural resources in the country's exports; democracy support FDI in countries where the share of natural resources is low but has adverse effects on FDI where natural resource dominate country's total exports. It corroborates with many of the nations in Sub-Saharan Africa region that seriously needs FDI but have weak democracies with a high share of primary commodities in their total exports. Jensen (2003) suggests that democratic governments attract higher levels of FDI as democracy lowers the country risk. The empirical evidence indicate that democratic regimes attract as much as 70 percent more FDI as a percentage of GDP than authoritarian regimes. The trustworthiness of a democratic institution depends on the veto players in a democracy who offer checks and balances and make abrupt policy reversal difficult. The government in democratic countries is more committed to market-friendly policies; therefore globally democracies are relatively more compatible with globalization (Jackobsen and Soysa 2006).

It is argued by Thies and Nieman (2017) that the authoritarian governments cannot protect property rights like the democratic regimes where transparent institutions are available. However, researchers point out weak correlations between democracy and property rights. Democracies enhance protection of property rights by designing appropriate institutions as also for resolving conflicts. Kugler and Coan (2009) explicitly modeled the interactive relationship between open market policy environments and relative political capacity (RPC). Based on the empirical study they argued that governments with open market policy frameworks and high levels of political capacity signal political environment favorable to sustained profitability. A small commitment to free-market policies is not enough hence the government should use its power to realize the policy goals. Incapable governments with open market policies are more likely to fail to induce FDI.

Sustainable Development Goals and FDI

In 2012, at the United Nations Conference on Sustainable Development in Rio de Janeiro, member states decided to establish an intergovernmental process to develop a set of "action-oriented, concise and easy to communicate" sustainable development goals (SDGs) to help drive the implementation of sustainable development.[1] The 17 Sustainable Development Goals (SDGs) which are the part of a broader 2030 Agenda for Sustainable Development built on the eight Millennium Development Goals (MDGs) set by the United Nations in 2000; to eradicate poverty, reduce child mortality, improve maternal health, and achieve universal primary education, hunger, illiteracy, disease and global partnership in development. The 17 SDGs support future development agenda and aims to end poverty, ensure universal access to clean water and sanitation, affordable and clean energy, responsible consumption and production patterns, improve health and education, reduce inequality, promote sustainable cities and communities, build resilient infrastructure and foster innovation, revitalize global partnerships and spur economic growth alongside managing climate change and preserving our oceans and forests. One of the key achievements of the UN conference was approving guidelines on green economy policies. Green economy in the milieu of sustainable development and poverty eradication was viewed as one of the fundamental tools to achieve sustainable development. The member states also agreed to strengthen the United Nations Environment Programme (UNEP) and establish a high-level political forum for sustainable development.[2] The UN 2030 SDGs aims at present and future peace and prosperity of people and planet. The goals included ending poverty and hunger, improving health and education, reducing inequality, and

---

[1] https://sustainabledevelopment.un.org/rio20
[2] https://sustainabledevelopment.un.org/index.php?menu=1225

spurring economic growth alongside combating climate change and pre-serving our oceans and forests.

Globalization is a key to development for most of the countries. It provides an opportunity for foreign investors to trade and invest in different countries per their discretion. FDI is largely viewed as a vital source of external capital that is capable of boosting the nation's growth on the premise of diffusing modern know-how, technology, management and their spillovers. However, nations are now largely replacing FDI with sustainable FDI.

World Association of Investment Promotion Agencies (WAIPA), a non-governmental organization founded in 1995 had the vision to serve as the engine of growth for global FDI. WAIPA besides facilitating global FDI is promoting IPAs to drive FDI.[3] The latest drive towards sustainable FDI is termed as 'the fourth generation' of investment promotion and WAIPA has introduced several methods to evaluate IPAs engagement towards sustainability.[4] Researchers believe that besides exploiting natural resources FDI is also a prime channel for the transfer of technology and know-how between countries boosting productivity and economic growth[5] but FDI needs to be sustainable itself to enable sustainable development. FDI is proficient of becoming an active vehicle promoting sustainable development provided the investing firms to change their perspective towards developing countries by integration environmental, social and economic considerations into FDI activities. Governments should also ensure a balanced global and ecologically responsive framework of environmental agreements and institutions besides integrating economic and social concerns to promote sustainable development.[6]

---

[3] Towards an Indicative List of FDI Sustainability Characteristics, Sauvant & Mann, concept paper, ICTSD and WET workshop for Sustainable development in Geneva, February 2017.

[4] http://www.waipa.org/wp-content/uploads/2017/02/22-Feb-Geneva-Round-Table-WAIPA-Short-Paper.pdf

[5] Foreign Direct Investment and Sustainable Development: Insights from Literature and Ideas for research, R. Echandi, handout at the ICTSD and WET workshop for Sustainable development in Geneva, February 2017.

[6] http://ic-associates.com/wp-content/uploads/2017/03/FDI-and-Sustainable-Development-Working-Paper-by-ICA-and-Wavteq.pdf

Stakeholder Theory and FDI

Stakeholder theory was discussed by Dr. F. Edward Freeman, a professor at the University of Virginia, in his landmark book, "Strategic Management: A Stakeholder Approach." The theory proposes that the stakeholder ecosystem entails of anyone and everyone that is directly or indirectly involved or impacted by the company's affair such as employees, customers, suppliers, environmentalists, communities, governmental agencies, political bodies and more. Freeman argues that the company's real success lies in satisfying not just its shareholders who have invested in the company but all its stakeholders and hence its bottom line.

Over the last couple of years developing and transition economies have been witnessing the promising flow of global FDI especially because of business opportunities which are mainly the size and growth potential of these markets. They are the most dominant drivers of foreign direct investment (Hornberger et al. 2011). MNEs expand their cross border presence through subsidiaries or undertaking Greenfield and Brownfield projects. According to Contessi and Weinberger (2009), FDI is an international venture where the foreign investor residing in the host country acquires the management right of its business. According to the stakeholder theory, the investor is responsible not only to the host country but to all the stakeholders directly or indirectly involved or impacted by the project. Globalization has eventually raised the concerns about the effect of foreign investments and their operations in the host countries mainly related to environmental and social consequences (Porras 2016).

The international project could have a diverse and contradicting interest of the participants such as the firm itself, the host country's government or even the local community (Laasonen 2010). International projects are often subjected to a complex and dynamic host country's environment where besides the shareholders there are numerous other stakeholders with their traditional values, norms, expectations, socio-cultural backgrounds, among others (Aaltonen et al. 2010) and may perhaps not align with the firms' interest. The firm thus needs to continuously interact with the local stakeholders in the host country to avoid any significant unexpected events which are mainly the situations not planned initially or expected during the project (Aaltonen et al. 2010).

Collaborative association between a firm and all the local stakeholders is vital for the successful operation of an international project in the host country (Bourne and Walker 2005). Internationalization and the expansion of MNEs to different nations have resulted in a significant rise of non-governmental organizations (NGOs) analyzing the activities of these international firms (Yaziji and Doh 2009).

The stakeholder theory has of-lately generated significant interest among academicians, researchers, policy-makers, NGO's and regulators on account of rising global concerns to attract and channelize sustainable FDI. The concept largely promotes the vision of the international firm and its key shareholders who are being confronted with unprecedented levels of environmental turbulence and climatic change to maximize all the stakeholders' value in a sustainable manner (Fontaine 2006).

For countries like India, the moot issue is whether the veto players are exercising a voice in matters of the relative impact of FDI. The evidence is mixed; on the one hand we have had the world's most significant industrial disaster—the Bhopal Gas Tragedy—in 1984 on the other, there have been sporadic but intense struggles by the environmentalists and NGO activists on the issues of resettlement and rehabilitation of indigenous people when the governments allot large land sites to FDI projects. (POSCO and Vedanta Resources, Orissa). The fact that it took the Bhopal tragedy of 1984 to make political executives pass legislation in 1986, that is, The Environmental (Protection) Act of India—the first of its kind, itself indicates a weak democratic system. The act authorized the central government to take measures to protect and improve environmental quality, set standards and inspect industrial units. It also laid down penalties for infringement of its provisions. The MNEs leverage their bargaining power over the governments when new legislation takes long lead time, and the enforcement is equally weak. The Courts in India have very active judicial activism in response to petitions filed by RTI and other activists, but then this process has its costs and benefits which may accrue over a more extended period. Even if one wants to apply the stakeholder theories, one is constrained because the stakeholders often do not know what they want and may be unduly influenced by certain activists who may present a different perspective on the likely costs and benefits of FDI.

We may also note that though we discussed the policy competition aspect the aspect of "competition policy" also deserves substantial attention from public policymakers. While in countries like India several researchers and scholars have analyzed competition policy; attention is required on the grey areas such as monitoring of performance by both the Greenfield and Brownfield FDI projects. The tasks of such monitoring rest with the designated authority—The Competition Commission of India (CCI). The tasks are to steer clear of monopolies, cartels, and other adverse effects on the market structure and the due process of competition.

The Indian government has further liberalized the FDI policy in many segments but has yet to simultaneously address the unresolved issues of innovative regulations and stringent enforcement or else the MNEs may tend to consolidate their monopolistic power in some fields and "the race to the top" may not happen at all.

References

Aaltonen, K., J. Kujala, P. Lehtonen, and I. Ruuska. 2010. "A Stakeholder Network Perspective on Unexpected Events and their Management in International Projects." *International Journal of Managing Projects in Business* 3, no. 4, pp. 564–88.

Ahlquist, J.S., and A. Prakash. 2010. "FDI and the Costs of Contract Enforcement in Developing Countries." *Policy Sciences* 43, no. 2, pp. 181–200.

Asiedu, E., and D. Lien. 2011. "Democracy, Foreign Direct Investment and Natural Resources." *Journal of International Economics* 84, no. 1, pp. 99–111.

Bourne, L., and D.H. Walker. 2005. "Visualising and Mapping Stakeholder Influence." *Management Decision* 43, no. 5, pp. 649–60.

Busse, M. 2003. "Democracy and FDI, HWWA Discussion Paper No. 220." Available at http://ssrn.com/abstract=384480 or http://dx.doi.org/10.2139/ssrn.384480 (accessed July 7, 2016).

Busse, M., and C. Hefeker. 2007. "Political Risk, Institutions, and Foreign Direct Investment." *European Journal of Political Economy* 23, no. 2, pp. 397–415.

Büthe, T., and H.V. Milner. 2008. "The Politics of Foreign Direct Investment into Developing Countries: Increasing FDI through International Trade Agreements?" *American Journal of Political Science* 52, no. 4, pp. 741–62.

Contessi, S., and A. Weinberger. 2009. "Foreign Direct Investment, Productivity, and Country Growth: An Overview: Federal Reserve Bank of St. Louis." *Review* 91, no. 2, pp. 61–78.

Dutta, N., and S. Roy. 2011. "Foreign Direct Investment, Financial Development and Political Risks." *The Journal of Developing Areas*, pp. 303–27.

Elkomy, S., H. Ingham, and R. Read. 2016. "Economic and Political Determinants of the Effects of FDI on Growth in Transition and Developing Countries." *Thunderbird International Business Review* 58, no. 4, pp. 347–62.

Fontaine, C., A. Haarman, and S. Schmid. 2006. "The Stakeholder Theory." *Edlays Education* 1, pp. 1–33.

Freedom House. 2014. *Freedom in the World 2014: The Annual Survey of Political Rights and Civil Liberties*. Rowman & Littlefield.

Freedom House. 2016. "Freedom in the World: Anxious Dictators, Wavering Democracies: Global Freedom Under Pressure." Available at https://freedomhouse.org/sites/default/files/FH_FITW_Report_2016.pdf

Gilpin, R. 1975. *US Power and the Multinational Corporation: The Political Economy of Foreign Direct Investment*, 2 Vols. Basic Books.

Gilpin, R. 2016. *The Political Economy of International Relations*. Princeton University Press.

Gonzalez Porras, L. 2016. *Stakeholder Opposition in a Foreign Direct Investment: Case Botnia's Pulp Mill in Uruguay* (Master's thesis).

Guerin, S., and S. Manzocchi. 2007. "Political Regime and Vertical vs. horizontal FDI." Available at http://eprints.luiss.it/99/1/Manzocchi_2006_03_OPEN.pdf (accessed July 7, 2016).

Guerin, S.S., and S. Manzocchi. 2009. "Political Regime and FDI from Advanced to Emerging Countries." *Review of World Economics* 145, no. 1, pp. 75–91.

Jakobsen, J., and I. De Soysa. 2006. "Do Foreign Investors Punish Democracy? Theory and Empirics, 1984–2001." *Kyklos* 59, no. 3, pp. 383–410.

Jakobsen, J., and T.G. Jakobsen. 2011. "Economic Nationalism and FDI: The Impact of Public Opinion on Foreign Direct Investment in Emerging Markets, 1990–2005." *Society and Business Review* 6, no. 1, pp. 61–76.

Jensen, N. 2008. "Political Risk, Democratic Institutions, and Foreign Direct Investment." *The Journal of Politics* 70, no. 4, pp. 1040–52.

Jensen, N.M. 2003. "Democratic Governance and Multinational Corporations: Political Regimes and Inflows of Foreign Direct Investment." *International Organization* 57, no. 3, pp. 587–616.

Jensen, N.M. 2006. "Democratic Institutions and Expropriation Risk for Multinational Investors." *Department of Political Science*. Washington University, mimeo.

Jensen, N.M., and N.P. Johnston. 2011. "Political Risk, Reputation, and the Resource Curse." *Comparative Political Studies* 44, no. 6, pp. 662–88.

Johnson, A.P., and Q. Li. 2017. *Regime Type and FDI: A Transaction Cost Economics Approach to the Debate.*

Kucera, D.C., and M. Principi. 2014. "Democracy and Foreign Direct Investment at the Industry Level: Evidence for US Multinationals." *Review of World Economics* 150, no. 3, pp. 595–617.

Kugler, T., and T. Coan. 2009. *Growth and Inequality within India: Government Efficiency, Policy Choice and FDI.*

Kusi, H., J. Battat, and P. Kusek. 2011. "Attracting FdI: How Much Does Investment Climate Matter?" The World Bank Group, available at http://worldbank.org/fpd/publicpolicyjournal

Laasonen, S. 2010. "The Role of Stakeholder Dialogue: NGOs and Foreign Direct Investments." *Corporate Governance: The International Journal of Business in Society* 10, no. 4, pp. 527–37.

Li, Q. 2006. "Democracy, Autocracy, and Tax Incentives to Foreign Direct Investors: A Cross-National Analysis." *Journal of Politics* 68, no. 1, pp. 62–74.

Li, Q. 2009. "Democracy, Autocracy, and Expropriation of Foreign Direct Investment." *Comparative Political Studies* 42, no. 8, pp. 1098–27.

Li, Q., and A. Resnick. 2003. "Reversal of Fortunes: Democratic Institutions and Foreign Direct Investment Inflows to Developing Countries." *International Organization* 57, no. 1, pp. 175–211.

Mansfield, E.D., H.V. Milner, and B.P. Rosendorff. 2000. "Free to Trade: Democracies, Autocracies, and International Trade." *American Political Science Review* 94, no. 2, pp. 305–21.

Manzocchi, S., and S. Salisoy Guerin. 2006. *Political Regime and Vertical vs. Horizontal FDI.*

MIGA. 2010. "World Investment and Political Risk 2009." 104. Available at http://miga.org/news/index_sv.cfm?aid=2486. doi:10.1596/978-0-8213-8213-8115-1

Milner, H.V., and K. Kubota. 2005. "Why the Move to Free Trade? Democracy and trade Policy in the Developing Countries." *International Organization* 59, no. 1, pp. 107–43.

Nieman, M.D., and C.G. Thies. 2012. "Democracy, Property Rights, and Foreign Direct Investment." *European Journal of Political Economy* 23, no. 2, pp. 376–96.

Rodrik, D. 1996. *Labor Standards in International Trade: Do They Matter and What Do We Do About Them?* Overseas Development Council.

Rudra, N. 2005. "Globalization and the Strengthening of Democracy in the Developing World." *American Journal of Political Science* 49, no. 4, pp. 704–30.

Schulz, H. 2009. *Political Institutions and Foreign Direct Investment in Developing Countries: Does the Sector Matter?* University of Pennsylvania. Available at http://ssrn.com/abstract=1403983

Sun, F. 2014. "The Dual Political Effects of Foreign Direct Investment in Developing Countries." *The Journal of Developing Areas* 48, no. 1, pp. 107–25.

Sunkel, O. 1969. "National Development Policy and External Dependence in Latin America." *The Journal of Development Studies* 6, no. 1, pp. 23–48.

Thies, C.G., and M.D. Nieman. 2017. *Rising Powers and Foreign Policy Revisionism: Understanding BRICS Identity and Behavior Through Time.* University of Michigan Press.

Wallerstein, I. 2011. *The Modern World-system I: Capitalist Agriculture and the Origins of the European World-Economy in the Sixteenth Century*, 1 Vols. University of California Press.

Yaziji, M., and J. Doh. 2009. *NGOs and Corporations: Conflict and Collaborations.* Cambridge University Press.

CHAPTER 3

Determinants of Foreign Direct Investment

There has been a large number of variables used as determinants of FDI by researchers across the globe. The study here attempts to identify the most significant determinants of FDI or else suggested other determinants because they make sense intuitively. Enabling institutional environment plays a very crucial role in attracting FDI. It reflects various dimensions of the political climate including national governmental policies, regulations, and so on; economic environments such as the structure of the domestic factor markets, market size, and so on, and socio-cultural environments such as informal norms, values, and beliefs. Several of the variables identified as determinants of FDI by researchers emerge in the UNCTAD's (1998) classification of the determinants of inward FDI. UNCTAD (1988) has also broadly classified determinants under three groups as economic factors, political factors, and business facilitation factors (Annexure I). The determinants in this chapter are also broadly classified under these three heads.

The Role of Institutional Environments for Foreign Direct Investment

The international debate mostly centers on economic determinants of FDI while analyzing FDI in developing countries. Since the 1980s, following major reforms, development along with economic growth became the primary concern in the West. Several countries adopted geopolitical changes and focused on the quality of domestic institutions to attract overseas investment. The United Nations Conference on Environment and Development (UNCED) in Rio de Janeiro in 1992 reinforced the growing concern for economic developments on the ground of increasing trade between the developed and developing economies. UN also supported establishment of the WTO in 1995. The vigilance by civil societies and NGOs also gained impetus on the pretext of rising international business. They inquired the cost-benefit ratios, and so on, associated with the business, especially in the context of an unprecedented challenge of development for the poor and underdeveloped economies.

FDI is preferred for much-needed technology transfer and managerial resources from the MNEs in the developing nations. Most of the developing economies do not have an appropriate institutional, legal and administrative device for incoming FDI into their core sectors rather public policy is somewhat based on the type of FDI project. The need of an hour is sound institutional environments including efficient public administration, legal systems, timely delivery of justice, economic freedom, political stability, protection of civil and political liberties, protection of property rights, lower level of corruption, and transparent financial markets, among others for the developing country to benefit from the FDI inflow.

Developing countries with different types of governance infrastructure, presenting certain business risks to the overseas investors, made it challenging to enter bilateral, regional or even multilateral trade agreements. MNEs indeed operate in the developing countries to take advantage of market imperfection nevertheless; they are cautious about the undue risks associated with numerous vital governance dimensions. In 1977, Coca Cola and IBM were driven out of India (though they returned in the mid-1990s) mainly due to the operating political ideology of nationalism prevalent during that time.

Institutional environment in the developing nations encourages FDI inflow through transparent rules and regulations, taxation, the ease of doing business and enforcement of contract among others. Several studies indicate that the institutional factors have positively impacted FDI inflow in Europe, ASEAN, and Africa countries though factors like corruption have a negative impact on FDI inflow. Development as Freedom (1999) was Amartya Sen's first and most widely read book after receiving the Nobel Prize. The book argues that development should not be viewed in terms of economic measures (e.g. GDP growth, average annual income) but in terms of the real freedoms that the people can enjoy such as economic facilities and social opportunities. He emphasized the relation between FDI and economic, political, and social opportunities. Stiglitz (1998) also believed that the process of development should ensure the transformation of society; focusing merely on economic growth was not enough instead non-market factors and spheres should also be given much weight-age. He also emphasized the role of institutions toward protecting property rights, the rule of law and social infrastructure.

Economic Determinants

The economic factors of any nation such as its market size, growth rate, and the quality of infrastructure, labor market, human capital, and exchange rate play a very crucial role in attracting inward FDI. The detailed descriptions of these variables are in this chapter.

Market Size

The economic literature on FDI and international trade considers the size of the host country market to be a fundamental determinant of investment and trade flows. Market size as measured by GDP or GDP per capita is an adequate and robust determinant of FDI. It's quite evident through statistical data that market size matters, because the world's 10 largest economies attracted 47 percent of FDI inflows in 2016 with the United States and China being the two top FDI destinations and this has been the case even in earlier times.

According to Kusi et al. (2011) market growth potential is more important than market size especially for developing and transition economies. The economic growth prospects driven by growing population and income offer high potential returns to foreign investors, leading to the FDI boom in the world's leading emerging markets. The emerging BRICS economies; Brazil, Russian Federation, India, China, and South Africa have experienced huge FDI inflow over the last couple of years. The market potential is an indicator of the future prosperity of any developing region. It also holds for Sub-Saharan Africa countries as well, given its high and relatively stable GDP growth in recent years. Researches argue that African countries have more high-return investment opportunities than any other developing region. It is a significant determinant for horizontal FDI unlike for vertical FDI. Market-seeking FDI that aims to serve local and regional markets, also called horizontal FDI, replicates the production facilities in the host country. Horizontal FDI targets to serve a local market by domestic production, making market size and market growth a critical determinant. The size-of-market hypothesis as proposed by Balassa (1966), and later by Scaperlanda and Mauer (1969), argues that the FDI is driven by the zeal of capture economies of scale in the broad markets. Countries with larger and expanding markets and higher purchasing power attract greater FDI on the presumption of receiving a higher return on the capital. Large markets primarily support efficient utilization of resources and exploitation of economies of scale; however, it might be the middle class in the host country that plays a significant role in attracting FDI. Consecutively, this also suggests that the distribution of income within the host country is also essential in determining inter-national investment and trade patterns. The high potential of the Indian market driven by an emerging middle class is one of the critical factors that attract FDI.

The higher GDP per capita or large market size implies better pros-pects for FDI in the host country though small countries can also attract FDI in a better manner through a coalition, that is, by achieving large market size. Regional economic co-operation also support FDI by enhancing political stability. They restrict membership only to select dem-ocratic government and ensure proper coordination of policies among member countries. Reduced corruption and implementation of sound and stable macroeconomic policies with investor friendly framework tend to attract more FDI. In the 1990s many developed and developing countries opted for regional trade agreements (RTAs). RTAs provide the benefits of free trade within the confined regional group including the exploitation of comparative advantage with partner countries, increased competition leading to greater efficiency, and a broader market allowing the exploitation of economies of scale. These efficiency gains result in boosting growth, apart from domestic and foreign investment. In many instances, FDI may act as an essential catalyst for these dynamic benefits to materialize. FDI is also valued for creating employment and generating incentives for domestic producers in terms of technology and knowhow to increase their efficiency.

Growth Rate

The net effect of economic growth on FDI is theoretically ambiguous as economic growth impacts FDI differently i.e., positively, negatively or may be neutral in different situations. Economic growth is an incentive for foreign investment as a higher economic growth rate leads to a higher level of aggregate demand and more excellent opportunities for making profits. A higher economic growth rate signals the size of the potential market, which could be expanded in the future. Cost efficiency of production and realization of economies of scale and scope in production are closely related to the market size especially in the country that is continually growing in terms of GDP. Economic growth motivates foreign firms to set off new projects or new production facilities. Regions that are experiencing rapid economic growth are generating more profitable opportunities and are quite promising in terms of market expansion and profit generation. FDI attracted by economic growth generally caters to the recipient nation's domestic market rather than for exports. It caters more to the horizontal FDI where economies of scale are more crucial, unlike vertical FDI.

Negative associations between FDI and growth results due to the scaling effect; economies that grow at a faster rate than the growth in FDI will experience a decrease in FDI as a percentage of GDP. In some instances, low economic growth is also associated with high FDI. The recession in early 1980, results in increased FDI flow to the number of industrialized nations. A negative association can also surface if low economic growth means more significant opportunities for future profits. For instance, an opportunist foreign investor would invest in a low growth economy with relatively poor capital but an abundant supply of cheap labor and natural resources to reap underutilized resources and realize unexploited future opportunities for profit. Instances were economic growth and FDI shows no relation indicates the export-oriented and extractive motives for FDI. It is quite likely that market size and market growth might not be important considerations for export-oriented and extractive motives for FDI as export-oriented FDI is motivated by factor-price differentials, such as labor cost and transportation cost while extractive FDI looks forward to mineral-rich countries. For example, in Africa, extractive FDI is located in several mineral-rich countries, where market size and growth rate are not the principal motivation for FDI. Growth rate could be one of the critical factors that attract foreign investments nevertheless foreign investment, in turn, could also lead to the growth of a nation, which is equally beneficial for the foreign investor and the host nation. A growing economy is home to burgeoning market and rising demand.

Modernization theories based on neo-classical and endogenous growth theories suggest that foreign investment is capable of promoting economic growth in developing nations. The neo-classical view argues that capital is required for growth and FDI facilitates capital flows and hence growth. The endogenous view suggests that there are technology and knowledge transfer via FDI which eventually develops absorptive capacity in the host economy (the efficiency effect). Dependency theorists, on the contrary, argue that FDI has an adverse impact on growth. According to them, FDI crowds out domestic investment as the local firms cannot compete in terms of financial resources, size and market power of the MNEs. Further, they believe that there are differences between the objectives of foreign investors and the host government on FDI involvement. There are instances when most of these theories are justified in some form or the other, but the most important take away lies in understanding the circumstances that a nation provides or creates when promoting FDI. The country needs to encourage absorptive capacities to benefit from foreign investments the most.

Several studies have also examined the impact on FDI on different sectors; for instance, there is ambiguity related to its effect on the services sector as compared to the manufacturing sector. Manufacturing sector seems to benefit largely on account of absorption effect. The focal point of debate is whether there is any linkage between FDI enhancing the absorptive capacity of the host country and thereby reaping additional benefits. It is quite likely that the FDI may promote growth through backward linkage yet other factors such as human capital and market size are equally crucial for such an effect to take place. The backward linkages may arise when the MNE procures intermediate inputs from the domestic suppliers whereas the forward linkages arise when the foreign supplier provide goods to the local firm in the upstream sector. FDI due to its inherent advantages would open up markets which otherwise would remain dormant. It may encourage local entrepreneurship and domestic investment and improve productivity levels in the host country. It is evident that in the 1980s, economies promoting export competitiveness were primarily benefitted by the FDI inflow, needless to say, that the host economies need to upgrade to the next level of absorptive capacity to reap benefits. Growth rate and market size of host economies are thus the prominent factors determining the locational aspect of FDI.

In developing counties, FDI is considered as a developmental tool to attain self-reliance in various sectors apart from the overall progress of the economy. India after liberalization in 1991, witnessed massive inflow of FDI where market size and economic growth have certainly played a vital role. Empirical work in the more recent times has documented specific effects of FDI on economic growth in the manufacturing, natural resource, and services sector. In the primary sector the evidence is contrary, in service sector too there are ambiguities, and some evidence of inconsequential impact has been indicated. Several researchers (Chen et al. 2015; Masron et al. 2012; Wong and Tang 2011) have reported a positive correlation between FDI and manufacturing sector and hence the overall economic growth. These studies also note that the relative capacities of the host economies as the primary recipients' of FDI vary considerably for a variety of reasons. They also seem to suggest that many segments of the host economies do not benefit in expected proportions due to the specific and unique constraints of public, institutional and regulatory policy, legal limitations and the particular political regimes in vogue.

Moreover, the studies also document the fact that public policies for FDI especially, in the context of poor and developing countries, resulting in some competition for attracting FDI without preparing the local segments of economies for absorbing the likely impact of FDI in the medium to long term. Industrial and trade policies along with appropriate governance structures (among other determinants) decide certain types of linkages and effects of FDI on economic growth. Furthermore, it is essential to identify the sector in which FDI is encouraged by the host economies as sector-specific FDI has a different impact on both in developing and developed economies. It requires a thorough understanding of the spillover effects related to productivity, technology, and knowledge.

We also note that FDI objectives are essential because FDI can be only one of the instruments of economic growth; it's not a panacea for several problems of development of particular countries.

Evidence supports that FDI facilitates the transfer of technology from the developed to the developing nations and the process of human capital formation. It improves the institutional environment; and foreign trade by promoting the production of goods in an economy endowed with specific resources surplus (comparative advantage). The neo-classists view that FDI can only augment the income levels without addressing long-run growth endogenous theorist suggests that FDI may generate increasing returns on production via externalities and spillover effects According to some studies, growth-enhancing effects of FDI are more visible in countries pursuing export promotion rather than import substitution. Export promotion facilitates foreign exchange earnings, trade openness, and a better investment climate. A minimum benchmark rate of human capital formation is essential for FDI to make growth-enhancing effects. However, as per the critique, this view is subject to the presence of good institutional environment.

An important issue that calls for deliberation as raised by dependency theorists is whether FDI crowds out domestic investment or is complimentary. The literature stresses the availability of sound macroeconomic policy and stability of the institutions for FDI to make any beneficial impact (fiscal and monetary policies). Studies have also documented that FDI may crowd-in domestic investment rather than crowding-out in the presence of enabling domestic policies. Dunning in its OLI paradigm pointed out that FDI contributes more to technological benefits rather than capital accumulation in the host economy. Further, there is evidence that FDI's productivity depends more on the extent of human capital formation which enhances the absorptive capacity of the host country compared to domestic investments. FDI promotes economic growth when financial markets are adequately developed. Literature supports the view that Greenfield FDI may augment the production capacity of the host economy by generating productivity spillovers.

The dependency school theory views foreign investment from the developed countries as harmful to the long-term economic growth of peripheral developing nations. It believes that the penetration of peripheral economies by large companies allows them to control resources that might otherwise have been used for national development. It asserts that First World nations became wealthy by extracting labor and material resources from the Third World nations. This kind of capitalism perpetuates a global division of labor that causes distortion, hinders growth, and increases income inequality in developing economies. Dependency theorists argue that developing countries are inadequately compensated for their natural resources and are thereby sentenced to conditions of continuing poverty. Countries on the periphery cannot be fully modernized as long as they remain in the capitalist world system. The Third World nations must develop independently of foreign capital and goods to get out of this economically debilitating relationship. Most recent papers advocating dependency theory perspectives use qualitative or statistical methods with a limited number of explanatory variables, in that case, the omitting of important variables leads to the potential for bias. Many do not even distinguish between the types of foreign investment, and mostly criticize direct investment and multinational companies.

The dependency theory was adopted by various countries in the 1970s, mostly by Latin American countries. A number of them chose an import substitution strategy and demonstrated a hostile attitude toward foreign investment. These inwardly oriented policies had a harmful effect on Latin American economies (Hein 1992). Their experiences contrast with some East and Southeast Asian economies whose policies were actively designed to attract foreign investment into their domestic economies. These policies correspond to a period of rapid economic growth in East Asia during the 1970s and 1980s (Hein 1992). This reality mostly curbed the popularity of the dependency theory, shifting attention to the study of FDI's contribution.

In Hymer's view, FDI is more than a process by which assets are exchanged internationally as it also involves international production. By putting forward the idea that FDI represents not merely a transfer of capital, but the transfer of a "'package" in which capital, management, and new technology are all combined, Hymer characterized FDI as an international extension of industrial organization theory. However, early theorists neither calculated the benefits and costs of technology transfers, nor explicitly analyzed their impact on a host country through spillover effects.

In the models of Koizumi and Kopecky (1977), Findlay (1978), and Das (1987), the superior technology possessed by foreign firms was considered to be a "public good" in nature that is transferred automatically. However, the growing importance of international patent agreements and the licensing of technology suggests that technological knowledge is frequently a private rather than a public good and that technology can rarely be automatically transferred. The model contributed by Wang and Blomstrom (1992) highlights the essential role played by competing host country firms in increasing the rate at which MNEs transfer technology. Both the MNE affiliate and the local firm can influence the extent of the technology transfer through their investment decisions. The spillover effect of foreign firms on domestic firms could be categorized into four types. First, the demonstration effect: local firms observe technology and management practices of foreign firms and imitate them for productivity enhancement. Second, developing domestic linkage: in this case the international firm develops backward and forward linkages with distributors and suppliers and knowledge is transmitted via these sources to the local firms. Third, employee turnover: when employees of foreign firms join domestic firms there are positive spillover effects. Fourth, competition effects: the increased competition from foreign firms makes local firms upgrade their technology and local management practices. Possibly this may also crowd out domestic investment if the international firm manages to divert market demand to its product or service. Researchers find diversity at the national level in terms of having a positive and significant relationship with the productivity of domestic firms in the same industry. The positive effects are stronger for larger local firms where the technology gap between foreign and domestic firms is at an intermediate stage.

Labor Market

A famous critique of globalization suggests that host countries lower tax rates, labor wages, and environmental standards attract FDI and hence the issue of race to the bottom. Foreign investors may prefer to invest in such countries and may engage in cut-throat competition for this purpose.

There are also implications for wages and equity; foreign affiliates will often pay lower wages than the domestic firms when low labor costs motivate the investment especially in an export processing zone (ICFTU 1999). Horton (1999) and Standing (1999) argued that some MNEs take advantage of segmentation in host labor markets, especially where the women are underpaid compared to men. However, UNCTAD (1999) reports that "there is no systematic evidence" to prove that MNEs actively seek inequity behavior and the empirical evidence on this aspect is relatively weak. The other prediction of the race to the bottom hypothesis is that countries lower their standards to undercut each other in attracting foreign investment. As the average labor standards by the competitors are reduced, the other external host countries will lower their labor standards in response. Countries generally attract vertical FDI by lowering these standards (Olney 2013). On the contrary, there is considerable evidence from both developed and developing nations that FDI increases the wage levels. Both unskilled and skilled workers benefit due to high premium wages; thus labors support FDI.

While the literature in general document that foreign-owned firms pay higher wages than local firms it is not necessarily true that they improve working conditions as the quality of the workforce may be different in developing counties. Again the issue has to be analyzed whether there are different implications for the types of FDI, that is, Brownfield versus Greenfield projects. The literature does not document much on the impact of FDI on non-wage conditions. There may be indirect effects of FDI on local firms by way of productivity spillovers as well transfer of knowledge effects in the labor market. Foreign investment could lower the supply of labor to domestic firms; in this case, the wages of local firms tend to go up. However, the evidence of positive wage spillover effects of foreign investment is limited. This may be due to the differences in labor market segments between the international and local firms or because of the limited absorptive capacity of the local firms. However, in some cases of skilled labor category wage spillover is evident. More recently more and more foreign companies are engaged in monitoring codes of labor practices in their supply chains to ensure compatibility of labor standards worldwide. Increase in labor costs arising from strong workers' rights varies between vertical and horizontal FDI. Increase in labor costs will hurt countries whose comparative advantage in attracting FDI is lower labor costs. At the same time if labor costs are lowered by weakening the right of freedom of association and collective bargaining or there are problems such as political and social instability it actually deters FDI (Kucera 2002). Foreign investment is also subjected to the job security issue, but it may be said that the MNEs are more resilient to uncertainties and shocks and therefore job security may not be an immediate effect and a concern in many instances (OECD 2008).

Human Capital

The neoclassical growth model by Solow (1956) recognized the importance of technical progress which was considered as an exogenous factor. It was indicated that the convergence in per capita income could only occur in the state when technologies converge. However, modern growth theory focuses on adaptation and indigenization of technical progress as a result of the accumulation of knowledge. Developing countries have potential to grow faster than developed economies for any given level of investment or R&D spending; however this growth is conditional to the economy's level of human capital. The human capital of a nation is largely determined in terms of the quality of labor force, experience, and the education level. Primary, secondary or tertiary education is generally considered as a proxy for human capital, as it highlights the skill enhancement initiatives within a country. Human capital signals the economy's ability to create new ideas and adapt old ones; therefore improvements in education and human capital are crucial for absorption and adaptation of foreign technology and to stimulate sustainable long-run growth.

Multinational firms exploit factor-price differences in the global economy by establishing skilled labor-intensive phases of operation in skilled labor-abundant locations and unskilled labor-intensive in relevant locations. The foreign investment flow to developing countries has drastically increased in the last few years; however, the bulk of the inflows have concentrated in only a few countries. Most of the developing countries aims at acquiring skills, management practices, and advanced technology through foreign investment for its long-run growth. However, on the other hand, foreign investors actively seek locations that provide them a multitude of location advantages with human skills as one of them and this could probably be one of the reasons for foreign investment being concentrated in a few developing countries. As human capital of the country impacts the locational distribution of FDI, government policies of enhancing local skills and building up human resource capabilities might play a significant role in attracting more FDI.

The human capabilities can be acquired and developed through education, training, health promotion and investment in social services. MNEs have a limited role to play in primary and secondary education however they distinctly impact the tertiary education in the host countries through the demand side. MNEs demand skilled labor, especially in natural sciences, engineering and business management, which creates demand for tertiary training and may also encourage governments to invest in higher education. Occasionally, MNEs also provide scholarships and sponsors the formal education of individual employee besides supporting the development of universities and related institutions in the host country. UNCTAD (1994) reports that the MNEs' "demand for highly trained graduates manifests itself in the form of financial support, particularly to business schools and science facilities, the provision of assistance and advice through membership of advisory boards, curriculum review committees, councils, and senates." In Thailand, several training programs are jointly driven by international chambers of commerce, MNEs, and the Thailand government. In Malaysia, several skill development centers are run jointly by the government, local business, and MNEs. Looking at the recent FDI trend, besides rudimentary education relatively skill-intensive training in production and services are crucial for the developing countries to attract high value-added MNEs hence it is indispensable to upgrade human capital way above the basic schooling level. Indian government too has initiated skill development programs for citizens to empower human capital and attract FDI in the manufacturing sector. The government believes that the future trajectory of Indian development depends on skilling India and boosting manufacturing within the country. The growth of India's software sector, ever since liberalization in 1991 is the result of the steady stream of trained graduates from several Indian engineering colleges who have been easily prepared for the job and has significantly contributed to both inwards and outwards foreign investments.

Employee development complements firm-specific advantages of foreign investments. The training and development of skills and knowledge are also extended to the other stakeholders of the MNEs such as suppliers, customers, and so on. The demand for skilled labor grows with higher levels of foreign investments. MNEs also support some higher level educational institutions in the host countries. Further, in the recent time there has also been a focus on capacity building in the services sector. Dunning believes that the collective action for problem-solving by the community is an essential measure of public participation and the role of civil society is critical in augmenting and defending social capital. Thus this view stresses both the role of formal and informal institutions in strengthening social capital.

The impact of foreign investment on human capital may be assessed in terms of host country capabilities to respond to the emerging needs. For instance, if technology transfer is of low to medium category, perhaps the local firms may not be able to react as the requirements are limited. However, if there is a vast technology gap the employees are unable to learn, or the difference is so broad that it deters the MNE from investing any further toward it hence; there is no prospect of human capital enhancement. Singapore, Thailand, and Malaysia are the prime examples where the government has invested in training and development of human capital concurrently while receiving foreign investment.

The issue of human capital assumed importance because FDI inflows to the developing world have increased in the last two decades. Mergers and acquisitions may not enhance human capital, but Greenfield investments are capable of doing so. Of course in conditions where FDI crowds out domestic investors, there are no learning benefits and human capital improvements. A well-educated workforce is probably looked upon by foreign investors as one of the location advantages. Human capital enhancement resulting in increased capacity of the employees to perform their tasks can lead to higher productivity and profitability. Nations benefit from foreign investment in new technologies and process innovations, as the employees are better equipped to absorb and utilize both the codified and tacit knowledge through which the benefits of such investment are primarily delivered. Human capital enhancement may also improve not only the ability of employees to achieve higher productivity but also their willingness, commitment, and motivation (Michie 2001).

According to the World Bank report (1991), a sample study of 60 developing countries during 1965–1987 highlighted the very significant positive relationship between economic growth rates and high levels of both education and macroeconomic stability and openness between countries. It indicates that the impact of trade and investment openness depends on people's absorption capacity and use the information and technology acquired. Analyzing a sample of 1,265 World Bank projects, Thomas and Wang (2007) reported the rate of return to be three percentage points higher in countries with both a more educated labor force and a more open economy than in countries that had only one or the other. To the extent FDI forces local firms to modernize and upgrade their technology, there are real technology and productivity gains. But in many developing countries only a few sectors exhibit this relationship. When MNEs and local firms are in direct competition, there are likely spillovers of positive nature, but this is turn also have implications for the host country's absorptive capacity. The positive effects of spillovers are not automatic; local firms are required to invest in R&D and capability building to reap the benefits.

Exchange Rates

An exchange rate is a rate at which one currency will be exchanged for another. It is also regarded as the value of one country's currency in relation to another currency and is an essential determinant of FDI. The exchange rates determine the amount of investment and its allocation across countries. If a particular nation's currency depreciates, the country's wages and domestic cost of production fall relative to the foreign country. In turn, this effect makes the host country more attractive for foreign investment. Depreciation increases the wealth of the source country's MNE lowering the relative cost of capital. Further depreciation in the host economy tends to improve FDI inflows in firm-specific assets.

Another view suggests that as the volatility of exchange rates increases firms will prefer to invest in local production rather than exports. But still the effects of exchange rates level and volatility are mixed for FDI projects. In the case of Horizontal FDI, foreign currency transactions are involved as home country replicates production in the host country; affecting the revenue and the cost side, however, in the vertical FDI only a part of the production is done in another location, so only the cost side is taken into account. Some studies indicate that depreciation in the host country's currency is negatively correlated to home country horizontal investor's profit, mainly when the firm is exporting goods to other destinations, well-established fact that depreciation boost exports whereas host country depreciation is positively correlated to home country vertical investors' profit, generally when the imports are involved.

Infrastructure

It is generally believed that a country with good infrastructures such as roads, ports, airports, and communication are likely to attract more foreign investment. Several researchers (Wheeler and Mody 1992; Asiedu 2002; Ancharaz 2003) acknowledged infrastructure as an essential determinant of inward FDI. Coughlin et al. (1991) and Wheeler and Mody (1992) in their studies identified transportation infrastructure along with other factors as the primary determinant of inward FDI in the United States. It has been widely argued that investors seek markets with a lower cost of production to maximize their benefits and a well-developed infrastructure with a potential of increasing productivity is often the sought-after destination (Jordan 2004). Studies conducted by many researchers including Asiedu (2002) and Ancharaz (2003) also highlighted telephone connectivity as a standard measurement for infrastructure development.

India allows 100 percent foreign investment in the e-commerce sector. Over the last couple of months, e-commerce in India has witnessed significant foreign investments such as Walmart, the world's largest retailer acquiring a 77 percent holding in Flipkart for $16 billion. According to a Deloitte report (2016) online retail is predicted to take a non-linear futuristic growth mainly due to exponential growth in mobile Internet and smartphone usage. Internet penetration in Urban India has grown from 60.6 percent in 2016 to 64.84 percent in 2017 whereas; rural Internet penetration was 20.26 percent in 2017 vis-a-vis 18 percent in 2016. It is evident that communication infrastructure has played a crucial role in attracting foreign investment in certain sectors in India. Poor infrastructure, however, can be seen both an obstacle and an opportunity for foreign investment (ODI 1997). It is often considered a significant constraint to foreign investment in low-income countries, but it is also capable of attracting investments provided the host governments permit more substantial international participation in the infrastructure sector (Demirhan and Masca 2008).

There's fire sale happening in Indian telecom during the last few years, and it has turned the sector into the hottest destination for FDI flowing into the country. One of the main reasons for telecom's prominence in FDI is the massive losses the industry has suffered in recent years, particularly since the disruptive entry of Reliance Jio in November 2016. Jio offered data and voice-calling services at meager rates that kicked off a brutal price war in the industry. In 2018, FDI inflows into communication services touched over $8.8 billion (around Rs. 63,000 crore), rising nearly 50 percent from the previous fiscal, according to the provisional numbers the Reserve Bank of India released in September 2018. This increase has for the first time helped the telecom sector to dethrone manufacturing, which had received the most significant share of FDI for the last nine years.

Declining profitability has forced many global players to quit the scene and other smaller ones to consolidate or shut shop. For instance, Telenor and Docomo have exited India. Aircel is filing for bankruptcy following its failed merger talks with Reliance Communications, which is also close to bankruptcy. Vodafone India and Idea Cellular have merged, leaving Airtel as the only major firm standing on its own. Companies are also putting their assets on the market to raise funds and absorb the heavy losses, This, in turn, has caught the attention of international giants. Boston-based ATC is looking forward to buying 20,000 towers from Vodafone and Idea. The two firms had put their standalone towers on sale after deciding to merge. Canadian investment group Brookfield had agreed to buy the telecom towers of the beleaguered Reliance Communications, but the deal fell apart after the latter called off its proposed merger with Aircel. Brookfield is now looking to buy towers from other players in the country.

Telecom's FDI share has also been growing steadily over the past four years since the Indian government lifted the 74 percent cap on FDI in the sector in 2013 and is expected to rise even in future attributing to the current sectoral conditions.

Business Facilitation Factors

Political Economy

A study by Pudington and Roylance (2017) analyzed the impact of governance dimensions of economic development, and the results were astonishing. According to the survey, populist and nationalist governments are capable of making significant gains in democratic states. The year 2016 marked the 11th consecutive year of decline in economic freedom. There was a setback in political and civil liberties and rights in many countries that reported themselves as free. Of the 195 countries assessed 87 (45 percent) were ranked free, 59 (30 percent) partly free; and 49 (25 percent) not free. The Middle Eastern and African countries had the worst ratings in the world followed by Eurasia. About 67 countries suffered a decline in political rights and civil liberties in 2016 compared to 36 that registered gains. In the past, the decline was mainly in autocratic and dictatorial regimes which merely went from bad to worst in the year 2016, and the relative performance of democracies was also on the decline. The free countries accounted for a larger share of the decline in 2016, and many of them were in Europe.

In the last few decades, the wave of nationalism has gathered momentum in several developed and developing economies as the political systems have experienced turbulence and popular pressures for macroeconomic reforms. Public protests against the MNEs in the developing countries in support of environments, health and child labor, and so on, are no more restricted to the NGOs and the civil society. However, the protest now represents a larger canvass of public views and beliefs that the MNEs conduct and operations in the host countries would be harmful to the domestic industries and the economies. In such a context the rules and regulations governing FDI would be stringent. In terms of political leanings, the left-leaning attitudes would welcome FDI for the positive effects on labor standards and employment as compared to the rightists who would want protection for the domestic industries. The moot issue is whether economic nationalism promotes economic independence. The trends of "expropriations" in the 60s and 70s and the prescription of "import substitution" indicated the firmly entrenched ideology that FDI projects would hurt the host countries' growth. But by the end of the previous century, there was widespread consensus that open trade could promote growth mainly due to the rapid process of globalization. But the bout of arguments for and against protectionist policies versus openness continued unabated after that. However, on the other hand, a view that gained popularity was economic nationalism by the political elites which included specific policies targeting MNEs as they control the definition of national interests. Since the 1990s there has been a wave of public opinion on the role of the state and its interactive implications for the society in general.

Individual attitudes may alter voters' perceptions about the role of the MNEs which in turn affect public policies of the host governments. The educated and skilled labor class, in general, may perceive the definite benefits of labor standards and high wages. But those favoring nationalist ideology will not subscribe to the likely positive effects of the FDI projects in the host countries. In general, the individuals' attitudes toward democracies lend more support toward FDI. More recently when the retired and the unemployed supported BREXIT in the UK the talk of economic nationalism was revived; but what about the other groups of voters and general people? What is the fate of FDI inflows and outflows to and from the UK to EU and vice versa after two years? The literature on the politics of FDI offers few explanations. A popular version relates to the merits of democracies versus authoritarian regimes as facilitators of FDI inflow; however, this view is contested by those who believe that autocrats provide more credible commitments to FDI. According to Li and Resnick (2003), constitutional constraints on elected representatives weaken the monopolistic position of the MNEs. The election rules on transparency do not permit the host governments to offer fiscal concessions and that the domestic investors may command far more comfortable access to the elected officials (for seeking favorable public policies) than the FDI, however, some have predicted that since democracies have lower political risks, they tend to facilitate FDI (Jensen 2003). Political risks are that of nationalization and expropriation, the possibility of tax rates revision, tariff rates, the imposition of capital controls and raising interest rates among others. These measures may hurt the profitability of the MNEs. It is also argued that democracy provides checks and balances on elected officials who in turn reduce arbitrary government intervention and thus the extent of policy uncertainty.

A particular group of political constraints is veto players-individuals or group of individuals whose consent is required to change the status quo. In countries where governments are constrained by governmental institutions such as those with a more significant number of veto players, investors are more comfortable in making investments. A study by Evans and Gereffi (1982) examines the link between foreign investment and politics through class conflicts. They highlighted the triple alliance hypothesis suggesting that the host governments, domestic and international capital owners collude to exploit workers. The traditional view suggests that local business would support foreign capital as it strengthens them, though the workers will oppose it. However, there is an alternate view which indicates that labor is more consistent in their support to foreign capital because FDI increases company's elasticity of demand for labor and due to this their wages and employment volatility also increases (Beitman 2015).

Incentives can be interpreted as direct government intervention in capital markets affecting the allocation of scarce financial resources and impacting government revenues. As per Li and Resnick (2003) incentives represent the transfer of benefits from domestic to foreign investors; however, contrarians view it as an indirect transfer of benefits from international to local investors. Further cherry picking by the government through incentives can give rise to rent-seeking behavior of foreign investors; also the MNEs have the market power to impact public policies.

India, an emerging country, has been globally recognized as an attractive FDI destination. Investors from all over the world have shown faith in the flexible Indian economy. Investor friendly legal and political environment has been one of the significant factors for a massive inflow of foreign capital and rapid economic growth in India after liberalization in 1991. The Indian government has undertaken various political and legal reforms to attract foreign investment, especially in the recent past. In 2014, almost all the sectors, barring few with specific caps, were opened for foreign investment through automatic route. The unprecedented growth of FDI since 2014, when major FDI reforms were initiated, indicate a positive relationship between foreign investments and the political environment of the country. In other words, the increase in foreign investment is also a function of a politically stable country, which overcomes the fear of policy alterations now and then, rendering more confidence among foreign investors.

Research and Development

New growth models stress the technological advantage of foreign investments in accelerating economic growth. While foreign firms may adopt Research & Development (R&D) to the local conditions: the domestic investors in the host countries also need to upgrade their technological capabilities. But the debate remains whether or not FDI induces more and innovative R&D activities in the host economy industries? Researchers studying the relationship between R&D and the process of acquiring it either by FDI means or technology import means suggest both complementary and substitution relationship. The view by Lall (1989) and Oxley (1995) indicate that technology import complement in-house R&D efforts whereas others including Mytelka (1987) suggest that technology import reduces the likelihood of domestic firms to undertake technological initiatives. Studies indicate that some local firms may also take R&D activities to enhance their absorptive capacities to benefit from FDI spillovers.

Ever since 1991 reforms, more firms are relying on technology imports rather than R&D investments. Maybe the Indian firms need more incentives to develop the required R&D to absorb benefits of spillovers of FDI? Post liberalization period witnessed many foreign establishments in R&D intensive industries, such as electrical, pharmaceuticals and electronics. Their subsidiaries in host countries had access to R&D facilities of their parent company hence focused more on adapting their products to local settings with relatively smaller expenditures. The FDI mode of investment will be considered as a substitution to R&D if the parent company of the MNE controls R&D then the FDI may not encourage R&D by the domestic investors in the host country. The relationship between technology imports and R&D is considered to be complementary when more imports of technology induce the local firms to adapt to the newer needs of R&D. The Indian government allows 100 percent FDI in defense industry; wherein 49 percent is permitted under automatic route and beyond 49 percent through Government route on the case to case basis, wherever it is likely to result in access to modern and state-of-art tech-nology. It is considering to further relax foreign direct investment norms to 74 percent in Defense sector through automatic route to attract more overseas inflows. During April 2000 and March 2018, the defense sector has attracted FDI worth only USD 5.12 million (Rs. 25.49 crore). The Government has opened up the Defense industry for private sector par-ticipation to provide impetus to domestic manufacturing. The opening up of the sector also paves the way for foreign original equipment manu-facturers to enter into strategic partnerships with Indian companies.

To overcome the various hurdles of defense sector development including measures to overcome import dependence, the government introduced several measures including defense FDI and promotion of private sector participation. A significant policy thrust in this direction is the defense offset policy which is expected to become a chief instru-ment for India to develop its indigenous defense manufacturing sector. According to the Defense offset policy of 2016, the defense purchases of over Rs. 2,000 crore will legally bound foreign company to guarantee 30 percent domestic value addition in India.

To fully exploit this opportunity and fulfill offset obligations, origi-nal equipment manufacturers and their suppliers should leverage Indian's competitive advantages in manufacturing and information technology by setting up units in India. A large number of Indian private companies and publicly funded research laboratories are looking for international partners. India has emerged as a global R&D hub with 150 of the Fortune 500 setting up R&D labs in India. A liberal Special Economic Zone pol-icy provides a competitive eco-system for exports through attractive fiscal incentives. Such a strategy would allow companies to fully participate in the Indian market as well as use India's competitive advantages to create a low cost regional/global manufacturing hub, as has been done success-fully in the auto sector.

Supply Chains

With the acceleration in the globalization process, the MNEs no longer view national markets as a standalone base to operate; instead, they tend to integrate with it the international production. As a result, we have vertical

FDI on the basis of fragmented production, and hence, the location factor has become a crucial determinant for global investment decisions. Also, the fact that FDI's focus has now shifted from market or resource seeking to efficiency-seeking implies the more prominent role for the global supply chains (GSCs) with benefits such as proximity to suppliers; reduced cycle time; competitiveness; innovativeness; improved quality; and better customer service, among others. The supply chain capability (SCC) is a measure of supply chain environments of an economy.

The quality of SCC is determined by countries infrastructure both physical and financial. Besides the quality of supply chain linkages the absorptive capacity of the supply chain network is also a significant part of overall supply chain environments. The improvement by way of SCC, in the productive capacity of low wage economies, attracts vertical FDI and the risk sharing alliances with the foreign partners promotes innovativeness.

The transaction cost theory, resourced-based view and network theories provide support for the SCC, in addition to the Porter's Diamond Framework. Dunning's OLI framework also discuss the competitive advantage of FDI. The supply side factors improve the attractiveness of the host country as a destination for FDI. Firms not only take advantage of reduced transport cost and international competition but also augment their knowledge capabilities globally for not only internalizing their operations but also build competencies. Production-related location characteristics matter more for vertical and export-platform FDI compared to Horizontal FDI. Further governance quality and the institutional environments also influence SCC of a host economy.

The rising importance of global value chain poses questions to the classic categories of motivations for international investment. In the last three decades due to increased complexity of international operations two new aspects need to be incorporated into the classic motivations-supply chain management and governance modes. MNEs bother more about managing knowledge within the suppliers' network so that their capabilities are upgraded.

Country's ability to participate in the GSC is a strong signal of its growing productive capacity; additionally, a strong relational linkage with the lead firm in a supply chain could also augment a transfer of knowledge, technology, and even financial capital into the suppliers' country. GSC participation of a developing country could enhance its productive capacity culminating into nation's economic growth however it is binding for a country to have some pre-requisite productive capacities which are mainly found in the middle to higher-middle income countries. Technology transfer within a GSC is not automatic as the lead firms, particularly those of products or production techniques with high intellectual property content may restrict technical and technological spillover to subcontracted suppliers. The investment strategy of MNEs also plays a significant role, for instance, studies suggest that during 1996–2006, a good deal of profits of America's lead firms' were financed through share buyback or a dividend increase to raise shareholder value, rather than investing in productive assets that boost productivity, growth, employment, and income (Winkler 2009).

Expropriation Risks

One of the political risks documented in the literature on FDI is that of expropriation by the host country government. FDI is vulnerable to expropriation in the resource-based industries; although the incidence of expropriation has come down since the 1980s. The timing of expropriation coincides with fluctuations in the mineral output prices. The act of expropriations is a deterrent for FDI. Though the frequency of expropriation across the world is fewer but countries like Latin America and Eastern Europe have reported many expropriations. Since the 1990s the less developed countries that have entered into trade agreements with mechanisms for dispute settlement have become more open to inviting FDI. Such a risk is more in mineral and petroleum projects. Even with such a threat, FDI is attracted to these countries because the host governments provide investment incentives such as compensation.

There are difficulties in valuing the assets seized by the host governments by way of expropriation as the data is not available easily; however the frequency of expropriations provides some measure. Sometimes the industry is nationalized so there are issues in counting firm level incidence of expropriations. The process of expropriations involves forced or involuntary disinvestment of assets by foreign firms though there are instances of "creeping expropriation" in terms of increase in property taxes, devaluation, fines, limitation on profits and withdrawal of licenses. But these are not accounted for when the transfer of ownership takes place.

The main determinants of expropriation are macroeconomic factors, political institutions, and external factors. Since 1980s IMF is actively guiding developing countries in public policy formulation. As a part of conditionality, the IMF insists on the adoption of market-oriented reforms by the developing nations. This, in turn, acts as a deterrent for the host developing country to engage in expropriations since they result in the violation of international property rights. Hence, there are minimal instances of expropriation by the host developing nations who are funded by the IMF (Duncan 2006).

According to Daniel and Healy (2012), the MIGA-EIU Political Risk Survey indicates that the majority of respondents in the survey denied withdrawal or cancelation of investments in developing countries despite prominent perceptions of political risk. Amongst the political risk factors; adverse regulatory changes followed by a breach of contract were the main concerns of foreign investors both in the short and medium term. Among those that do plan to withdraw or cancel investments, it was again mostly due to adverse regulatory changes or breach of contract. These two political actions were responsible for many withdrawal and cancellation of foreign investments in developing countries besides the losses suffered by foreign investors. The political risk that increases the most perceived significance between the short and medium term is expropriation.

According to Daniel and Healy (2012), authoritarian political regimes were linked to increased risk of expropriation. Sovereign defaults often caused by adverse economic shocks, were also related to the political risk of non-honoring the sovereign financial obligations. Both these risks remain significant issues for foreign investors amid the global economic slowdown and continued political instability. Historical, these events usually occur in waves and are typically associated with a shift of a country's external liability position in the balance between equity and debt. Following the wave of expropriations during the 1970s, a change to sovereign debt as a source of financing for developing countries culminated in sovereign defaults of the 1980s. Consequently, the defaulted countries lost access to international capital markets hence FDI became the dominant form of foreign capital flowing into developing countries. Off-lately, developing countries have relied more on FDI and portfolio equity compared to sovereign debt, suggesting the prize for expropriating private assets is more significant in the current scenario.

Corruption

Bureaucratic, administrative and political corruption can dampen foreign investments by diminishing investors' confidence and adversely impacting the reputation of the nation. Corruption represents unethical business practices, non-disclosures of the required information, market manipulation and lack of respect for local laws, predatory marketing methods, lack of accountability and transparency and absence of faith in the essential dimensions of good governance. During 1960s FDI projects in extractive industries of the authoritarian regimes in Africa, mainly flourished due to high levels of corruption in the political system. FDI projects in these countries exploited natural resources available in the nation, putting at stake the economic and social benefits of local stakeholders. Later in the 1970s and 1980s, these events gave rise to a different FDI debate: democracy versus authorization regimes and their impact on FDI. In the resource-rich countries which were otherwise ironically poor countries, the lack of institutional resources led to adverse resource curse effects. Nevertheless, smaller countries like Norway also managed to neutralize the resource curse effects by way of upgraded institutional environments (Odenthal and Zimmy 1999).

Besides corruption-related issues, there were also certain other issues about MNEs corporate power which mostly pertained to their supremacy in technological, financial and managerial resources. Corporate power is often abused when the host country lacks proper regulation mechanism, or their enforcement is weak; for instance, there have been doubts on the quality of some FMCG products, for example, Maggie of Nestle India in 2015 which led to an active intervention of the judiciary and the government of India. The MNE lost considerable revenue and corporate reputation after selling this popular fast food snack for over two decades in India. However; the worst example of absolute abuse of power was the cumulative neglect of the Union Carbide Corporation in India of their old and depleted plant which was known to be leaking dangerous chemicals. This resulted in the Bhopal Gas Tragedy on December 2, 1984. Further, the corporation which fought bitter legal battles in India and the United States considered some financial compensation for the loss of lives and the irreversible health damages inflicted on the citizens of Bhopal. The corporate accountability in industrial disasters across the world over is weak or absent; this can be seen in the oil spill cases (the Shell in Nigeria and elsewhere).

As the previous episodes reveal, corruption is not only financial but also non-financial, for instance when an MNEs project does not follow voluntary guidelines of the OECD, ILO, WHO and the UN on labor standards, human rights, health, and safety, and so on. They are then engaged in non-financial corruption which has a lot of long term financial liability for the stakeholders, regulators and the governments of the host country. Another form of non-financial corruption is deliberate default on the legally required disclosures and reporting for corporate sustainability. In the case of Vedanta Resources in Eastern India (Odisha), the forest land acquired for the project was resisted by the tribal's of the Niyamgiri Hills. This land acquisition deprived them of their economic, cultural and religious rights; the Indian Supreme Court in their judgment has upheld the appeal of the tribal's and directed the Gram Sabhas (village councils) to take prior consent of the indigenous communities before the FDI project acquires forest land. Corporate power is also abused by some FDI projects when they do not provide for adequate waste disposal of chemicals and other effluents into the rivers superseding economic considerations over the environmental damage.

Thus corruption means higher FDI costs with the necessity to bribe, which acts like an imposed tax. Moreover, there is an increase in uncertainty even after bribing related to the outcomes as expected by the MNEs. In the last few decades, there has been considerable NGO activism, with the print and electronic media exerting pressures on the MNEs. Therefore, the FDI projects need to be extra careful in dealing with corruption: there have been reported kickback scandals in military spending on the procurement of equipment both in India and other developing nations. However, corruption cannot be contained by a mere design of a public policy instrument. The actual incidence of corruption can be higher in the project implementation period: for instance, when any FDI project has an Indian corporation as a strategic partner it gets all approvals done by the partner firm but the major implementation issues are under their control which may lead to questionable business practices.

Some analysts argue that if the bribes expedite the clearances and administrative approvals, then corruption is beneficial in some context, however, in the long run, if the bureaucracy changes incentives and rules it may result in higher costs for the foreign investors. Further because of NGO activism and media noise if the foreign investor is caught in litigation, the costs may be substantially higher, and the damage to corporate reputation will be more significant. Corruption reduces the transparency of deals within the bureaucracy, and there is little guarantee that in the event of a dispute settlement the administration will be fair.

The Economist Intelligence published the first indices of corruption in 1984; this was followed by the World Competitiveness Report of the World Economic Forum. Since 1955 Transparency International has been releasing Corruption Perception Indices. These serve the purpose of making the stakeholders aware of the extent and implications of corruption for economic development in general. There is also an issue as to whether the corruption reduces the attractiveness of investment location. The evidence of China and Indonesia do not support this view but still the popular notion that corruption reduces the incidence of FDI persists. Remedying corruption requires fundamental changes in the institutional structure of an economy. According to Dunning, corruption is associated with other bad governance practices, and the FDI flows are highly concentrated in countries that are mostly not very corrupt, but there is a negative relationship between corruption and FDI. Studies suggest that MNEs used short term contracting and joint ventures to reduce the effects of corruption in telecom projects. Corruption also implies less or no transfer of knowledge and technology to the host economies. On the other hand, the pollution-haven hypothesis suggests that the lack of environmental standards would attract FDI as it might be cost effective with no binding regulations by the government. However, there is no empirical support for this hypothesis.

Policy Factors

Trade Openness

Foreign investments have provided strong momentum for economic development across countries over the last three decades. The funds supplied by foreign investors promote capital formation in the host country and trade openness is a significant factor affecting FDI inflows. Studies suggest that trade openness induces export-oriented FDI, whereas trade restriction attracts tariff-jumping FDI which aims to take advantage of the domestic market. Theoretically, trade restrictions or openness may affect FDI inflows both positively or negatively. Some policies on trade openness might produce a significant impact in attracting FDI. For instance, several Latin American countries were able to attract greater foreign investment through the implementation of free trade agreements (FTA) however FTA may not attract FDI in cases where external equilibrium tariffs are too low to induce foreign investment or because there are numerous equilibrium and countries are caught in one that does not support FDI.

The impact of openness on FDI depends on the type of investment. The foreign firms aiming to serve local markets may decide to set up subsidiaries in the host country if it is difficult to import their products to the country. On the contrary, MNEs engaged in export-oriented investments may prefer to invest in a more open economy to overcome trade protection and reduce transaction costs associated with exporting. Most widely accepted economic beliefs favor openness in international trade as a means to accelerate development. It suggests that countries with lower barriers to international trade or practicing "outer-oriented" trade strategies have better access to developmental benefits compared to restrictive culture experience faster economic growth. Solow's neoclassical growth model advocate technological change (an exogenous factor) is unaffected by a country's openness to world trade nevertheless new growth theories pioneered by Romer (1986) and Lucas (1988) provides powerful intellectual support to link trade openness to nations growth positively. They argued that the openness of the economy generates a greater ability to absorb technological advances from the leading countries. It provides access to imported inputs and new technology; increases the effective size of the market and promotes innovation and research development.

International Investment Agreements and Bilateral Agreements (IIAs and BITs)

Do these agreements promote FDI? The evidence is somewhat mixed. Despite strict investment rules why do developing nations want to include IIAs and BITs? Competing host nations see benefits of BITs and plurilateral agreements. Also, the fact that most counties are increasingly signing such agreements induces developing nations to follow suit. Thus competition among the host developing countries is the main stimulating factor. The developing countries are concerned about other developing countries signing such agreements if the agreements contain strict investor-state dispute settlement or pre-established national treatment provisions because these pose the greatest threat of potential FDI diversion away from the country (Neumayer et al. 2014).

According to the survey conducted by Zimny and El-Kady (2009) investors' confirms the importance of BITs and other IIAs in attracting the foreign investments as they are highly significant for MNEs in terms of investment protection and enhancing stability and predictability for FDI projects. The survey indicates that BITs coverage in host developing countries and transition economies play a crucial role in MNEs decision-making irrespective of the sector they choose for investment. In the recent past, the numbers of MNEs investment arbitration cases have increased many folds, where MNEs are relying on BITs for justice.

Developing countries with IIA's increase the likelihood of attracting FDI though at times the restrictions imposed through IIAs could prove costly to developing countries. They may constrict the respective nation's sovereignty by particularly limiting their ability to take decisive legislative and administrative actions to advance and protect their national interests (Salacuse and Sullivan 2005). IIAs need to be more influential and should aim to cover most of the host country determinants of foreign investment. Nevertheless, there seems to be a possibility to further strengthen the role of IIAs as an investment promotion instrument.

Developing countries can attract more foreign investors by making their FDI regulatory framework more transparent, stable, and predictable and secure (UNCTAD 2003). With a substantial rise in both inward and outward FDI flows from developing nations, IIAs are now being considered not only a device aimed at stimulating inward FDI from developed countries, but also as a means to encourage and protect their own outward FDI in developed and other developing countries. Apart from the growing South-South trade co-operation, several new IIAs have also been surfaced that cover trade and other issues. Many nations have renegotiated their BITs to promote investment conditions further.

Policy determinants such as IIAs, BITs along with economic determinants like market size, cost of resources, availability of natural resources and business facilitation plays a crucial role in attracting specific FDI to the nation. For instance, the combination of FDI determinants required to draw efficiency-seeking FDI is different from the ones needed to attract market-seeking FDI (Annexure 1). Determinants also vary depending on the economic sector involved, for instance, the primary sector, manufacturing, or services furthermore, MNEs, even from the same industry, may react differently to the same FDI determinants (UNCTAD 1998). For example, market size and growth may not matter for efficiency-seeking investors, which usually export goods and tradable services from host countries instead for them open trade policy, exchange rate policy and other policies affecting the quality and cost of infrastructure services and human resources are more significant. On the contrary, the restrictive trade policies with high import barriers especially in Brazil during the 1970s significantly attracted market-seeking FDI. Privatization policies are crucial for investors in infrastructure services such as telecommunication or electricity, as it determines the conditions of entry and operations.

Trade liberalization was expected to dampen the significance of market size especially for the domestic market-seeking and efficiency-seeking FDI in favor of larger international or regional markets, however; studies claim that market-related factors continue to remain a key determinant of inward FDI. The positive interaction between trade openness and FDI gives rise to efficiency-seeking FDI which is mostly limited to the manufacturing sector, in particular to tradable goods and services. The global FDI boom has primarily taken place in non-tradable services which is mostly market-seeking FDI (UNCTAD 1998; Nunnenkamp and Spatz 2002). Economic variables such as cost differences among locations, the quality of infrastructure, the ease of doing business, the availability of complementary local factors of production and the availability of skills remain the second most important group of economic determinants for inward FDI, especially in developing and transition economies. India is among the most favored emerging economy to attract FDI mainly because of its market size especially the mostly untapped rural segment, however; it is also working to strengthen the second most sought-after determinates such as infrastructure, skills, and so on, India has climbed 23 notches in World Bank's ease of doing business index to 77th place, becoming the top-ranked country in South Asia for the first time and third among the BRICS.

The majority of IIAs and BITs promote foreign investment by protecting foreign investors against certain political risks in the host country (Table 3.1). IIAs may impact FDI inflows by improving individual components of the FDI policy and institutional framework in the host country which in turn enhances the investment climate. IIAs also mitigate risks associated with investment in developing countries by guaranteeing foreign investors a certain standard of treatment and a mechanism for international dispute settlement. The IIAs of some countries like Canada, Japan, and the United States also grant foreign investors certain rights

Table 3.1 Key provisions of IIAs

General standards of treatment (after entry)

- Fair and equitable treatment in accordance with international law;
- National treatment—foreign investors must not be treated less favorably than their domestic counterparts;
- Most favored nation (MFN) treatment—that is, non-discrimination among investors of different foreign nationality;

Protection of foreign investors

- Guarantees of compensation based on international standards in case of expropriation of foreign property;
- Guarantees of the free transfer and repatriation of capital and profits;

Dispute settlement

- In case of an investment dispute, the right of the foreign investor to challenge the host country measure before an international arbitration tribunal.

Source: UNCTAD (2009).

concerning their establishment in the host country. IIAs possibly lead to more transparency; predictability and stability of the investment framework of host countries, and to some extent, they also serve as an alternative for weak institutional quality in the host country concerning the protection of property rights.

Taxation

The international debate on corporate taxation revolves around the issue of whether or not lower corporate taxes facilitate FDI? In other words as per the OECD: how does FDI react to corporate taxation? As per the OECD report, it is necessary to carry out a cost-benefit analysis of tax reliefs given for FDI and estimate its impact on revenues to the host authorities. As per the report, on an average, FDI decreases by 3.7 percent following a 1 percent increase in tax on FDI. But there are variations between and among countries of these estimates, although in the more recent times FDI is becoming more sensitive to taxation. The optimal tax rate on business reduces with a decline in trade costs and relatively more capital mobility though the extent of international tax competition cannot be ignored. If a higher tax burden matched by good governance and sound infrastructure conditions, may not constitute a disincentive for FDI.

On the contrary, tax reliefs and weaker investment climate are conflicting in nature hence generally do not promote foreign investments. The OECD also notes that there is a limited treatment of taxation to outbound FDI as compared to inbound FDI. Tax neutrality deals with imposing the same tax rates for inbound and outbound FDI acts as an important policy goal for some countries.

The Policy Framework for Investment (OECD 2005) has proposed guidance on 10 fields including tax for the developing and transition economies. As per these guidelines, the policymakers need to assess if the host country offers risk and return opportunities by meeting conditions such as public governance, political stability, fiscal and monetary steadiness and the prevalence of location-specific profit. The frequently used framework by the public finance economist regarding tax on FDI focuses on the parameter based marginal and effective tax rates (METRS and

AETRS) derived from the neoclassical investment model. This helps in measuring the percentage change in tax burden from a single or a package of corporate tax policy adjustments. Favorable tax treatment to outbound FDI may result in efficient access to foreign markets, production scale economies and spillover effects leading to an increase in net domestic income without impacting local investment activity. The local stock of capital should be maintained even in the absence of outbound investment (OECD 2007).

The costs of tax incentives could be the foregone revenue, resource allocation (neutrality) costs, compliance, and enforcement costs and lack of transparency. In some countries such as Ireland, Malaysia, and Costa Rica tax incentives are not found to be enough to attract FDI inflows. Uganda and Indonesia eliminated tax incentives in favor of a more general tax regime to draw (Clark et al. 2007). Tax is recognized as one of the essential determinants though not the prime determinant of investment decisions. MNEs share their income with the respective nation's government through taxes on wages, profits, property, and so on, hence policymakers try to formulate foreign investment-friendly tax rules to attract inbound FDI. The competitive tax environment of the host country ensures that an appropriate share of domestic tax is collected from multinationals. FDI is capable of boosting local income through spillover effects, that is, by introducing new technologies and the enhancement of human capital, that is, skills. Most of the nations are keen to attract FDI due to their positive impact on employment generation and growth of the country. Taxation policies also ease outward investment for firms seeking access to foreign markets and production scale economies resulting in increased net domestic income.

The tax incentives aimed at promoting regional and sectoral investments, performance enhancement, and transfer of technology. However, assessing the relative advantages and disadvantages of tax incentives is a complicated and controversial issue. The main difficulty lies in determining whether the incremental investment is indeed the result of incentives. For assessing the same, governments can develop an incentive system by clearly listing and analyzing the market imperfections along with the extent they believe these imperfections could be reduced or eliminated through incentives (Table 3.2). The costs of granting an incentive can then be compared to the benefits of removing or reducing

Table 3.2 Governmental objectives and tax incentives use offered

Objectives	Rationale	Incentives offered
Performance enhance- ment: Export promotion	Economies of scale in export- ing, country image building, differences between the actual exchange rate and the equilibrium exchange rate	Exemption from import duties on capital goods, equipment or raw materials, parts and inputs related to the production process; exemption from export duties; preferential treatment of income from exports, income tax reduction for foreign exchange earnings; tax credits for domestic sales in return for export performance; duty drawbacks, tax credits for duties paid on imported materi- als; income tax credits on net local content in exports; deduction of overseas expenditure and capital allowance for export industries; income tax reduction or credits for net value added, exemption from import duties on capital goods, equipment or raw materials, parts and inputs related to the production process; exemption from export duties preferential treatment of income from exports, income tax reduction for foreign exchange earn- ings; tax credits for domestic sales in return for export performance; duty drawbacks, tax credits for duties paid on imported materials income tax credits on net local content in exports; deduction of overseas expenditure and capital allowance for export industries; income tax reduction or credits for net value added
Technology transfer	Spillover effects, risk aversion	Accelerated depreciation on machinery; income tax reduction/tax holiday; investment and rein- vestment allowances; allowances for skills training; reduction in tax for royalties/dividends
Performance enhancement: Domestic value addition	Problems of supplier develop- ment, spillover effects to down- stream industries	Tax holidays; reduction from standard rate of income tax; loss carry forward and carry back for income tax purpose; deductions in income tax based on marketing and promotion; reductions in income tax based on total sales
Sectoral investment	Spillover effects, industrial strategy and policy, national security	Exemption from import duties on capital goods, equipment or raw materials, parts and inputs related to the production process; accelerated depreciation on machinery; income tax reduc- tion/tax holiday; investment and reinvestment allowance; allowances for skills training; loss carry forward and carry back for income tax purpose; preferential treatment of capital gains
Regional incentives	Shared infra- structure; equity considerations	Same as the aforementioned

Source: UNCTAD (2000).

that imperfection. Timely assessment of these incentive regimes will not only help Governments prevent revenue leakage by eliminating excessive incentives or unnecessary tax breaks to investors but also assist them in updating incentives packages to provide real value to investors and attract more investment.

The chapter attempts to explore various economic, business facilitation and policy factors, based on the literature review, which is considered significant in attracting foreign investment to a nation. Several empirical studies show a positive relationship between FDI and macroeconomic factors such as GDP, growth rate, labor market, and so on. The ever-changing factors that influence globalization have also affected the way MNEs pursue their objective of overseas investment. Openness to trade, FDI, technology, innovation, changes in government policies, improved firms access to markets for goods and services and factors of production and increased domestic competition has forced firms to seek new markets and resources overseas. Technological advances have motivated firms quest to expand their international production networks and explore promising markets across the globe. Through overseas investment, firms aim to develop a portfolio of locational assets that complement their competitive strengths. Besides the traditional determinants of FDI, several new factors are also given importance by the firms due to the changing global dynamics. The traditional motives for FDI are also reflected in the strategies pursued by firms for their internationalization processes. This book includes several case studies which will help you explore various discussed factors and determinants influencing both inward and outward foreign investment.

As FDI is considered a vital component of the world's growth engine, it motivates countries to attract foreign investors by creating favorable conditions or by providing ease of doing business. World Bank's, ease of doing business index ranks economies on their ease of doing business environment from 1 to 190. High ease of doing business ranking means the regulatory environment of the nation is more conducive to start and run an operation of a foreign firm compared to a lower ranking country. This index indicates better and simpler regulations for businesses and stronger protections of property rights. Empirical research funded by the World Bank suggests that the economic growth impact of improving these regulations play a significant role in driving FDI. Policymakers also facilitate FDI inflow by understanding the requirement of the investors. India recently improved its World Bank's Ease of doing business ranking by moving from 130th position to 100th position. It implemented GST and Insolvency and Bankruptcy reforms which are capable of substantially improving "doing business condition" for foreign investors. Hence, enabling institutional environment plays a very crucial role in attracting FDI.

The factors identified in this chapter are exhaustive and significant however many more could be considered as the requirement of the firms seeking overseas investment.

Annexure I Host country determinates of FDI

Host Country Determinants	Types of FDI Classified by Motives of MNCs	Principal Economic Determinants in the Host Countries
I. Policy Framework of FDI • Economic, Social and Political stability • Rules regarding entry and operations • Standard of treatment of foreign affiliates • Policies on functioning and structure of market • International agreement on FDI • Privatization Policy • Trade Policy (tariffs and NBTs) and coherence of FDI and trade policies • Tax policy	A. Market Seeking • Market size and per capita income • Market growth • Access to regional and global markets • Country-specific consumer preferences • Structure of Markets	
II. Economic determinants	B. Resource/Asset–seeking • Raw materials • Low cost unskilled labor • Skilled labor • Technological, innovatory and other created assets • Physical infrastructure (ports, roads, power, telecommunication)	
III. Business Facilitation • Investment promotion • Investment incentives • Hassle cost (related to corruption, administrative efficiency, and so on) • Social amenities (quality of life, bilingual schools, and so on) • After investment services	C. Efficiency Seeking • Cost of resources and asset listed under B, adjusted for productivity for labor resources • Other input costs of Transport and communication, cost of intermediate products • Membership of are regional integration agreement conductive to the establishment of regional corporate office	

Source: World Investment Report 1998: Trends and Determinants, table IV.1, p. 91.

References

Ancharaz, V.D. 2003. "Determinants of Trade Policy Reform in Sub-Saharan Africa." *Journal of African Economies* 12, no. 3, pp. 417–43.

Asiedu, E. 2002. "On the Determinants of Foreign Direct Investment to Developing Countries: Is Africa Different?" *World Development* 30, no. 1, pp. 107–19,

Balassa, B. 1966. "Tariff Reductions and Trade in Manufacturers Among the Industrial Countries." *The American Economic Review* 56, no. 3, pp. 466–73.

Beitman, A.L. 2015. *Distributional Consequences and Executive Regime Types: The Politics of Foreign Direct Investment Incentives* [Doctoral dissertation]. University of Minnesota.

Caves, R.E. 1971. "International Corporations: The Industrial Economics of Foreign Investment." *Economica* 38, no. 149, pp. 1–27.

Caves, R.E. 1974. "Multinational Firms, Competition, and Productivity In Host-Country Markets." *Economica* 41, no. 162, pp. 176–93.

Chen, G., M. Geiger, and M. Fu. 2015. "Manufacturing FDI in Sub-Saharan Africa." *World Bank Group*, available at http://worldbank.org/content/dam/Worldbank/Event/Africa/Investingpercentage20inpercentage20Africapercentage20Forum/2015/investing-in-africa-forum-fdi-and-manufacturing-in-africa.pdf

Clark, S., A. Cebreiro, and A. Böhmer. 2007. "Tax Incentives for Investment–A Global Perspective: Experiences in MENA and non-MENA Countries." *MENA-OECD Investment Programme.*

Coughlin, C.C., J.V. Terza, and V. Arromdee. 1991. "State Characteristics and the Location of Foreign Direct Investment Within the United States." *The Review of Economics and Statistics*, pp. 675–83.

Das, S. 1987. "Externalities, and Technology Transfer through Multinational Corporations A Theoretical Analysis." *Journal of International Economics* 22, nos. 1–2, pp. 171–82.

Delloit Report. 2016. "Retail FDI in India-Towards a Brighter Tomorrow." Available at https://deloitte.com/content/dam/Deloitte/in/Documents/CIP/in-cip-retail-fdi-india-noexp.pdf

Demirhan, E., and M. Masca. 2008. "Determinants of Foreign Direct Investment Flows to Developing Countries: A Cross-Sectional Analysis." *Prague Economic Papers* 4, no. 4, pp. 356–69.

Duncan, R. January, 2006. "Costs and Consequences of the Expropriation of FDI by Host Governments." In *2006 Conference* (50th), *February* 8–10, 2006, *Sydney, Australia* (No. 139524). Australian Agricultural and Resource Economics Society.

Evans, P., and G. Gereffi. 1982. "Foreign investment and dependent development: comparing Brazil and Mexico." *Brazil and Mexico: patterns in Late Development*, pp. 111–68.

Findlay, R. 1978. "Relative Backwardness, Direct Foreign Investment, and the Transfer of Technology: A Simple Dynamic Model." *The Quarterly Journal of Economics* 92, no. 1, pp. 1–16.

Hornberger, K., J. Battat, and P. Kusek. 2011. "Attractive FDI: How Much Does Investment Climate Matter?" Available at http://siteresources.worldbank.org/FINANCIALSECTOR/Resources/327-Attracting-FDI.pdf

Horton, S. 1999. "Marginalization Revisited: Women's Market Work and Pay, and Economic Development." *World Development* 27, no. 3, pp. 571–82.

International Confederation of Free Trade Unions (ICFTU). 1999. "Behind the Wire: Anti-Union repression in the Export Processing Zones." *ICFTU*, available at www.icftu.org/english/tncs

Jensen, N.M. 2003. "Democratic Governance and Multinational Corporations: Political Regimes and Inflows of Foreign Direct Investment." *International Organization* 57, no. 3, pp. 587–616.

Jordaan, J.C. 2004. *Foreign Direct Investment and Neighboring Influences* [Doctoral thesis]. Unpublished University of Pretoria.

Kindleberger, C.P. 1984. *Multinational Excursions*. MIT Press Books.

Koizumi, T., and K.J. Kopecky. 1977. "Economic Growth, Capital Movements and the International Transfer of Technical Knowledge." *Journal of International Economics* 7, no. 1, pp. 45–65.

Kucera, D. 2002. "Core Labour Standards and Foreign Direct Investment." *International Labour Review* 141, nos. 1–2, pp. 31–69.

Li, Q., and A. Resnick. 2003. "Reversal of Fortunes: Democratic Institutions and Foreign Direct Investment Inflows to Developing Countries." *International Organization* 57, no. 1, pp. 175–211.

Lucas, R.E., Jr. 1988. "On the Mechanics of Economic Development." *Journal of Monetary Economics* 22, no. 1, pp. 3–42.

Masron, T.A., A.H. Zulkafli, and H. Ibrahim. 2012. "Spillover Effects of FDI Within Manufacturing Sector in Malaysia." *Procedia-Social and Behavioral Sciences* 58, pp. 1204–11.

Michie, J. 2001. "The Impact of Foreign Direct Investment on Human Capital Enhancement in Developing Countries." *Report for the Organization for Economic Co-operation and Development (OECD)*.

Neumayer, E., P. Nunnenkamp, and M. Roy. 2016. "Are Stricter Investment Rules Contagious? Host Country Competition for Foreign Direct Investment through International Agreements." *Review of World Economics* 152, no. 1, pp. 177–213.

Nicita, A., V. Ognivtsev, and M. Shirotori. 2013. "Global Supply Chains: Trade and Economic Policies for Developing Countries." *United Nations Conference on Trade and Development*, available at http://unctad.org/en/PublicationsLibrary/diae2013d1_en.pdf

Nyen Wong, K., and T. Cheong Tang. 2011. "Foreign Direct Investment and Employment in Manufacturing and Services Sectors: Fresh Empirical Evidence from Singapore." *Journal of Economic Studies* 38, no. 3, pp. 313–30.

Odenthal, L., and Z. Zimny. 1999. "Foreign Direct Investment in Africa: Performance and Potential." *UNCTAD, Geneva*, available at http://unctad.org/en/Docs/poiteiitm15.pdf

ODI. 1997. "Foreign Direct Investment Flows to Low-Income Countries: A Review of the Evidence." http://odi.org.uk/publications/briefing/3_97.html

OECD Annual Report. 2005. Available at https://oecd.org/about/34711139.pdf

OECD, WTO and World Bank Group. 2014. "Global Value Chains: Challenges, Opportunities, and Implications for Policy, OECD, WTO And World Bank Group." Available at https://oecd.org/tad/gvc_report_g20_july_2014.pdf

OECD. 2007. "Tax Effects on Foreign Direct Investment—No. 17, Recent Evidence and Policy Analysis." Available at http://oecd.org/ctp/tax-policy/39866155.pdf

OECD. 2008. "The Impact of Foreign Direct Investment on Wages and Working Conditions." *OECD Conference Centre, Paris, France*, available at https://oecd.org/investment/mne/40848277.pdf

Olney, W.W. 2013. "A Race to the Bottom? Employment Protection and Foreign Direct Investment." *Journal of International Economics* 91, no. 2, pp. 191–203.

Puddington, A., and T. Roylance. 2017. "Populists and Autocrats: Dual Threats to Global Democracy." *Freedom House Freedom in the World*, 1–11. Available at https://freedomhouse.org/sites/default/files/FH_FIW_2017_Report_Final.pdf

Romer, P.M. 1986. "Increasing Returns and Long-run Growth." *Journal of Political Economy* 94, no. 5, 1002–37.

Salacuse, J.W., and N.P. Sullivan. 2005. "Do BITs Really Work: An Evaluation of Bilateral Investment Treaties and their Grand Bargain." *Harv. Int'l LJ* 46, p. 67.

Scaperlanda, A.E., and L.J. Mauer. 1969. "The Determinants of US Direct Investment in the EEC." *The American Economic Review* 59, no. 4, pp. 558–68.

Sen, A. 1999. *Freedom as Development*. Oxford University Press, Oxford.

Solow, R.M. 1956. "A Contribution to the Theory of Economic Growth." *The Quarterly Journal of Economics* 70, no. 1, pp. 65–94.

Standing, G. 1999. "Global Feminization through Flexible Labor: A Theme Revisited." *World Development* 27, no. 3, pp. 583–602.

Stiglitz, J.E. October, 1998. *Towards a New Paradigm for Development*. Geneva: United Nations Conference on Trade and Development.

Thomas, V., and T. Belt. 1997. "Growth and the Environment: Allies or Foes?" *The Journal of Social, Political, and Economic Studies* 22, no. 3, p. 327.

UNCTAD. 1994. "Trade And Development Report." *Geneva*, available at http://unctad.org/en/PublicationsLibrary/tdr14_en.pdf

UNCTAD. 1999. *World Investment Report 1999: Foreign Direct Investment and the Challenge of Development*.

UNCTAD. 2000. "Tax Incentives and Foreign Direct Investment: A Global Survey, ASIT Advisory Studies No. 16." *Geneva*, available at http://unctad.org/en/Docs/iteipcmisc3_en.pdf

UNCTAD. 2003. *World Investment Report: FDI Policies for Development: National and International Perspectives*. New York and Geneva. United Nations. United Nations publication, Sales No. E.03.II.D.8.

United Nations Conference on Trade and Development (UNCTAD). 1998a. *World Investment Report 1998: Trends and Determinants*. New York and Geneva. United Nations. United Nations publication, Sales No. E. 98.II.D.5.

Villar, D., and H. Conor.2012. *World Investment and Political Risk 2012*. Washington, DC: World Bank. Available at https://miga.org/documents/wipr12.pdf

Wang, J.Y., and M. Blomström. 1992. "Foreign Investment and Technology Transfer: A Simple Model." *European Economic Review* 36, no. 1, pp. 137–55.

Wheeler, D., and A. Mody. 1992. "International Investment Location Decisions: The Case of US Firms." *Journal of International Economics* 33, nos. 1–2, pp. 57–76.

Winkler, D. 2009. *WP 2009-5 Financialization and the Dynamics of Offshoring in the US* (No. 2009-5). Schwartz Center for Economic Policy Analysis (SCEPA), The New School.

World Bank. 1991. *World Development Report 1990: The Challenge of Development*. New York, NY: Oxford University Press.

World Investment Report. 1998. "Trends and Determinants." Table 9.10, p. 286. Available at http://unctad.org/en/docs/wir1998overview_en.pdf

Zimny, Z., and H. El-Kady. 2009. *The Role of International Investment Agreements in Attracting Foreign Direct Investment to Developing Countries*, 9 Vols. United Nations Publications.

CHAPTER 4

Public Policy and Regulation

The evolution of FDI policy is a consequence of the interplay of many macroeconomic policies such as industrial, trade, financial sector, labor market and fiscal policy. Each policy subset defines the broad contours of the economic growth process. As the growth process unfolds the economy experiences various kinds of shocks and problems caused by both internal and external factors. The magnitude of such disturbance is larger for an economy where regulations and institutions for economic development are not yet in place or else they do not have the core competencies to deliver growth. While tracing the modern economic history of the 20th century, it revealed that different model of industrial policies was evolved across developed and developing countries. For instance, while most developing economies in the 1970s and 1980s were struggling to evolve appropriate legal and regulatory framework together with conservative import substitution policies, the UK and the United States in the 1980s initiated a series of policy measures for privatization and deregulation. Similarly, the credit of East Asian miracle of the 1990s goes to successful export orientated growth models.

Further, the Japanese model of industrialization focusing on innovation and technological excellence in the 1980s introduced a new dimension to industrial competitiveness. Some Latin American and East Asian economies too introduced industrial policies changes in the 1990s. China accelerated its drive for FDI regime since the 1980s and achieved a record share of nearly 30 percent of global FDI by the end of the previous century.

In the case of developing economies mostly, inward-looking protectionist policies were followed in the initial post-colonial phase of development. Trade policies too were restrictive because the model was import substitution for most of them. It was only after acquiring technology for manufacturing and solving the productivity problems that these developing countries managed to export and earn the much needed foreign exchange. Similarly, most developing economies also had underdeveloped labor and financial markets which were some of the principal barriers to trade openness. Fiscal policy constraints also prevented many developing economies to liberalize their economies as the incidence of cumulative fiscal deficit was very high in many cases. Therefore, when we trace the evolution of FDI policy for any economy, it is essential to analyze the strategic choices made by that country's government against a backdrop of legal, institutional, regulatory and political economy constraints. Also, we may note that there is no particular sequence for the developing nations in terms of economic reforms through public policy. Most developing nation's liberalized industrial policies much faster than trade, fiscal or financial sector policies because in many of the sub-segments of industrial policy (barring privatization and rehabilitation of sick industries) they did not have to go through the parliamentary approval route as many decisions were taken by the empowered political executive.

But on the other hand, ticklish issues of labor market reforms need legislative restructuring and hence the parliamentary approvals, as is the case of India. In respect of trade policy, the agenda that was decided earlier to 1995 at the national level in the developing countries was shifted to international level as most countries became members of the WTO. The protracted negotiations of the successive rounds of WTO on many vital issues of trade implied a higher bargaining power of the developed nations over the developing nations. Through taxation treaties, regional and bilateral trade agreements have proliferated over the last three decades which have impacted FDI policies of the respective member countries. We may further note that the fundamental geopolitical changes since the 1970s have also impacted the macroeconomic and regional investment policies.

It is pertinent to note one more aspect of the links between FDI and macroeconomic policies, for instance; as a result of the Washington Consensus since the 1990s many developing countries had to undertake macroeconomic reforms; however, there were leads and lags in the timing of setting up institutions and preparing legislative changes for implementing many economic reforms. India, for instance, introduced reforms in 1991 but many significant enactments followed much later such as the patent act, disinvestment policies, banking reforms, tax reforms and policies for privatization. Therefore, the policy cycle displays as in the case of India uneven and sometimes very tardy progress as compared to already industrialized countries which are the sources of FDI. Also, issues like contract enforcement, transparency and accountability, good governance, and populism in policy among others are also responsible for the somewhat slower introduction of newer rules for FDI inflows.

The government in the developing economies has to be careful in avoiding the "winners curse" in the sense that the eventual cost-benefit rational of inviting FDI should not turn out to be adverse for the host economy. Without the potential threat of expropriation the governments, like India should develop mechanisms to monitor the MNEs. Countries like India also need to contend with issues such as land acquisition which is more often than thought the root cause of litigation between the MNEs and local community and also with the state governments at the decentralized levels. The government in the developing economies also have to worry about policy choices in dealing with the MNEs; for instance, fiscal incentives and other concessions should not end up suggesting "race to the bottom" policy (relaxation of taxation or labor standards or environmental standards) compounding the incidence of the "winners curse."

We are mentioning few observations on policy choices for countries like India which is more fortunate than many poor and transition economies and which has developed a certain benchmark human capital in many critical fields like science and technology. However, even with this comparative advantage, there are ideological biases and opposition to FDI in certain fields and the fact that appropriately handled FDI has the potential to improve the relative absorptive capacity of the economy, is still less appreciated. The Indian entrepreneurial actions both in respect of overseas investments (OFDI) as well as domestic enterprises in the manufacturing and services sectors have proved this beyond any iota of doubt. However, how this advantage should interact with trade liberalization and other macroeconomic policies is a vital question. The advantages of FDI are not automatic, and hence symbiosis needs to be developed as per a coherent and consistent policy framework. For instance, one of the public policy issues is to identify the extent to which the Indian government should develop its policy design to attract FDI in research and development (R&D) intensive projects? Similar are the issues in the agriculture and service industries.

An Overview of Macroeconomic Policy Reforms in India

Industrial Policy

Pandit Jawaharlal Nehru, the first Prime Minister of independent India, laid the foundation of modern India with a strong and diversified industrial base. He emphasized the rapid agricultural and industrial development of the country. The Government of India immediately after independence in 1948 introduced the industrial policy resolution emphasizing the continuous increase in production and equitable distribution. Following the adoption of the constitution and the socio-economic goals, the industrial policy was extensively revised and adopted in 1956.

The industrial policy resolution of 1956 laid emphasis on increasing the economic growth rate and pace of industrialization to achieve a socialist pattern of society. Acknowledging the state of capital and entrepreneurship base, the Indian states lead the direct responsibility for industrial development. Apart from other agendas, the industrial policy statement of 1973 identified high-priority industries to attract investment from large industrial houses and foreign companies. The industrial policy statement of 1977 along with decentralization emphasized the contribution of small-scale, tiny and cottage industries in economy's growth.

The main concerns raised by the industrial policy statement of 1980 were regarding the promotion of domestic competition, technological advancement, and modernization. The policy laid the foundation for a competitive export base and foreign investment in high-technology areas. The Indian government announced a new industrial policy in July 1991 to deregulate industry and promote the growth of a more efficient and competitive industrial economy. The government removed more than 80 percent of the industries from the gambit of licensing framework. The monopolies and restrictive trade practices (MRTP) Act was repealed to purge the need for prior approval for capacity expansion or diversification by large firms. The policy promoted disinvestment of government holdings of the equity share capital of public sector enterprises and narrowed down the public sector control to encourage more private sector participation in the core and primary industries.

Reforms in the 1990s

The economic reforms in India started in 1991 in the wake of serious balance of payment crisis when the government signaled a systemic shift to a more open economy and a larger role for the private sector including foreign investment. India followed a restrictive foreign private investment policy until 1991 and relied largely on bilateral and multilateral loans with long maturities. Inward FDI was the means to acquire industrial technology that was not accessible through licensing agreements and importing capital goods but foreign investment was permitted only in selected industries, subject to conditions imposed on setting up joint ventures with domestic partners, local content clauses, export obligations, promotion of local research and development, and so on, quite similar to practices of industrializing Asian economies.

Liberalization in FDI was imperative to attract a considerable volume of investments improving production technology and India's access to the global market. The policy then allowed 100 percent foreign ownership in various sectors except in banks, insurance companies, telecommunications and airlines. Automatic approval was granted to the listed industries up to a specific level of foreign equity, that is, 100 percent, 74 percent, and 51 percent. Foreign investment promotion board (FIPB) was established to deal with investment requests in other industries or for a higher share of equity other than the ones permitted through the automatic approval route. Later in 1993, the government permitted portfolio investment in existing companies and allowed foreign institutional investors to purchase shares of listed Indian companies in the stock market.

In 2014, the investor friendly FDI policy was executed permitting 100 percent FDI through automatic route in several sectors. Over the last four years (2014–2018) Indian government has undertaken several reforms in different economic areas. During this period 21 sectors covering 87 areas of FDI policy have undergone reforms which have resulted in increased FDI inflows over the last few years, setting up new records.

India recorded $55.6 billion FDI inflow in 2015–2016 which further peaked to $60.08 billion inflow in the financial year 2016–2017. The Government has liberalized FDI policy in sectors like defense, railway infrastructure, construction, and pharmaceuticals, and so on, but the sectors that attracted highest FDI equity inflows include services sector, construction development, computer software and hardware and tele-communications among others.

Trade Policy

The trade policy reforms being outward-oriented greatly emphasized the openness of the nation. Initiatives were taken to create an environment providing stimulus to export and reduce the degree of regulation and licensing control of foreign trade.

Prior to 1991, the imports in India were regulated by a positive list of freely importable items, whereas post-1992, imports were regulated by a limited negative list of 71 restricted items; however, all interme-diate and capital goods were freely tradable. During the 1992 budget, import duty was slashed from the peak rate of more than 300 percent to 150 percent and the initiative continued in the successive budgets. Government not only allowed export houses to import a wide range of products but also permitted the establishment of trading houses with 51 percent foreign equity to promote exports. During the 1992–1997 trade policy, export and trading houses were permitted through self-cer-tification under the advance license system to import duty-free items for export purpose.

During the post reform period, the government took several initia-tives to promote foreign investment in India. The government initially allowed 51 percent FDI in the specified list of high technology and high-investment priority industries through the automatic route, which was subsequently raised to 74 and 100 percent incorporating several more industries. Apart from the automatic route that required no prior approval from the government, FIPB was additionally set up to negotiate with international firms and approve direct foreign investment in select areas. Steps were also taken periodically to promote foreign institutional investment (FII) in India.

The main focus of 1991 reforms was on the formal sector; thus the sectors like telecom and aviation mostly benefited from deregulation and subsequent reforms. However, the informal sector comprising of small and medium enterprises (MSMEs) and agricultural sector needs equally more attention.

Fiscal Policy

During 1950 and 1980, both state and central governments had moderate fiscal deficits instead by and large reported revenue surplus. RBI initiated automatic monetization of government deficit during the mid-1950s. Nationalization of major commercial banks distinctively changed the management of the financial sector during 1969 and 1980. These two developments radically impacted the relationship between the monetary authority (RBI) and the fiscal authority (Government).

Automatic monetization of government deficits significantly deteriorated the fiscal situation in the 1980s. The monetization of large government deficits resulted in excess liquidity in the system followed by increased cash reserve ratio (CRR) by the monetary authorities to wipe up the excess liquidity in the market. The monetary authority, being the debt manager of the government, also hiked statutory liquidity ratio (SLR) to ease the central government borrowing requirements. The large fiscal deficit and its monetization widened the external sector's current account deficit in the late 1980s and early 1990s. The balance of payment crises in the early 1990s initiated the reform process in 1991–1992 when the stock of foreign currency depleted to support imports for barely two weeks.

The tax reforms, expenditure management, institutional reforms and financial sector reforms in the first half of the 1990s significantly reduced the magnitude of fiscal deficit and the proportion of debt to GDP during the period 1991 to 1997. The fiscal policy during the last couple of years, aimed at increasing investments to promote nations growth. The government focused mainly on infrastructure, agricultural and rural sectors by laying down the core developmental schemes and making higher budgetary provisions. The government aimed at improving the productive capacity of the economy and reviving growth momentum along with the upliftment of rural social sectors, where the majority of the population resides. However, the fiscal policy strategy stays rigid on the path of fiscal consolidation.

Fiscal responsibility and budget management (FRBM) Act was implemented in 2004 with the primary objective to control the fiscal deficit. The fiscal deficit was considered the major threat to the economic growth of a country by increasing inflation and debt burden. The government of India had been setting ambitious targets, such as eliminating revenue deficit by March 2009, reducing fiscal deficit to 3 percent of GDP by March 2008, and so on, however, they have been mostly breached. The present government, constituted a committee in 2016, under the supervision of Mr. N.K. Singh, to review the fitness of the act in aiding fiscal consolidation, the first time since its implementation. Fiscal deficits can be contained only through greater resource mobilization or by reducing expenditure. Resource mobilization is not very effective with plodding progress in narrowing India's tax to GDP ratio it has barely increased from 15.25 percent in 2004–2005 to 17.5 percent in 2014–2015.

How important is this fiscal target of 3 percent when the Economic Survey 2016 points that India's tax collection and spending potential are less than OECD countries and even its emerging market peers? It stated that India's spending to GDP ratio (spending on human capital, that is, health and education) is lowest among BRICS nations. Targeting fiscal deficit at 3 percent was indicated as a pre-condition for the member countries to join the European Union (EU) formation in 1992. Historically, even the EU's most fiscally prudent countries have struggled to achieve it, for instance, France breached it for seven years and Germany for five during 1999–2011. The review of FRBM act became even more crucial due to the turbulent current international arena signaling weak prospects of trade and external investments. Certain useful suggestions could help rationalize the expenditure and improve the tax capacity, that is, India's tax to GDP ratio.

The World Bank's Global Economic Prospects report (June, 2017) highlights the escalating fiscal vulnerabilities in some emerging and developing economies. The debt in more than half of the emerging economies has gone beyond 10 percent of GDP and the fiscal balance between 2007 and 2016 has recorded 5 percent depreciation in one-third of these economies. However, the tightening of the fiscal policy could impact both the private sector and government finances which in turn could slow down the growth prospects of these countries. India is credited for reducing its fiscal deficit in the recent past and is also working on the new fiscal framework to reduce both fiscal and debt stock in the near future.

Financial Sector Reforms

Why, when and how does the public policy for FDI in an economy evolve? These are interrelated questions. Before we discuss these questions, a few observations on the "why" part of public policy for FDI needs to be answered.

Countries at different stages of economic growth need different types of physical, financial, technological inputs to initiate and maintain a certain growth rate. Depending upon the political system, governments at certain development path may decide to "open" their respective economies to international trade in an incremental manner. In the case of most developing economies, the initial policy of import substitution and a closed economy model did not produce expected results which necessitated a review of macroeconomic policies making a prominent place for FDI. With the evolution of industrial development policy, governments acknowledged the need to broad base the ownership patterns and structures of enterprises both for the public and private sector. Governments created a necessary institutional environment facilitating basic regulatory and legal framework to achieve growth objectives.

The need for an economy to participate in international trade depends on many factors, though not in any particular sequence but some critical factors in the case of developing countries include balance of payments, capital account controls, current account convertibility, balance of trade, need for technology, need to achieve minimum export targets and a certain levels of foreign exchange. Theoretically, a country producing goods with certain cost advantages arising from relative factor endowments enables export, but there are also certain goods in which a country lacks comparative advantage need to be imported which in turn require adequate foreign exchange reserves building. Trade liberalization and the corresponding realities of globalization also reinforced the need for FDI, both greenfield and brownfield investments.

By the time India opened up in 1991, the country had already developed some industrial infrastructure besides skilled workforce (the relative human capital advantage), and with all the apparent limits to democracy, Indian economy produced global level enterprises in the public sector which enabled the private investors to capitalize on the same for further development. The relative quantum and types of FDI needed is assessed time to time by the government, and accordingly, a guarded FDI policy evolves. Indian economy faced several difficulties in legal enforcement of contracts and had limited sphere of government influence in monitoring the Indian private sector and the MNEs operating in India.

However, there are certain constraints responsible for the evolution of FDI policy in the manner it did. For instance, depending on the notion of economic nationalism at a given point in time, a particular government may be against encouraging foreign private investment endorsing a widespread perception that the MNEs are harmful to the indigenous economy. This resulted in the outright rejection of the role of MNEs in India. The tone and tenor of a "Swadeshi campaign" by any political party is consistent with their limited or negligible understanding of the process and content of globalization. In part this attitude also arises because the Indian government continued to be unprepared for proper policy posture from time to time; at least this was the case until the late 1990s. The true costs and benefits are not assessed objectively due to the political economy considerations: the costs are exaggerated, and the benefits underestimated to suit a certain political stance of the day which may have long term consequences. One consequence has been that in many segments India could not demonstrate that it has upgraded its relative "absorptive capacity," especially where the "technology gap" was large.

The "why" question can also be explained in terms of the Indian government's inability to align and realign industrial and trade policies including FDI policy consistent with changing facets of globalization. In the last two decades Indian government could give more emphasis on the services sector, especially the IT sector because of its human capital advantage but in the manufacturing sector, it needed certain lead time to capture benefits of globalization and FDI. Further, it is not the sheer volume of policy content but the need for a corresponding legal, regulatory and institutional framework that is the foundation of long term policies on foreign private investment.

Now we turn to the "how" part of policy evolution on FDI. The developing nations like India embarked upon economic liberalization policy based on the "Washington Consensus" of the 1990s. So in this sense, it was externally induced package for macroeconomic reforms as part of the "conditionality" of the package by the World Bank and IMF. Such "conditionality" focused among other things on the reduction in fiscal deficit, current and capital account convertibility, public sector reforms, and generating foreign exchange reserves. This was a formidable list of reforms in 1992 when the Indian government was precariously poised concerning foreign exchange reserves. The "conditionality" also emphasized on privatization and the Indian government's commitment to the process and content of globalization. Here lies the real problem, as in the absence of well thought out labor market and financial market reforms, the Indian economy was unprepared for any significant process of privatization though some initial disinvestment processes started around that period.

Also, the "how" part can be explained in terms of the cumulative evidence of international entrepreneurship by the Indian family businesses during 1960s–1990s. During this phase inward looking industrial and trade policies placed too many restrictions on the expansion of domestic capacity. Some family groups like the Birla's went out and set up foreign joint ventures in the nearby developing economies but this implied availability of domestic entrepreneurship, an important part of human capital, was not only capable of attracting FDI but also forming global partnerships after economic reforms. For instance, during 2000–2010, Tata's could set up many brown-field projects in the world. These examples also explain the "when" part of emerging FDI policies.

Special economic zone (SEZ) is another policy angle to analyze inflow of FDI. Asia's first export processing zone (EPZ) was set up in Kandla in 1965 followed by seven more, however; due to the array of control and clearances, the absence of world-class infrastructure and unstable fiscal regime these zones could not be developed as effective instruments for export promotion. In order to overcome the shortcoming of the EPZs SEZ policy came into force in 2000. To instill confidence among investors and signal Government's commitment to a stable SEZ policy regime, a comprehensive Special Economic Zones Act, 2005, was passed by Parliament in May 2005. It was expected that SEZs would attract substantial FDI in infrastructure and production capacity leading to generation of additional economic activity, export and employment opportunities.

The aim of setting up the SEZs was to attract FDI, which is crucial for economic development besides being a non-debt financial resource. India has liberal FDI policies allowing 100 percent investment through automatic route in most of the manufacturing activities except few like defense, nuclear energy, and so on. Compared to the North-Eastern Indian states, the coastal states like Maharashtra, Karnataka, Gujarat, Tamil Nadu, and Andhra Pradesh have attracted more FDI due to its locational advantage.

In the following section, we answer the next question: who influences public policy for FDI in the host developing economies?

Factors Influencing Public Policy on FDI

The Multilateral Institutions

The organization for economic cooperation and development (OECD) forum provides opportunities to the governments of 30 democracies to work together to tackle the economic, social and environmental challenges of globalization. The OECD helps governments to execute new developments and overcome apprehensions. The organization facilitates governments to compare policy experiences, seek solutions to frequent problems, discover good practices and collaborate with domestic and international policies.

The OECD guidelines for multinational enterprises are recommendations addressed by the concerned nation's government to multinational enterprises. They recommend voluntary principles and standards consistent with the applicable laws for executing business. The guidelines ensure that the operations of MNEs are synchronized with government policies, strengthen confidence between enterprises and the societies and fortify the foreign investment climate to boost sustainable development.

According to the OECD guidelines, the enterprises should adhere to the established policies in host countries where they are operating apart from acknowledging the views of other stakeholders. The enterprises are responsible for contributing to the economic, social and environmental progress in sync with sustainable development. They should respect the human rights of the people affected by their activities and adhere to the host government's international obligations and commitments. MNEs should encourage local capacity building through close co-operation with the local community and develop the enterprise's activities in domestic and foreign markets by ensuring sound commercial practices. They should also encourage human capital formation by creating employment opportunities and facilitating training opportunities for employees and encourage good corporate governance principles and practices. The enterprise should firmly adhere to the statutory or regulatory framework related to environmental, health, safety, labor, taxation, financial incentives, or other issues in the host country. MNEs should develop and apply effective self-regulatory practices and management systems to promote confidence and common trust between enterprises and the societies. They should promote employee awareness of company's policies through training programs and should not take disciplinary action against employees submitting bona fide reports to management or other competent public authorities. Encourage business partners, including suppliers and sub-contractors, to adhere to the principles of corporate conduct compatible with the guidelines and refrain from involvement in local political activities.

As defined by UN, "transnational corporation" is an economic entity that operates in more than one country or a cluster of economic entities operating in two or more countries. UN norms emphasize that transnational corporations and other business enterprises concerning human rights, 2003, are responsible for carrying out their activities under national laws, regulations, administrative practices and policies relating to the preservation of the environment of the countries in which they operate. They are also required to adhere to the relevant international agreements, principles, objectives, responsibilities, and standards concerning the environment as well as human rights, public health and safety, bioethics and the precautionary principle. They are supposed to conduct their activities in a manner facilitating attainment of the broader goal of sustainable development. UN also stresses on adhering to necessary legal and administrative framework ensuring compliance to relevant national and international laws.

The world commission on the social dimension of globalization was established by the International Labor Organization (ILO) in February

2002. The commission was formed to address the needs of people whose lives were impacted by globalization. The commission considered various aspects of globalization including the diversity in public perceptions of the process, and its implications for economic and social progress. It used extensive expertise to make recommendations concerning the economic, social and environmental objectives of the nation.

Multilateral Investment Guarantee Agency

Due to markets failures, innovation and entrepreneurship suffer the most and private benefits possibly lag behind social benefits. The involvement of public sector displaces private activity and unnecessarily dissipates limited public funds that could have been deployed for a different purpose. Seeking public support should ensure that benefits exceed the cost.

International Finance Corporation (IFC), a multilateral investment guarantee agency (MIGA) identifies six types of market failures (supply side failures, risk aversion, lack of competition, informational asymmetries, externalities and credit market imperfections) for innovation projects that supports innovation and entrepreneurship. Amongst them, the credit market imperfection is the most frequently cited failure. IFC aims to fix market and government failures that restrict the flow of FDI to developing countries. FDI is viewed as an important channel for the transfer of technology and a significant source of innovation in developing countries. MIGA's articles of agreement specify that its key mandate is to support the flow of capital and technology to the developing countries hence they aim to improve market failures associated with the lack of a private source of political risk insurance.

Most of the World Bank's projects on innovation and entrepreneurship needs World Bank's support to correct some market or government failure. World Bank interventions addresses four main categories of market or government failures: lack of supporting public services, incentive problems, information asymmetry, and poor business enabling environment (Table 4.1). These market and government failures vary across sectors and regions.

Table 4.1 Failures addressed by World Bank interventions

Failure	World Bank Group response
GOVERNMENT FAILURES	
Enabling Environment Restricted access to global knowledge. This includes overly restrictive trade policy, limitations on FDI, high taxes or prohibition of technology licensing agreements, foreign travel, and foreign education. A third dimension of government failure is corruption and or government capture by the groups it is trying to support	• Support to basic education, including higher education. • Reform of trade policies to encourage entry of and to decrease costs of imported products or services • Increased entrepreneurship and innovation to boost competition policies and regulation • Overall legal and regulatory environment
S&T policies Allocating government R&D effort to the wrong areas or industries, as well as using other government innovation instruments such as subsidized loans, venture capital, procurement, and so on. or to encourage private sector R&D through grants and subsidies in the wrong areas.	Support to S&T projects
Corruption and or government capture by the groups it is trying to support The first is a common problem in most countries. There are no clear solutions for this except for the citizens of the country to demand more accountability of their government and government officials. The second is also quite common in many countries but this is not generally the case with innovation support.	AAA
Incentive issues Innovators unable to protect their innovations from replication by others,	• Establishment or improvement of support of a country's intellectual property rights regime consisting of licensing agencies, patent institutes, and a general regulatory system for licensing and transferring innovation from elsewhere • Subsidization of research and development activities using fiscal incentives, grants, and matching grants • Helping entrepreneurs in the commercialization of their innovation

Information asymmetry Financiers unable to invest to bring innovations to the market because of lack of necessary information about potential markets *Incorrect perception of risks* Coordination failures when the profitability of one investment depends on an initial investment being in place	• Operation or subsidization of business incubators to help start-ups. • Sponsorship and support of enterprises for upgrading and innovation using matching grants, competition, soft loans, skills development, product upgrading, or export promotion Financing or support of venture capital funds using loans and grants • Support for enterprise upgrading and innovation by strengthening S&T information services
Lack of support for public services Inadequate public goods and services for the stimulation and absorption of innovation	Support to • Public research institutions and S&T parks for basic and applied research • Public research universities, particularly the science and mathematics departments and research labs • Metrology, standards, and quality control infrastructure including institutions, laws, and regulation

Source: IEG, World Bank

Note: AAA = analytic and advisory activity; FDI = foreign direct investment; R&D = research and development; S&T = science and technology

The objective of IFC and MIGA is to regulate market and government failures that curb the flow of FDI to developing countries which is vital for transmitting technology and innovation to the developing countries.

Policies Toward FDI in Developing Countries

The governments in developing countries are constantly on a lookout for best-practice policies toward FDI. The positive benefits of FDI concerning economic development and poverty re-enforced confidence in many countries to liberalize their FDI regimes toward the 1990s compared to their restrictive stand in 1960s, 1970s, and 1980s. However; the high-quality FDI does not guarantee the improvement of local capabilities hence it is imperative for governments to ensure maximum benefits for nation and society by encouraging linkages between local suppliers and foreign multinationals through various efforts such as linkage program or a cluster development strategy. Theoretical developments and empirical evidence show that the development of local capabilities is crucial to exploit benefits from FDI.

In order to attract more FDI, several nations link their FDI promotion strategy to industrial and macro-economic policies, withstanding their limited control over external factors such as natural resource endowments, international agreements, and so on. FDI policies could be a part of a broad developmental strategy based on pre-conditions such as the presence of local capabilities, endowments of production factors such as labor, natural resources and capital, and so on, and the degree of permitted state intervention. Once the country plans to liberalize the FDI regime, there is a multitude of policies by which a country can maximize profit and minimize costs.

Most of the developing countries have designated investment promotion agencies (IPAs) to deal with multinationals. The government organizations often being short of skills and experience to facilitate FDI engage autonomous organizations, quasi-governmental organizations or private organizations to assist in the screening and approval of foreign investments. They are responsible for building an image, generating investment and providing investor services and policy support. Apart from IPA's various other ministries and government agencies also coordinate with these organizations in the investment approval process. Countries generally adopt various lucrative policies to attract multinationals and improve the linkages with them.

Transparent Trade and Investment Policy

The EU trade policy broadly focuses on the interest and objectives of European countries and large firms. The focus on regulatory issues in the Transatlantic Trade and Investment Partnership (TTIP) negotiations highlights some threats to the EU's social and regulatory model. In the current circumstances, consumers all over the world are progressively more informed and apprehensive about the social and environmental impact of trade and investment along with their human rights. The effect of free trade agreements (FTAs) on countries other than the partner, especially the low developed countries (LDCs) has been increasingly examined.

Policymaking needs to be transparent and adequately respond to people's concerns regarding the EU's social model. The European Commission promotes a policy for society with universal standards and values besides fundamental economic interests. It emphasizes sustainable development, human rights, tax evasion, consumer protection, and fair trade. Impact assessments and evaluations are deemed vital for the formulation of sound, transparent and evidence-based trade policies therefore besides pre-screening; Commission also undertakes ex-post evaluations to analyze the economic impact of agreements after their conclusion.

Transparency enhances regulation and authenticity of the EU policy and generates public trust. It is crucial during trade negotiations especially involving domestic policy concerns like regulation. The commission adequately responds to these concerns by publishing EU's negotiation proposals, meeting details, and so on. The policymakers believe that trade is not an end in itself instead it is a tool to benefit people hence the EU trade policy aims to maximize these benefits. It also insists that in future the policies guiding Europe's integration into the world economy, like investment and regulatory cooperation, must align with the EU's broader objectives of protecting people and the planet.

Geopolitical Scenario

This note joins the worldwide debate assessing the political system which is best suited to FDI as there are different regime types with differing effects on FDI and therefore, economic development. The moot issue is whether the two frames: democracy and totalitarian system adequately explain the presence or absence of FDI and more recent literature extends this debate further. In the last few decades, unprecedented geopolitical changes have changed the nature, types and direction of international trade and commerce. There is an exhaustive list, but to name a few, the end of the cold war, the formation of EU, the fall of the Berlin Wall, China's entry into WTO and the rise of emerging competitive markets and newly found democracies in South Asia and South East Asia. More recently the world is witnessing civil unrest and social protests against regimes in Venezuela and Turkey. The considerable political unrest in Greece was due to the debt crisis; not to mention conflict zones of the

Middle East and West Asia; these, in turn, have affected international investment climate unfavorably. The tensions in the South China Sea and the impending political conflicts the United States has with North Korea loom large on investment horizons in the near future with irreversible consequences.

As we prepare this backgrounder, BREXIT falls out effects loom large on England and other economies dealing with EU and England. The main contention of this note is that political regime types and political environments are one of the most crucial determinants of FDI inflows and outflow. As per the FDI Intelligence's independent data, the Green-field FDI in the UK has been witnessing a negative trend with project numbers and volumes declining over the past two years.[1]

Policy Competition for FDI

The advent of globalization has implications for public finances both in developed and developing economies. Economies generally attract MNEs by providing tax and investment incentives. So in other words, when a country's government engages in incentives based policy competition, it is known as FDI competition or policy competition for attracting FDI. However, what are the effects of such policy competition based on incentives and tax reliefs? This type of public finance decision represents government intervention which may distort resource allocation in the economy which in turn may have welfare implications.

Further from the host country's perspective providing generous incentives implies extra-budgetary constraints and lack of commensurate rate of return to the state; which results in welfare loss to the society. Such a situation is known as the "winners curse" indicating harmful effects on the state finances. Many countries suffer from a "demonstration effect"— since other countries are also providing such incentives the host economy in question also should do so without regard to the future consequences which may be colossal and irreversible. Another moot question that

---

[1] https://fdiintelligence.com/Inside-fDi/Inside-fDi-An-FDI-Brexodus-edges-towards-reality?utm_campaign=August+2018+e-news+2&utm_source=emailCampaign&utm_medium=email&utm_content

arises is whether such type of incentives to the MNEs leads to the race to the bottom effects? As per the OECD analysis while in general the tax or incentives based policy competition is intense; but the intensity is evidenced only in certain groups of industries. Also, much of such investments are intra-regional, but at times these "distortionary effects" may go against the local firms.

Moreover, not all host country governments are capable of improving their infrastructure and other macroeconomic factors that may make foreign investment sustainable; in such a scenario the investors may not perceive the incentives to be sustainable in the long run. The adverse effects of tax incentives can be moderated by international cooperation that impacts the trade agreements; this in turn also can moderate the undesirable outcomes of the race to the bottom effects. For the host countries in the developing world, there is logic in following rule-based competition than a discretionary competition. Since in the last two decades many host developing nations adopted decentralization, it is evident that many sub-national governments also engaged in intense fiscal competition. As per the notion and practice of fiscal competition we may note that FDI does respond to fiscal incentives in developing countries.

The economic integration of regions through regional trade agreements (RTAs) has made tax incentives an important determinant for choosing FDI location. In 2007, several non-OECD countries including Bulgaria, Turkey, South Africa, Colombia, Israel, and Malaysia slashed their corporate income tax rates to attract FDI (World Bank 2008). Asian countries, including China, Korea, Taiwan, and Hong Kong, are also quite aggressive on this front. Tax incentives are quite popular instruments used by developing countries as they do not require direct payments of scarce public funds instead it is a tax provision granted to a qualified investment project that is deemed favorable for the country. The supporters of fiscal incentives for FDI believe that such investments would create jobs and generates economic and social benefits through positive spillovers however the arguments against such incentives are also numerous. Such tax regimes are expensive to administer, vulnerable to corruption, lead to transfer pricing and several other distortions.

Most of the developing countries offer fiscal intensives such as tax holidays to attract FDI; hence a better strategy could be to offer a low and stable corporate income tax rate to attract FDI from developed countries which could result in better governance and development of the labor force.

Trade Agreements

One of the moot issues debated in the international business literature is the implications of various types of trade agreements for FDI as agreements form one of the central planks of trade policy for both developed developing economies.

Why are trade agreements necessary? Historically, FDI has been between and among the developed economies. As the pace and content of globalization gathered momentum since the 1980s, the developing economies also started relying on trade agreements as a means to attract FDI. This facilitated internationalization of MNEs operations especially from the developed countries who were seeking markets globally. Further, economic liberalization implied trade reforms emphasized the need for an open economy framework, especially for the developing and the transition economies. Since 1995, more and more countries started joining the WTO which resulted in an ongoing series of negotiations on trade policy between the developed nations and the rest of the world. One of the advantages claimed for trade agreements is that they tend to reduce business uncertainties and investment risks for foreign investors. Trade agreements guarantee certain rights to foreign investors and contain appropriate provisions for dispute resolution and therefore afford a certain degree of investor protection. However, the present literature notes that such agreements in segments such as natural resources and infrastructure are exposed to the risks of "obsolescing bargain." Once the investments are made the relative bargaining power of the MNEs decline the host country's government policies and may alter the terms of contracts (changes in rules, regulations, tariffs, pricing, and so on) for appropriating more returns from the FDI projects. Conceptually such agreements ensure equitable treatment of foreign and domestic investors, in addition to protecting the contractual rights. The agreements also permit recourse to international arbitration.

RTAs assist the developing economies toward a higher degree of trade openness through their subsequent process of integrating with the world economy. RTAs promote most-favored-nations (MFN) liberalization which is trade creating and increasing the volume of inter-regional trade. The effects of RTAs can be better analyzed by studying the degree of fulfillment of the economic, social and political objectives. It may be further noted that regional integration is subject to reduction in tariffs for all the participating countries. Moreover, many such RTAs cover non-trade issues such as services or labor which can have significant long term consequences for the economic growth of the member countries.

Do the RTAs stimulate trade? The literature notes that the RTAs are trade creating rather than trade diverting, but there may be some exceptions to this effect. Moreover, RTAs alone cannot promote exports of the participating nations; hence trade and macroeconomic policies are considered as the other essential factors. RTAs ensure the benefits of technology transfer along with market expansion for the member nations. By and large, trade creation, terms of trade effect, market and competition enhancement effect are considered as the main economic effects of FTAs. Since the 1990s the RTAs have proliferated suggesting a certain priority over multilateral trade objectives. They promote regulations over and above multilateral agreements and promote South-South cooperation. One of the main reasons why the RTAs are preferred is the difficulty of obtaining consensus among the reasonably large number of members of the WTO. Also, there is logic in the argument that the RTAs better promote the regional interests than multilateral agreements. The objective of securing peace and stability in the region to achieve economic growth emphasizes the need to improve social and economic governance of the regions.

Countries promote vertical FDI to explore specific advantages of the factor price differential. A country with low trade barriers has more of vertical FDI than horizontal FDI. FTAs bring more benefits from vertical FDI than horizontal FDI. In the case of vertical FDI production and sales involve exporting and importing intermediate and final goods. Tariff charges on transportation add up to the cost of production however after agreement tariffs are reduced to minimize costs of vertical FDI enabling member states to enjoy a comparative advantage over the non-member states. Due to the FTA between two countries, there is a substantial decline in horizontal FDI as trade agreements reduce the cost of goods.

Nevertheless, vertical FDI also depends on the extent of human capital and trade openness. According to the WTO Report (2011), "the explosion of preferential trade agreements (PTAs) is not matched by an expansion of trade flows that receive preferential treatment. Further, the proliferation of PTAs means that the difference between the MFN rate and the PTA rate overstates the competitive advantage of a PTA member, since increasingly its competitors will also enjoy preferential access to the market therefore, one has to look beyond tariffs to explain why countries enter into PTAs." PTAs now include issues such as service, investments, intellectual property protection and competition policy which involves domestic regulation. As per the WTO Report almost 300 PTAs-notified and non-notified were in force in 2010 (Table 4.2). WTO member is party to an average 13 PTAs however only 16 percent of global merchandise trade receives preferential treatment, and less than 2 percent of the world trade is eligible for preference margins above 10 percent The first wave of regionalism appeared in the 1960s in Europe. The European Economic Community (EEC) formed in 1957 was a regional organization that aimed to bring about economic integration among its member states. Besides this other countries like Africa and the United States also started forming their free trade associations and the intra and cross-regional PTAs increased year on year (Table 4.3).The second wave was during the 1980s–1990s when Europe established a single market program, and BITs emerged as a prominent policy choice. EU then expanded into other regions. It is quite evident looking at the number of bilateral and plurilateral PTAs in force by 2010 (Table 4.4).

World Bank Guidelines on Treatment of FDI

In April 1991, the Development Committee, which was a Joint Ministerial Committee of the Boards of Governors of the International Monetary Fund and the World Bank, requested the MIGA to prepare a legal framework to promote FDI. The development committee believed that a higher flow of FDI would substantially promote efficiency of the world economy, especially the developing countries through greater competition, transfer

Table 4.2 Total and Average PTA in force by 2010

Total and average number of PTAs in force, 2010, notified and non-notified PTAs, by region, regional type and country group

		Africa	CIS	Europe	South America	Central America	Caribbean	West Asia	Middle East	Oceania	East Asia	North America
Intra regional	Total	24	29	36	13	7	0	7	7	5	17	1
	Avg/country	0.4	2.4	0.9	1.1	1	0	0.9	0.5	0.2	0.9	0.2
Cross-regional	Total	31	4	42	52	34	19	14	30	10	34	37
	Avg/country	0.5	0.3	1.1	4.3	4.9	0.8	1.8	2.3	0.3	1.8	7.4
Developed-Developed	Total	0	0	21	0	0	0	0	0	2	1	2
	Avg/country	0	0	0.5	0	0	0	0	0	0.1	0.1	0.4
Developed-Developing	Total	12	2	41	11	3	3	1	15	11	22	18
	Avg/country	0.2	0.2	1	0.9	0.4	0.1	0.1	1.2	0.4	1.2	3.6
Developing-Developing	Total	43	31	16	54	38	16	20	22	2	28	18
	Avg/country	0.7	2.6	0.4	4.5	5.4	0.7	2.5	1.7	0.1	1.5	3.6

Source: World Trade Report (2011).

Table 4.3 Intra and Cross-regional PTA in force by 2010

Intra- and cross-regional PTAs in force, 2010, notified and non-notified PTAs, by region and time period

Period	Type	Africa	CIS	Europe	South America	Central America	Caribbean	West Asia	Middle East	Oceania	East Asia	North America
	Intra-regional	2	0	2	0	0	0	0	0	0	0	0
1950-59	Cross-regional	0	0	0	0	0	0	0	0	0	0	0
	Intra-regional	1	0	1	0	1	1	0	0	0	0	0
1960-69	Cross-regional	0	0	0	0	0	0	0	0	0	0	0
	Intra-regional	1	0	5	0	1	1	0	0	0	1	0
1970-79	Cross-regional	2	0	3	3	1	2	2	2	2	1	2
	Intra-regional	5	0	1	1	1	0	0	0	2	2	2
1980-89	Cross-regional	1	0	1	11	9	4	0	1	2	0	6
1990-99	Intra-regional	12	25	10	9	0	0	0	2	2	1	1
	Cross-regional	11	1	12	10	8	3	1	1	14	0	8
2000-10	Intra-regional	3	4	7	3	5	0	5	5	5	15	0
	Cross-regional	17	3	3	26	28	16	10	10	12	9	21

Source: World Trade Report (2011).

Table 4.4 *Number of Bilateral and Plurilateral PTAs in force by 2010*

	Bilateral	Plurilateral	Plurilateral, atleast one party is a PTA
Number of bilateral PTAs and types of plurilateral PTAs in force, 2010 notified and non-notified PTAs, by country group and regional types			
Developed-Developed	6	9	8
Developed-Developing	29	6	41
Developing-Developing	135	36	18
Intra regional	81	39	26
Cross-regional	89	12	41

Source: World Trade Report (2011).

of capital, technology and managerial skills and enhancement of market access and international trade.

The framework lays down a set of guidelines which are not legally binding but significantly influence the development of international law in this field. These guidelines aim at boosting the confidence of international investors by minimizing non-commercial investment risks across countries. The guidelines recommend norms for member countries of the World Bank Group toward the treatment of private foreign investment in their respective territories, apart from the relevant bilateral and multilateral treaties and other international instruments. These guidelines are not final standards; however, they are generally accepted international standards which complement and not substitute bilateral investment treaties. The guidelines covered the four main areas frequently dealt with investment treaties, that is, the admission, treatment, and expropriation of foreign investments and the settlement of disputes between governments and foreign investors.

Performance of FDI in India

According to UNCTAD report in 2015 India stood at 10th position in attracting global FDI and was sixth most preferred investment destination. However report indentifies United States, China, and India as the top three prospective host countries preferred by MNEs for overseas investments. During the 2016 survey, the two developing nations, Philippines and Myanmar, were the new entrants to make place in the list of top 14 prospective host economies (Table 4.5). Among the top 14 host countries, eight belongs to developing economies in Asia and Latin America and the Caribbean, reflecting the longer term prospects of these two regions. Contrary to the list in 2015, Belgium, Canada, Ireland, Luxembourg, Netherlands, Hong Kong (China) and Singapore are not included in the list.

The world inward FDI stock has witnessed surge during the last two decade increasing from $3,565,318 million in 1995 to $24,983,214 million in 2015, however, the world outward FDI stock increased from $ 3,992,701 million in 1995 to $25,044,916 million in 2015. Developing Asia is the world's largest recipient of FDI and third highest outward investor with 22.5 percent share in the world's OFDI, though witnessed

Table 4.5 MNE's Top prospective Host Economies for 2016–2018

Rank	Country	Economy Type
1	United States	Developed Country
2	China	Developing Country
3	India	Developing Country
4	UK	Developed Country
5	Germany	Developed Country
6	Japan	Developed Country
7	Brazil	Developing Country
8	Mexico	Developing Country
9	Indonesia	Developing Country
10	Philippines	Developing Country
11	France	Developed Country
12	Australia	Developed Country
13	Singapore	Developing Country
14	Myanmar	Developing Country
15	Vietnam	Developing Country

Source: World Investment Report (2016).

a recent decline in the outflows (UNCTAD 2016). India has been a key contributor to these outflows by continuously increasing its share from $495 million in 1995 to $138,967 million in 2015 reflecting the increasing competitiveness of the firms (Table 4.6).

The inward and outward flow of investments reflects an integration of the world economies; inward FDI signals attractiveness of the country for foreign investors whereas outward FDI signals the country's competence to venture beyond national boundary. The subsequent rise in OFDI by the developing Asian economies is attributed to the growth of Asian firms. The surge in export revenues from manufactured products and natural resources have also partially fuelled the overseas investments which encompass a broad spectrum of developing countries such as China, India, Chile, Malaysia, South Africa, Venezuela among others.

The Indian government aims to attract FDI to supplement domestic capital, technical know-how and generate employment and skills to provide impetus to economic growth. Besides being a significant driver of economic growth, FDI is also a primary source of non-debt financial

Table 4.6 FDI Stock* overview

FDI Flow	FDI stock (US$ Millions)					FDI (% of Gross Fixed Capital Formation)			
	1995	2012	2013	2014	2015	1995	2013	2014	2015
Developing Economies*									
Inward	843 340	7 207 807	7 657 342	8 172 034	8 374 428	13	26.4	26.9	28.5
Outward	311 398	3 965 290	4 413 431	5 015 372	5 296 346	5.2	15.5	16.8	18.3
World*									
Inward	3 565 318	22 639 110	24 532 733	25 112 800	24 983 214	11.2	31.9	31.8	33.6
Outward	3 992 701	22 701 815	24 664 815	24 809 704	25 044 916	12.9	32.3	31.7	34
Developing Asia									
Inward	571 680	4 789 651	5 172 855	5 658 064	5 886 453	14.6	25.4	26.1	27
Outward	211 482	3 246 382	3 654 828	4 239 327	4 481 478	6	18.1	19.7	20.7
India									
Inward	5 641	224 985	226 549	252 817	282 273	1.5	12.2	12.4	13.5
Outward	495	118 072	119 838	131 524	138 967	0.1	6.4	6.4	6.6

Source: Exim Bank, Occasional Paper No.165.

* FDI stocks are presented at book value or historical cost, reflecting prices at the time when the investment was made. For a large number of economies, FDI stocks are estimated by either cumulating FDI flows over a period of time or adding flows to an FDI stock that has been obtained for a particular year from national official sources or the IMF data series on assets and liabilities of direct investment. UNCTAD, 2016.

resource for the economic development of India. The Indian government's favorable policy regime and healthy business environment ensure inflow of FDI into the country. MNEs mostly invest in India to benefit from relatively lower wages, special investment privileges such as tax exemptions, and so on. In the recent past, FDI norms have been relaxed across sectors such as defense, PSU oil refineries, telecom, power exchanges, and stock exchanges, among others to promote more investments. According to Department of Industrial Policy and Promotion (DIPP), government's effort to improve ease of doing business and relaxed FDI norms resulted in 30 percent year-on-year rise in inward FDI flow amounting to $21.6 billion in April–September 2016 compared to 2015.

India need more than $1 trillion to fund infrastructure growth covering sectors such as highways, ports and airways and requires support from FDI inflows. India's growth rate, along with competitive location in terms of wages and policies like Stand-up India, is expected to boost FDI in the coming future.

The government of India recently abolished FIPB, an inter-ministerial body housed in the Department of Economic Affairs in the finance ministry. It was responsible for processing and recommending FDI proposals for approvals to the finance minister and subsequently to the Cabinet Committee on Economic Affairs if the investment amount exceeded Rs. 3,000 crore. Abolition aims to simplify and expedite the existing procedure of seeking clearance on FDI proposals enabling individual departments of the government to clear FDI proposals in consultation with DIPP. The FIPB offered a single window clearance for FDI applications in India that were under the approval route however the sectors under automatic route did not require any prior approval from the FIPB and were subjected to only sectoral laws. The abolition of FIPB is a positive step by the government to liberalize FDI policy framework and alleviate regulatory hurdles in attracting investments.

FDI both inwards and outwards is the reflection of a country's growing competence. India is among the world top 10 recipients of FDI inflows and fourth in developing Asia.[2] Being the fastest growing economy in

---

[2] India ranks 10th in FDI inflows: UNCTAD report http://livemint.com/Money/K1BnZ0ZQV6FhJKsZWcMHVL/India-ranks-10th-in-FDI-inflows-UNCTAD-report.html

the world it offers vast potential for foreign investors, accounting for $44 billion of FDI inflow in 2015 compared to $35 billion in 2014 (UNCTAD 2016). In the current context, the surge in OFDI from India in terms of magnitude and cross border acquisition deals have brought it to the limelight especially among developing nations. The globalization and liberalization of trade and investment policies have gradually led to the openness of the Indian economy. During the 1990s, India being at the developmental phase was more reliant on export for venturing off-shores. The investment policy then focused on attracting inward FDI, but today the Indian firms are competitive enough to influence the world market by even acquiring overseas assets. Over the past two decades, India has witnessed a substantial rise in the OFDI stock from 0.1 percent in 1995 to 6.6 percent of GDP in 2015 (UNCTAD 2016).

Traditionally, Indian firms focused on organic growth as opposed to inorganic growth of venturing out for mergers and acquisitions. Nevertheless, post-liberalization the firms aimed at penetrating the international markets across continents and gain prominence as global market leaders through inorganic growth. Many Indian firms have engaged in overseas mergers, acquisitions, and strategic alliances to gain a competitive advantage in terms of technology, brand, goodwill or intellectual property rights. Indian knowledge-based industries like—pharmaceuticals, information technology, telecommunications, software, and automobiles witnessed an upsurge in OFDI as they managed to position themselves in the new competitive market-setting by upgrading the quality and improving productivity. Pradhan (2005) and Sauvant (2005) broadly classified Indian OFDI into two major phases. The "early phase" runs across the early 1970s till 1990 and the second "start-up phase" runs from 1991 to early 2000s. Hansen (2008) recommended that there also exist third "the take-off phase" in the Indian OFDI path that begins in the early 2000s till present.

The third "take-off phase" differed from earlier phases on account of four key features. In the early phase Indian investments, in the form of joint ventures, were largely governed by political and regulatory constraints in developing Asian and African countries. Post liberalization, during the "start-up phase," liberal foreign investments reforms facilitated cross-border acquisitions by the Indian corporate sector. However, 2004–2015, marked the era of India's remarkable overseas foreign investments termed as the "take-off phase" on account of capital and current account liberalization undertaken by Foreign Exchange Management Act 1999 (FEMA). Since 1991 Indian OFDI witnessed incremental growth but the second phase of liberalization aided exponential growth. The OFDI stock during the period 2000–2008 grew more than 30 times compared to the 7 percent inward FDI, narrowing the inward, outward foreign investment gap (UNCTAD 2010). Manufacturing sector dominated the "early phase" of OFDI but during the "start-up" phase focus eventually shifted toward the service sector. During the "take-off phase," Indian manufacturing sector outshined due to significant merger and acquisitions (M&A) activities along with service sector owing to outward investment by IT and software firms like Tata Consulting Services, Satyam, Wipro Technologies, Daksh Services, Hinduja and TMT Ltd among others. During this period, natural resource seeking firms (chemicals, energy, and steel) also internationalized in countries like Canada, Russia, Australia, Sudan, and so on, for exploration, refining and retailing activities.

Before the "take off phase," OFDI by Indian firms was primarily driven by pull and push factors. The pull factors were majorly resource-seeking or market-seeking in nature whereas push factors encouraged overseas investments to avoid restrictive domestic regulation such as labor laws, licenses, anti-trust regulation, and so on. OFDI after liberalization was directed more toward developed countries, majorly market-seeking investments into pharmaceuticals, steel, and engineering sector. The "take off phase" is not driven by push or pull factors instead it is strategic asset-seeking in nature through M&A. The strategic asset seeking firms acquires complementary foreign assets along with brands and market distribution system to overcome entry barriers in the developed countries. The structural reforms facilitated competiveness and confidence among Indian firms to compete globally and acquire overseas resources and strategic assets.

The OFDI though picked up pace after the liberalization in the early 1990s, but during the last decade, it recorded exponential growth through overseas acquisitions, aided by the liberal capital transfer reforms. The overseas direct investment stock increased from $495 million in 1995 to $118,072 million in 2012 and $138,975 million in 2015 (UNCTAD 2016).

The economic reforms along with the magnitude also changed the geographical spread and sectoral composition of the OFDI by aligning to the motives of overseas investing firms. During the mid-1970s, Indian Government aided the knowledge-based industries like pharmaceutical and software to create capabilities which later graduated to the next level of learning by capitalizing technological advantage through the liberalized regime. India witnessed a surge in the domestic market driven investments in this phase, accumulated technological skills and later explored dynamic links between the process of growth and technological up-gradation through strategic joint ventures and acquisition of technology portfolios in developed countries yielding better stock returns. Indian firms largely seek technological assets in developed countries and natural resources in developing countries. Host market attractiveness in terms of resources, strategic assets, market expansion, bilateral investment treaties, and FDI openness are the most sought-after motives of internationalization.

During 2002–2014, direct investments gained momentum; FDI inflow grew at a CAGR of 21 percent whereas FDI outflows registered a higher growth rate of CAGR 35.1 percent. During the first half, overseas investments were directed to resource-rich countries such as Australia, UAE, and Sudan, while in the latter half, ODI was channeled into countries seeking higher tax benefits such as Mauritius, Singapore, British Virgin Islands, and the Netherlands. There has been a perceptible change in the direction of India's ODI during the last decade (Table 4.7).

Table 4.7 Region wise ODI in 2001–02 (Total: US$ 999 mn) and 2011–12 (Total: US$ 30863 mn)

Region	2001–02	2011–12
North America	25.7	7.3
Africa	3.9	24.3
Asia Pacific	6.8	31.4
CIS	40.9	0.4
Europe	16.7	21.7
Latin America & Caribbean	5.2	12.4
Middle East	1	3.8

Source: Exim Bank, Occasional Paper No. 165.

In 2001–2002, Commonwealth of Independent States[3] (CIS) region accounted for 41 percent of India's ODI but declined in 2011–2012; instead, Africa and the Asia Pacific emerged as significant destinations in 2001–2002, respectively. During 2001–2002, Russia and the United States attracted maximum ODI whereas, in 2011–2012, Singapore and Mauritius surfaced as the major destinations (Exim 2014). However, the years 2001–2012, manufacturing sector attracted the most substantial overseas investments.

In early 2000s Indian ODI was primarily directed toward traditional mature markets, but during mid-2000, resource rich nations like Sudan also emerged as an important investment destination. During 2011–2012, ODI was more directed toward tax haven nations like Mauritius, Singapore, Netherland and, British Virgin (UNCTAD 2015). Over the years, manufacturing has been the most favored choice for Indian overseas investments, but the share of the manufacturing sector is gradually declining from 59.8 percent in 2003–2004 to 31.5 percent in 2011–2012.

India has emerged as one of the strongest performers in the deal-street across the world in Mergers and Acquisitions (M&A). M&A activity increased in 2014 with deals worth US$ 38.1 billion, compared to US$ 28.2 billion in 2013 and US$ 35.4 billion in 2012. In 2015, India became the third largest source of FDI for UK contributing 65 percent of the total investments and 9,000 new job creations (IBEF 2016). Indian MNEs are active acquirers in global M&A markets, particularly in developed countries such as the UK and the United States. Indian IT service providers have long been important players in M&A markets however in the recent years, firms from service industries such as banking and food services have also become increasingly active in overseas markets (UNCTAD 2013).

To conclude, public policy and regulations largely influence both inward and outward FDI. As emphasized earlier, the evolution of FDI policy is a consequence of the interplay of many macroeconomic policies,

---

[3] Commonwealth of Independent States (CIS) was created in December 1991. In the adopted Declaration the participants of the Commonwealth declared their interaction on the basis of sovereign equality. At present the CIS unites: Azerbaijan, Armenia, Belarus, Georgia, Kazakhstan, Kyrgyzstan, Moldova, Russia, Tajikistan, Turkmenistan, Uzbekistan and Ukraine.

and each policy subset defines the broad contours of the economic growth process. The global trade relationships are mainly regulated and influenced by these policies.

References

Budget. 2017. "Revamp FRBM Act to Balance the Budget." http://hindustantimes. com/union-budget/budget-2017-revamp-frbm-act-to-balance-the-budget/ story-TaBjBw0Lquc6OdpVDxp3WI.html

Borensztein, E., J. De Gregorio, and J.W. Lee. 1998. "How Does Foreign Direct Investment Affect Economic Growth?" *Journal of International Economics* 45, no. 1, pp. 115–35.

Brown, O., F.H. Shaheen, S.R. Khan, and M. Yusuf. 2000. "Regional Trade Agreements: Promoting Conflict Or Building Peace?" *International Institute for Sustainable Development*, https://Iisd.org/pdf/2005/security-rta-confllict. pdf

Chakraborty, T., H. Gundimeda, and V. Kathuria. 2017. "Have the Special Economic Zones Succeeded in Attracting FDI?—Analysis for India." *Theoretical Economics Letters* 7, no. 3, p. 623

Economic Survey 2016–17. January, 2017. "Government of India Ministry of Finance Department of Economic Affairs Economic Division." https:// indiabudget.gov.in/es2016-17/echapter.pdf

Export-Import Bank of India (EXIM). 2014. "Outward Direct Investment from India: Trends, Objectives and Policy Perspectives." Occasional Paper No. 165, http://gbv.de/dms/zbw/815934823.pdf

Economic Reforms. 1991. http://indiabefore91.in/1991-economic-reforms

European Commission. 2015. "Trade for All: Towards a More Responsible Trade and Investment Policy." Available at http://trade.ec.europa.eu/doclib/ docs/2015/october/tradoc_153846.pdf

Foreign Direct Investment Inflows-A Success Story Press Information Bureau: http://pib.nic.in/newsite/PrintRelease.aspx?relid=161955 (accessed May 19, 2017).

Foreign Exchange Management Act 1999. http://dor.gov.in/Foreign_Exchange

Fiscal Policy Strategy Statement. http://indiabudget.nic.in/ub2017-18/frbm/ frbm3.pdf

Reddy, Y.V. n.d. "Fiscal Policy and Economic Reforms." Working Paper 2008-53 http://nipfp.org.in/media/medialibrary/2013/04/wp_2008_53.pdf (accessed May 2008).

Investment Policy in India Performance and Perceptions, CUTS Centre for Competition. "Investment & Economic Regulation Discussion Paper." http://cuts-ccier.org/pdf/Investment_Policy_in_IndiapercentageE2 percentage80percentage93Performance_and_Perceptions.pdf

FDI Policy as a Part of Development Strategy. Available at https://odi.org/sites/odi.org.uk/files/odi-assets/publications-opinion-files/5543.pdf

Government of India Ministry of Industry Statement on Industrial Policy New Delhi. "An Overview of Macroeconomic Policy Reforms in India." http://dipp.nic.in/English/Policies/Industrial_policy_statement.pdf (accessed July 24, 1991).

Growth of Indian Multinationals In the World Economy-Implications for Development. 2007. http://isid.org.in/pdf/WP0704.pdf

IEG, World Bank, World Bank group response to market and government failures http://ieg.worldbankgroup.org/sites/default/files/Data/reports/chapters/innovation_app_a.pdf

IBEF 2017. "Foreign Direct Investment." https://ibef.org/economy/foreign-direct-investment.aspx

"India's Outward FDI: A Giant Awakening?" 2004. Available at http://unctad.org/sections/dite_dir/docs/diteiiab20041_en.pdf

Lall, S. 2000a. "FDI and Development: Research Issues in the Emerging Context." Policy Discussion Paper 20, Centre for International Economic Studies, University of Adelaide.

NCAER. 2015. Principal Gaps in India's FDI Statistics: User Perspectives Findings from Interviews with Indian Policy-makers and FDI Researchers. Available at www.ncaer.org/free-download.php?pID=243

OECD Guidelines For Multinational Enterprises. 2008. Available at http://www.oecd.org/investment/mne/1922428.pdf

Pradhan, J.P. 2005. "Outward Foreign Direct Investment from India: Recent Trends and Patterns." Gujarat Institute of Development Research Working Paper.

Sahoo, P., G. Nataraj, and R.K. Dash. 2014. "Foreign Direct Investment in South Asia." *New Delhi: Springer India* 10, pp. 978–81.

Safarian, A.E. 1999. "Host Country Policies Towards Inward Foreign Direct Investment in the 1950s and 1990s." *Transnational Corporations* 8, no. 2, pp. 93–112.

Sauvant, K.P. "New Sources of FDI: The BRICs-outward FDI from Brazil, Russia, India and China." *J. World Investment and Trade* 6, p. 639.

State and Market Failures. https://ieg.worldbankgroup.org/Data/reports/chapters/innovation_app_a.pdf

Summer 2011. "The Rise of Indian Multinationals: Perspective of Indian Outward Foreign Direct Investment." *Reserve Bank of India Occasional Papers* 32, no. 1, https://rbi.org.in/scripts/bs_viewcontent.aspx?Id=2490

"Transparent Trade and Investment." policy.http://trade.ec.europa.eu/doclib/docs/2015/october/tradoc_153846.pdf

Te Velde, D.W. 2001. *Policies Towards Foreign Direct Investment in Developing Countries: Emerging Best-practices and Outstanding Issues.* London: Overseas Development Institute. https://odi.org/sites/odi.org.uk/files/odi-assets/publications-opinion-files/5543.pdf

UNCTAD. 2010. "World Investment Report." Available at http://unctad.org/en/docs/wir2010_en.pdf

UNCTAD. 2013. "World Investment Report." Available at http://unctad.org/en/PublicationsLibrary/webdiaeia2013d4_en.pdf

UNCTAD. 2015. "World Investment Report." Available at http://uctad.org/en/PublicationsLibrary/wir2015_en.pdf

UNCTAD. 2016. "World Investment Report, Investor Nationality: Policy Challenges." http://unctad.org/en/pages/PublicationWebflyer.aspx?publication id =1610

Urata, S. 2002. "Globalization and the Growth in Free Trade Agreements." *Asia Pacific Review* 9, no. 1, pp. 20–32.

World Trade Report. 2011. Available at https://wto.org/english/res_e/booksp_e/anrep_e/world_trade_report11_e.pdf

World Bank. 2008. "Doing Business." *Fifth Report*, Washington D.C.

Wells, L.T.J., and A.G. Wint. 1990. *Marketing a Country: Promotion as a Tool for Attracting Foreign Investment.* The World Bank.

World Bank's Global Economic Prospects report. 2017. Available at https://openknowledge.worldbank.org/bitstream/handle/10986/26800/9781464810244.pdf

World Commission on the Social Dimension of Globalization. 2004. "A Fair Globalization: Creating Opportunities for All." http://ilo.org/fairglobalization/lang--en/index.htm

World Bank Guidelines on the Treatment of Foreign Direct Investment. http://documents.worldbank.org/curated/pt/955221468766167766/pdf/multipage.pdf

CHAPTER 5

Foreign Direct Investment and Sustainable Development

In the 1970s and 1980s, the bulk of foreign investments were confined among the developed economies. However, post-1990s there was a substantial increase in the share of capital flowing into developing countries and ever since developing countries have exhibited a reduction in the aid flows and rise in FDI flows. FDI takes place in an institutional context that influences its structure and effects, which include international and multilateral agreements and has an ongoing agenda for liberalizing international trade and international environmental agreements. In the current circumstances mobilizing investment that ensures sustainable development is of prime significance for the majority of countries. The new generations of investment policies are largely aiming at inclusive growth with sustainable development.

Sustainable Development

The concept of sustainable development was popularized by the Brundtland Commission Report in 1987 but was earlier also advocated in the World Conservation Strategy (IUCN 1980). The Brundtland Commission relates sustainable development to human welfare. Sustainable development was defined as one that meets the needs of the present without compromising the ability of future generations to meet their own needs (World Commission on Environment and Development 1987). The early themes of sustainable development emerged soon after World War II in response to the unprecedented needs of rehabilitation and reconstruction of economies ravaged by the War. World Bank Group, UN and other multilateral institutions came together in the search for viable policy options to tackle human developmental issues. Sustainable development focuses on the needs of the poor people and acknowledges the limits of the state in addressing the intra and inter-generational human needs. Sustainable development is a part of the environment and development policies that stimulate and changes the quality of growth. It emphasizes meeting indispensable needs for jobs, food, energy, water, and sanitation among others. It advocates a sustainable level of population, conservation, and enhancement of the resource base besides technology reorientation and risk management. There is a fundamental requirement to integrate environment and economics in decision making.

The theoretical framework for sustainable development is the result of several international conferences and initiatives held during 1972–1992. Sustainability at the global scale was discussed for the very first time at the UN Conference on the Human Environment organized in 1972 in Stockholm. It was the first major international gathering to discuss sustainability at the global scale. The conference created considerable momentum, and a series of recommendations led to the establishment of the UN Environment Programme (UNEP) and formation of various national environmental protection agencies at the national level. In 1980, World Conservation Strategy—a collaboration between the International Union for the Conservation of Nature, the World Wildlife Fund (WWF), and UNEP further advanced sustainable development by recognizing priority conservation issues and key policy options.

The 1992 Rio Summit laid the foundations for the global institutionalization of sustainable development based on the Brundtland report (1987). The 20th anniversary of the Stockholm Conference was declared as the Earth Summit when Rio adopted a declaration on environment and development and agenda 21 as a global plan of action for sustainable development. The Rio Declaration contains 27 principles of sustainable development. The developed countries acknowledged the responsibility of sustainable development in international pursuits related to the global environment, technologies and financial resources. Agenda 21 outlines actions concerning the social and economic dimensions of sustainable development, conservation, and management of natural resources. It aims at integrating global environmental considerations into an accelerated development process.

Sustainable Foreign Direct Investment

Sauvant and Mann (2017) defined sustainable FDI as "commercially viable investment that makes a maximum contribution to the economic, social and environmental development of host countries and takes place in the framework of fair governance mechanisms," which signifies sustainable FDI for sustainable development. Globally, sustainability has become a catchphrase, especially during environmental and developmental debates. After the announcement of Brundtland Commission formally known as World Commission on Environment and Development in 1985, the work on theories of sustainable development received substantial attention. Sustainability emphasizes on reconciliation of society's development goals with its long term environmental limits. It re-iterates on achieving economic prosperity, a healthy environment and social equity for present and future generations. Faced with the challenge of achieving sustainable development goals (SDGs), policymakers have become progressively more concerned about the sustainability aspect of foreign investment. Sustainable FDI is widely defined as investments in environmentally friendly industries, technologies, infrastructure, and practices that directly pave the way for environmental progress also termed as "green FDI." Green FDI is crucial for sustainable societies and the governments worldwide are aiming to leverage all FDI in support of a more sustainable future. Green growth is defined by the OECD as the quest for economic growth and development while averting costly environmental degradation, climate change, biodiversity loss, and unsustainable natural resource use.[1] FDI could genuinely translate into global value chain sustainability, provided governments put in place the right policies and institutional frameworks.

OECD's policy framework for investment enables governments to formulate domestic policy frameworks that encourage and support sustainable FDI. These Guidelines recommend firms to follow standards of responsible business conduct during their operations regardless of the strength of local, legal and governance frameworks. Quintessentially, the guidelines highlight the importance of domestic policy frameworks to influence sustainability outcomes through a multilateral approach.

---

[1] Interim Report of the Green Growth Strategy: oecd.org/greengrowth

The investment required to meet SDGs and climate change obligations runs in trillions of dollars of investment. FDI can certainly contribute toward these agendas provided it is considerably increased. In 2016, global FDI amounted to the US $1.8 trillion (UNCTAD 2017) which will probably grow significantly in the coming years. What we are concerned here is just not the FDI but the sustainable FDI. Most of the FDI is capable of contributing to sustainable development subject to the nation's specific surrounding environment. Few nations permit certain types of FDI such as mergers and acquisitions (Australia and Canada) or Greenfield investments (United States) based on net benefit tests or national security tests. Many countries even adhere to limit or restrict the FDI inflow to shield certain services, manufacturing industry, natural resources, and so on. This strategy may be adopted to promote domestic industry, small or medium-size firms or for security reasons.

Most of the nations now are sensitive toward the environmental and social impact of foreign investments including human rights. They aim to maximize economic and social benefits to the community, especially in the natural resources sectors, for instance in mining through the shared value concept. It is generally believed that certain foreign investments backed by national and international policies explicitly contribute toward the development objectives in the respective host economies. It is most evident that the investment promotion agencies (IPAs) in both developed and developing countries are attracting industry-specific FDI that they believe could contribute to their development priorities. United Kingdom (UK) evaluates the FDI project based on quantitative and qualitative indicators. Quantitative indicators, for instance, identifying the total value of an investment and number of new jobs created, are imperative to evaluate big investment projects that are expected to deliver higher economic, social and other multiplier benefits. Qualitative indicators include, for instance, salary level of newly created jobs, R&D focus, the presence of global or regional headquarters, quality of the investor, export potential, and so on. The IPA of The Republic of Korea emphasizes the development of domestic economic competitiveness. IPAs of different countries provides industry or sector-specific investment incentives, for instance, Nigeria in telecommunications, electricity and transport industries; Chile's in food, infrastructure, and tourism industries; Hungary in automotive and electronics industries and shared service centers while

Vietnam in new technologies, agriculture, and forestry, and environmentally friendly technology.

Investment Policy Framework for Sustainable Development

With the changing times, increasing social and environmental challenges need special attention in order to harness economic growth for sustainable and inclusive development. Investments being the primary driver of growth for all countries and especially the developing ones should contribute to sustainable development objectives. UNCTAD's Investment Policy Framework for Sustainable Development (2015) provides guidance for FDI. It takes into account policies related to the establishment, treatment, and promotion of investment.

The policy related to cross-border investments are subjected to regular changes. At the country level, governments continuously implement investment policy measures to attract foreign investments whereas at the international level new investment agreements are concluded at a rate of more than one per fortnight over the past few years. Soft Law (unenforceable, voluntary standards) that governs the behavior of corporate investors is also expanding at a faster pace. All these changes have given rise to a new generation of investment policies that promote a favorable investment climate while ensuring a broader development policy agenda. They aim to promote concrete measures and mechanisms for sustainable development in policymaking and implementation at both national and international levels.

The core principles for investment policymaking serve as design criteria for UNCTAD's Investment Policy Framework (2015). It comprises three sets of operational guidelines:

(a) Guidelines for national investment policies.
(b) Guidance to design and use International Investment Policies (IIAs).
(c) Action menu for promoting sustainable investment in key sectors.

The national investment policy guidelines assist in formulating effective investment policies. At the strategic level, policymakers are responsible for developing investment policies that judiciously addresses economic growth and sustainable development. The roles of public-private partners along with domestic and especially foreign investment should be clearly defined in the development strategy. The investment policies should aim at utilizing FDI to enhance productive capacity building and international competitiveness with critical elements including human resources and skills development, technology and know-how, infrastructure development, and enterprise development.

At the normative level, policymakers can support and control sustainable investment through a set of laws and regulations. FDI is capable of reaping both negative and positive effects; however, regulations covering areas beyond investment policies, such as trade, taxation, intellectual property, competition, labor market regulation, environmental policies and access to land can help in maximizing developmental benefits. The government can complement these regulations with soft laws such as voluntary CSR initiatives and standards that may increasingly influence corporate practices, behavior and investment decisions and maximize the developmental benefits of investment. At the administrative level, importance and efficacy of the investment policies could be ensured through proper execution. They should be executed based on overtly formulated policy objectives with clear priorities and time frames.

UNCTAD's IIA policy framework provides options to design provisions in investment agreements or treaties. The treaties should integrate investment commitment for sustainable development. Certain major initiatives and mechanisms that a nation should target for sustainable investment are precise facilitation mechanism which includes information sharing and investment promotion forums; outward investment promotion initiatives which include insurances and guarantees; joint promotion investment initiative; technical assistance initiative; and capacity building initiatives. The investor should be obliged to match the state's commitment to promoting responsible investment. In the case of non-compliance, the investor could be subjected to domestic laws. Nations can ensure a proper balance between commitments and space for development besides shielding host countries from unjustified and high procedural costs in investment dispute settlement through proper provisions made in the treaty.

UNCTAD's action menu promotes investment in priority sectors for sustainable development. It encourages sustainability-based incentives instead of location-based incentives. It promotes regional initiatives toward sustainable investment especially into cross-border infrastructure development and regional firms' clusters in sectors such as green zones. UNCTADs investment policy framework for sustainable development intends to serve as a point of reference for policymakers in formulating, negotiating or reviewing IIAs and design policies to promote sustainability in priority sectors. Since its commencement in 2012, it has been used by several nations and regional groups to review and revise national investment rules and regulations besides negotiating international investment agreements. It is quite challenging to encourage investment in areas that contribute immensely to sustainable development, however; the new generation of investment promotion and facilitation strategies, institutions and partnership are aiming to provide favorable investment climate to mobilize investment into such sectors.

FDI is an integral part of every country's economic development, but it deserves further contemplation for a developing country like India where economic growth and poverty elevation are both equally crucial elements for the nation's progress. The government of India endorses liberal economic framework but disallows 100 percent FDI in the multi-brand retail sector, the most controversial area of FDI, on the grounds of safeguarding small indigenous retailers or corner shops commonly known as "Kirana stores" and poor farmers who supply goods to them. The government opines that permitting FDI in organized multi-brand retail sector will increase competition for the small indigenous retailers and might push them out of business which in turn will impact the poor farmers, leading to more unemployment and poverty. MNEs competitive pricing strategy is also a point of concern posing business losses for indigenous retailers. However, the question arises here is, "Is this the best possible way to help poor farmers and corner shops or is there any other possible approach?" The following section of the chapter will attempt to throw some light on this concern.

Countries aim to strengthen the weaker sections of the economy, uplift their living standards and empower them to join the growing middle-income group. Indian government too, over the past few years, has been busy framing sustainable investment policy framework to attract FDI in various sectors. The present Indian government has initiated the biggest ever reform termed as "radical liberalization" of the Foreign Direct Investment regime by easing norms for a host of important sectors including defense, single brand retail, food processing, telecommunication, and so on. Foreign investment promotion board (FIPB) was abolished in February 2017 to sets the stage for more reforms in the FDI policy. More than 90 percent of the total FDI inflows are now through the automatic route. The government allows 100 percent FDI through automatic route in food processing sector where the foreign investors are free to sell food products manufactured and produced in India. Food processing industry is fundamental for India's development due to its crucial linkages and synergies with industry and agriculture sector. Fast growing food processing sector supported with the improved value chain could significantly impact agricultural business growth both domestically and internationally. Indian agriculture sector though has a long way to go nevertheless the efficient food processing industry seems competent of tackling nation's food security issue by preventing post-harvest losses of fruits and vegetables by 25 to 30 percent approximately. Marginal reductions in losses are also capable of giving good returns and considerably improving farmers' income levels in the long run (Grant Thornton-Assocham 2017). As per these new FDI guidelines in the e-commerce sector, 100 percent FDI under automatic route is permitted in the marketplace model of e-commerce, although FDI is not permitted in inventory based model of e-commerce.

Well, looking at the FDI policies in both food processing and e-commerce sector, it is evident that the government seems to have a sustainable strategic approach in mobilizing foreign investment that immensely contributes to sustainable development. Investment in food processing sector ensures the development of the value chain up to the farmer, cutting down on the waste of agricultural produce and getting more food to be processed for consumers thereby leading to better returns for farmers. Food processing is considered to be a sunrise sector for India capable of contributing to the income of farmers and processors. Integration with the global economy would add gleam to the success of this sector and would create many new jobs at different levels of skills.[2] On the other hand, permitting 100 percent FDI in the marketplace model of e-commerce apparently, indicate the government's motive to strengthen the indigenous retailers. The collaboration with e-commerce companies can boost up their business as they are then eligible to list themselves as sellers on their website. The big players of online grocery segment like Grofers, Bigbasket, and so on, are operating with the help of these indigenous retailers, and they are their selling partners besides their inventory setup. The government has not permitted FDI in inventory based model of e-commerce to safeguard the interests of domestic brick-and-mortar stores especially the indigenous retailers and Kirana shops. The policies very well reflect policymakers support and acknowledgment of SDGs.

Therefore, to address the question raised earlier, about the best possible approach to safeguard farmers and indigenous retailers, it seems that by mobilizing investments in areas especially food processing and e-commerce sector, particularly in this case, the government is trying to promote responsible investment that could maximize developmental benefits and sustainable development. Restricting 100 percent FDI in the multi-brand sector until the farmers and indigenous retailers equip themselves to face competition and align themselves to the changing market conditions by far seem to be a good decision to achieve sustainability. The Government reviews FDI policy on an ongoing basis for further liberalization and simplification. It aims to provide ease of doing business and attract larger FDI inflows. Indian Government has been proactively involved in opening up of different sectors for FDI with a vision to alleviate poverty, strengthen the poor to face the growing completion across the globe and to gear up the economic growth.

FDI and Human Rights

MNEs are responsible for promoting and protecting human rights. In today's globalized economy, MNEs action and decisions directly impact

---

[2] Rajesh, C., and J. Laxmi. 2017. "A Solution at Last for Low Farmer Incomes? Why the Food Processing Sector is Critical for a Developing India." http://ncaer.org/news_details.php?nID=240

government policies and human rights. Firms being an integral part of society regularly interact with consumers, shareholders, and communities and it is vital to ensure their respective rights. The Universal Declaration of Human Rights (UDHR) plays an integral role in securing universal observance of human rights and is a milestone document in the history of human rights. It is drafted by people representing different legal and cultural backgrounds from all regions of the world. The Declaration was proclaimed by the United Nations General Assembly in Paris on 10 December 1948 as a common standard of achievements for all peoples and all nations. It sets out, for the first time, fundamental human rights to be universally protected and have been translated into over 500 languages.

Amnesty International is a London-based non-governmental organization that focuses on human rights. It promotes all the human rights preserved in the UDHR and other international standards. The organization is impartial and independent of any government, political persuasion or religious creed. It neither supports nor opposes any government or political system or views of the victims whose rights it seeks to protect. According to the human rights principles for companies (Amnesty International 1998) every company should adopt an explicit company policy on human rights which includes public support for UHDR. Employees should be entitled to rights to freedom from discrimination, the right to life and security, freedom from slavery, freedom of association, right to form trade unions, and fair working conditions. Security arrangements to protect human rights should be consistent with international standards for law enforcement. Procedures should be consistent with the United Nations basic principles on the use of force and firearms by law enforcement officials and the UN code of conduct for law enforcement officials. Companies should ensure that their operations do not adversely impact the human rights of the communities in which they operate. They should be willing to meet community leaders and voluntary organizations to discuss the role of the company within the broader community. The policies should prevent discrimination based on ethnic origin, sex, color, language, and so on. Should prohibit slavery in terms of forced labor, bonded child laborers and provide safe and healthy working conditions by enabling rights to freedom of expression for employees. MNEs should adhere to fair means of collective bargaining without discrimination and not condemn formation of a trade union. Companies should ensure just and favorable conditions of work, reasonable job security and fair and adequate remuneration and benefits besides establishing mechanisms to monitor effectively that all their operations comply with codes of conduct and international human rights standards.

There are a number of instances of human rights violations by mega-corporations despite UN declaration, ILO social policy, OECD guidelines and other international voluntary codes like UN global compact. Examples galore such as Shell in Nigeria, Enron in India, Chevron in Sudan, Mike, Reebok, and plantation industry in Latin America, energy trading company in Burma and conflict diamond (mining) in Africa, among others. These corporations damaged their corporate image and incurred fury of the NGOs, activists, and regulators.

Globally, FDI is highly attributed for inducing growth and has become tantamount with the term "spillover" which could though be either positive or negative. Policymakers generally consider FDI as an integral tool to promote growth and curb poverty, which is well reflected by the liberal FDI policies of the nations and the remarkable surge in FDI flows. Besides other factors, the abundance of natural resources in many developing countries has also been the prime motivation for FDI. There has been substantial growth in FDI to major oil producing African countries (World Bank 2005). Economists generally believe that resource abundance can hasten economic development by increasing the rate of foreign investment in resource-rich economies compared to the rate in resource-poor economies. FDI is also believed to financially stabilize the economy by making it capable of importing capital goods needed further development. Several studies suggest that the adequate policy framework adopted by resource—abundant nations can correct market failure and curb potential environmental damage leading to sustainable development (Auty 2007). However, there are contrarian views that suggest FDI channeled to the natural resource industries; neither creates positive spillovers of job creation nor technology transfers in the host country. The resource curse also known as the paradox of plenty, is one of the most mystifying economic paradoxes which explains that the nations with an abundance of non-renewable natural resources like fossil fuels and certain minerals tend to have slower long term economic growth, lesser democratic, environment, and inferior development outcomes compared to countries with fewer natural resources (Sachs and Warner 1997).

The Dutch disease and rent-seeking activities are assumed to be the primary cause of the resource curse. Dutch disease is the apparent causal relationship between economic development of a particular sector like natural resources and a decline in other sectors like manufacturing and agriculture. In this case, the manufacturing and non-resource sectors collapse as resources are being diverted toward natural resource production. The considerable investment in the natural sector crowds-out domestic investment, thereby hampering the growth of the nation.

Rent-seeking activities are another component of a resource curse where the poor state of institutions results in high economic rents. High rents are the cause for high corruption, red-tapism, and poor government efficiency which in turn, discourage investment demand in others sectors leading to an economic slowdown. Resource curse thus relates to the failure of many resource-rich countries to benefit fully from their natural resource wealth, and for governments in these countries to respond effectively to public welfare needs. Discovery of natural resources in a country is often linked to accelerated growth and development, but the resource-rich countries tend to have higher rates of conflict and authoritarianism, and lower rates of economic stability and economic growth, compared to their non-resource-rich neighbors.[3]

It has been widely noticed that in the case of resource-seeking FDI human rights are generally violated by repression of the workforce. Some of the illustrations of mega FDI projects in the Indian economy suggest a number of unresolved issues in policy formulation and implementation for foreign investment. POSCO's and Vedanta's operations in Orissa are the cases of failed resource seeking FDI due to non-compliance with international human rights standards. In 2005, Pohang Steel Company (POSCO), the world's fourth-largest steelmaker from South Korea, signed a memorandum of understanding (MOU) with the Odisha

---

[3] Munich Personal RePEc Archive (MPRA). November 2009. "Foreign Direct Investment and the Natural Resource Curse; What is the Relationship to Economic Development, Income Inequality and Poverty? Do Institutions and Good Governance Matter?" MPRA Paper No. 18254, https://mpra.ub.uni-muenchen. de/18254/1/FDINRCECONDEV.pdf

government to set up a 12-million-ton-capacity steel project in Jagatsing-hpur district. It was the first biggest FDI in India of its time with $12 billion (Rs. 52,000 crores) of investment. It was considered a very significant project for the future growth and development of Odisha, which was a weak and underdeveloped state and makes India a steel superpower. The company signed the MOU with the state government but was unable to start construction because of social and environmental controversies. After 12 years of several twists and turns on account of protests from the local community and public resistance to the project and regulatory hurdles, the South Korean steel major officially withdrew from the project in 2017. The case raises some fundamental questions from the angle of public policy, regulatory and institutional framework. Besides questioning the 90s public policy framework of Indian government regarding FDI in the steel industry, it also indicates inefficiency on the part of state government to monitor such a large FDI. This case also has significant implications on the trade-off between foreign investment and the environmental impact. International Human Rights Clinic (IHRC) also suggested suspending POSCO's operations in India on account of non-compliance with international human rights standards.

The global concern today is not about attracting more FDI but sustainable FDI. In the present scenario, many countries are scrutinizing inward FDI on the basis of various considerations such as net benefit tests or national security tests. As mentioned earlier Australia and Canada use net benefit tests whereas the United States consider national security tests before allowing inward FDI. Various governments cap or entirely restrict inward FDI in certain services, manufacturing industries, natural resources, and infrastructure. Increasingly the developed and developing countries are adopting this approach for a variety of reasons, such as to promote the development of domestic firms in the specific sectors, for strategic security reasons, or to protect specific cultural industries, public services or small and medium-sized firms (Sauvant and Mann 2017).

Sustainable Development and Multinational Business

Globally, governments are busy crafting frameworks incorporating reduced tariffs and investor-friendly agreements to attract FDI. However; on the other hand, few MNEs are also taking responsibility and leading the way for sustainable development through their investment. They are expected to transfer environmentally sound technologies, environmental management schemes and follow international codes of conduct such as the OECD Guidelines for Multinational Enterprises to contribute to sustainable development.

Tata Motors from India, operate in the overseas market. In partnership with reputed NGOs and their distributor partners in various countries, they work to support marginalized communities.

The SkillPro program, launched by Tata Motor's international business division, trains talented youth across several countries. The youth are identified by the collaborative effort of both Tata motors and their distributor partners. They provide them meticulously planned nine-month mechanic motor vehicle training at Jamshedpur training center followed by on-the-job training in their respective countries at their channel partners' workshops. During 2016–2017, Tata Motors trained 22 youth, including two women participants, from eight countries—Bangladesh, Mozambique, Sudan, Tanzania, Kenya, Nigeria, Ghana, and Sri Lanka. All the 22 participants are now part of the distributor network and the Tata Motors extended family in their countries.

MNEs like PepsiCo and Hindustan Unilever Limited (HUL) operating in India are genuinely contributing to addressing sustainable development along with their profit-making motive. PepsiCo, a global food and beverage leader, is operating in India through 100 percent FDI route in food processing sector with the product portfolio of 22 brands and annual retail sales of over $1 billion. In India, PepsiCo operates with 38 beverages and three food plants and proposes to invest 33,000 Crore by 2020 toward upgrading innovation, supply chain mechanism, market infrastructure, and manufacturing capacity. Since inception in 1989, PepsiCo has been working with farmers through contract farming. Contract farming is an agreement between farmers and the buyers, where farmer promises to timely supply specific commodity at a pre-agreed price, quality and quantity to the buyer. According to the terms of a contract, the farmer is not only required to plant contractor's crop, harvest and deliver the product at the pre-agreed price but will also receive the required inputs, technical advice or expertise for plantation. Contract farming is a powerful means to introduce new crops and farm technologies when marketing and production uncertainties pre-dominate the economy and are highly effective when it offers a fair price and adequate risk coverage (Chaturvedi 2007). PepsiCo first contracted with farmers for tomato cultivation to export tomato paste to foreign countries. The advanced agricultural practice and technical support resulted in increased agricultural yield by threefold and doubled the length of season for growing tomatoes (Seth 2003). The improved yield increased farmers income and lowered prices for the consumers.

PepsiCo is associated with more than 12,000 farmers across various states like Punjab, Uttar Pradesh, Karnataka, Bihar, West Bengal, Gujarat, and Maharashtra for the production of world-class chip-grade potatoes. PepsiCo as a development partner reaches out to more than 22,000 farmers to produce potato, barley, tomato, paddy, and chilies through contract farming and supplies them higher quality seeds, suitable agricultural inputs and tools to raise productivity free of cost. The company's guaranteed buy-back mechanism at a pre-determined rate shields the farmer from losses due to market price fluctuations. PepsiCo has brought together world-class agricultural practices to increase farm productivity and earnings and managed to reform the lives of thousands of poor farmers in India. The research and development efforts undertaken by the MNEs and training of local employees in the foreign affiliates demonstrates an important channel of spillover of FDI on local firms.

PepsiCo ensures best inputs to farmers for quality produce procured at a pre-agreed price, facilitating company's long term planning and investments and raising the living standard of farmers. PepsiCo has emerged as a development partner by aiding farmers in creating cost-effective, localized agriculture-supply chain for its business and raise their earnings. Karnani (2007) believes that private sector can play a strategic role in alleviating poverty by considering poor as producers from whom they can buy and increase their real income rather than looking at them as potential buyers and selling to them. Once their income increases, this section of the population will possibly join the mainstream consumer group and eventually the growing middle-income group of the nation. PepsiCo seems to have been working in this direction and sets an example for other MNEs to follow. PepsiCo along with the farmers and State governments is collaborating to upturn agricultural-sustainability and crop diversification and provides customized solutions suitable to specific geographies and locations.

The present Indian government has rightly initiated Private-Public Partnerships (PPP's) in training and skill up-gradation for the rural India population through Skill India initiative program. The government can largely impact the business decisions and activities of MNEs to carve out the most appropriate development frameworks for the society without disturbing their profit-making business. PepsiCo's initiative lead to spill-over from improved social sectors to reach the broader population enhancing the overall human capital; hence FDI could also be seen as a tool to strengthen specific absorptive capacities in a nation with the help of government's effective trade policies (Kaushal 2016).

HUL is a subsidiary of Unilever, a British-Dutch company. It is a Fortune 500 multinational company with a worldwide presence across 100 countries. It was established in 1933 by Lever brothers but was later in 1956 merged with Hindustan Vanaspati Manufacturing Company Ltd. and United Traders Ltd. It is the market leader in Indian fast moving consumer products with its presence in over 20 product categories like food and beverages, cleaning agents and personal care products. They operated through a public-private partnership in promoting personal hygiene campaign such as regular hand washing with their soap-lifebuoy and incorporated hygiene and child health as an integral part of their business activity. HUL (Unilever India) initiated the drive to educate people about hand washing as a method to keep bacterial infections at bay. The company hired local people for campaigning in rural areas so that they can communicate well with the indigenous people. The campaign ran successfully across several rural states of India. This was hence a win-win situation for the poor consumers and the company. The Nobel laureate Amartya Sen also suggest that poverty can be capability-deprivation and could be tackled by increasing people's choices and enhancing human capabilities. UNDP developed three main human development indices based on the capabilities approach namely, Gender Development Index (GDI), the Human Development Index (HDI) and the Human Poverty Index (HPI). Majorly these indices measure human well being in terms of longevity, health, awareness, knowledge, the standard of living and gender inequality. These are fundamental measures to gauge the success of poverty reduction measures and the development of the rural poor population. MNE's can thus contribute to the development front when the investment and business strategies are directed to involve them and increase their earnings along with addressing the human wellbeing concerns about education, longevity, health, awareness, and so on.

Unilever India continuously works on developing grass root marketing initiatives to reach the poor and rural population. Hence; as suggested by Karnani (2007) MNEs general course of business activities could tackle a social problem by collaborating with local partners to ease poverty, enhance development and generate jobs through skill up-gradation. Unilever India believes that empowering women will transform individual lives which will, in turn, transform societies and contributes significantly to the United Nations 2030 sustainable development agenda and its SDGs. Unilever aims to empower women and girls as a means to achieve gender equality and the need to work in partnership. Empowering women leads to skill improvement and employability; finally enabling economic empowerment. Empowered women play an essential role in reaching potential consumers and enabling Unilever's business to grow. By building skills among their small-scale distributors and retailers, they create new opportunities for women and at the same time strengthen their business. Studies indicate that the narrowing gender gap in employment in emerging markets could lead to a 30 percent rise in per capita by 2030. Unilever believes that by creating opportunities for employment and entrepreneurship and addressing gender barriers, they can help women achieve greater control over their incomes. Simultaneously, they are also helping Unilever to build stronger supply chains, distribution networks, and markets as part of their drive to create a genuinely inclusive business (Scott 2014). Unilever also empowers women farmers who can make a significant difference to their livelihoods and to the broader communities in which they live. Their agricultural workforce comprises of approximately 43 percent of women workforce and the proportion significantly growing.

Marks and Spencer's financial literacy program in India educates female factory workers to manage their own money. They educate them about the concepts of loans, savings, pay slip deductions and many other benefits. M&S co-ordinates with factory management in developing payroll efficiency and credit salary directly into the woman's bank account. The workers are now open to use mobile and community kiosks to access their funds. The program has resulted in a 30 percent increase in the number of workers who have savings (Scott 2014).

There are linkages between FDI and SDGs (which the UN has identified for 2015–2030). Some of these who deserve urgent attention are poverty, sanitation and drinking water, public health and climate change and it is evident that FDI projects can help achieve some of these objectives to a great extent. Of course much remains to be done in countries like India in the areas of rulemaking and legal enforcement to achieve SDGs. It is essential for governments to craft investment policies and frameworks that enable sustainable development because it is evident that growing number of MNEs are starting to take this responsibly but in case of those not voluntarily adopting to such practices, enforcement, regulations and enabling environments should be the key.

References

Amnesty International. 1998. "Human Rights Principles for Companies." Available at https://amnesty.org/download/Documents/148000/act700011 998en.pdf (accessed January 1998).

Auty, R.M. 2007. "13 The Resource Curse and Sustainable Development." *Handbook of Sustainable Development*, p. 207.

Chaturvedi, R. 2007. "Contract Farming and Frito-Lay's Model of Contract Farming for Potato." *Potato Journal* 34, nos. 1–2, pp. 16–19.

Karnani, A. 2005. "Misfortune at the Bottom of the Pyramid." *Greener Management International* 51, pp. 99–111.

Kaushal, L.A. 2016. "Multinational Corporations: A Boon or Bane for a Developing Economy–A Study in Indian Context." In *Handbook of Research on Impacts of International Business and Political Affairs on the Global Economy*, 154–72, IGI Global.

Rio Declaration on Environment and Development. 1992. "United Nations Conference on Environment and Development." Available at http://unep. org/Documents

Sachs, J.D., and A.M. Warner. 1997. "Sources of Slow Growth in African Economies." *Journal of African Economies* 6, no. 3, pp. 335–76.

Sauvant, K.P., and H. Mann. 2017. *Strengthening the Global Trade and Investment System for Sustainable Development*. International Centre for Trade and Sustainable Development (ICTSD), World Economic Forum.

Scott, L.M. 2014. "Private Sector Engagement with Women's Economic Empowerment-Lessons Learned from Years of Practice." Available at https://sbs.ox.ac.uk/sites/default/files/research-projects/GBCWEE/RES-0054-GBCWEE-Report-171123.pdf

Seth, A. 2003. "Marketing Led Extension Services: The Challenge of Contract Farming." Retrieved September 30, 2014, from http://info.worldbank.org/etools/docs/library/51025/ZipAgExtension1/ag_extension1/Materials/May7Session2/ContractFarming-A.Seth.pdf

Tata Motors. "International Initiatives." https://tatamotors.com/corporate-social-responsibility/international-initiatives/

Thornton, G., and Assocham India Report. 2017. *An Instinct for Growth-Food Processing Sector Challenges and Growth Enablers.*

"Unilever's Work on opportunities for women supports—5 of the UN Sustainable Development Goals." Available at https://unilever.com/sustainable-living/enhancing-livelihoods/opportunities-for-women/

UN Documents Our Common Future. "Chapter 2: Towards Sustainable Development." Available at http://un-documents.net/ocf-02.htm

UNCTAD. 2015. "Investment Policy Framework-For Sustainable Development." Available at unctad.org/en/PublicationsLibrary/diaepcb2015d5_en.pdf

United Nations. 1987. "Report of the World Commission on Environment and Development." Available at http://worldinbalance.net/pdf/1987-brundtland.pdf

World Bank. 2011. "The Changing Wealth of Nations: Measuring Sustainable Development in the New Millennium." *Environment and Development.* World Bank. ©World Bank. https://openknowledge.worldbank.org/handle/10986/2252 License: CC BY 3.0 IGO

CHAPTER 6

Case Studies

The case studies in this chapter indicate various shortcomings of public policy, regulations, and institutional environment related to FDI. These case studies serve the purpose of identifying core issues that arise in liberalizing the Indian economy and integrating specific policies related to FDI, technology transfer, etc. These case studies in no way are a reflection of effective or ineffective handling of any managerial situation. Many other case studies and examples highlight specific areas of impact of FDI activities in the select segment of the Indian economy; however, we have identified only a few cases that are well documented in secondary resources. Through these case studies we are not attempting any measurement of success or failure of FDI operations but merely analyzing the actual effects as they occur in some of these projects, with a view to reflect on the emerging scale for improvement in the scope and content of public policy for FDI. The main purpose of these illustrations and those mentioned in the preceding text is to draw some lessons and future directions from the angle of public policy, regulation and institutional environments; especially since the year 2000 the international debate focused on sustainable development and presently on sustainable development goals (SDGs). It is pertinent to note that CSR and Corporate Philanthropy are useful in initiating community and social welfare measures; however, SDGs can be achieved only by way of sustainable development practices of large multinational and national level enterprises. What is more critical is the fact that the process and content of sustainable development policy and practices involve and engage the primary and to some extent secondary

---

Disclaimer: The case studies in this chapter serves the purpose of identifying core issues that arise in liberalizing the Indian economy and integrating specific policies such as FDI and so on. The studies do not intent to illustrate either effective or ineffective handling of any managerial situation.

stakeholders to meet various SDGs and FDI as a source of external funding can go a long way in helping governments and industry achieve some of the SDGs. In addition, the lessons from theses illustrations demonstrate that both the governments and industry (inclusive of agriculture and services sectors) can develop unique capabilities to formulate programs of action for achieving specific objectives of SDGs. Sustainable development being a complex mix of legal, regulatory, policy, and institutional requirements demand dynamic capability from multi-stakeholder groups to conceive and implement sustainable development programs. Apart from these we need to note that two other specific determinants of FDI–international economic relations (inclusive of multilateral, bilateral and regional trade arrangements and agreements) and the political economy framework- are very important if a host country like India wants to promote a time bound program of action to achieve some of the SDGs.

Daiichi Sanyo and Ranbaxy Laboratories

The pharmaceutical industry deals in developing, producing, and marketing drugs that are licensed to medical usage. Pharmaceutical companies mainly deal in generic and branded medications apart from medical devices and are governed by country-specific laws and regulations regarding the patenting, testing and ensuring safety and efficacy and marketing of drugs.

India enjoys a prominent position in the global pharmaceutical sector. The Indian pharmaceuticals market globally ranks third in terms of volume and 13th in terms of value. India is also the largest exporter of generic drugs globally, accounting for 20 percent of exports in terms of volume. Indian pharmaceutical firms are currently supplying over 80 percent of the antiretroviral drugs used globally to combat acquired immunodeficiency syndrome (AIDS). The UN-backed Medicines Patent Pool has signed six sublicenses with Aurobindo, Cipla, Desano, Emcure, Hetero Labs and Laurus Labs, allowing them to make generic anti-AIDS medicine Tenofovir Alafenamide (TAF) for 112 developing countries. Off-lately, owing to the highly fragmented nature of the Indian pharmaceutical industry, consolidation has become an important characteristic.

The Indian pharma industry is expected to grow over 15 percent per annum between 2015 and 2020 and would outperform the global pharma industry that is expected to grow at an annual rate of 5 percent between the same periods. India is leading ahead of China in pharmaceutical exports with 11.44 percent year-on-year growth accounting to US$ 12.91 billion in FY 2015–2016. There has been a marginal year-on-year growth of 80 percent restricting total imports at $1,641.15 million.

Total drug approvals given to Indian companies by the US Food and Drug Administration (USFDA) have nearly doubled to 201 in FY 2015–2016 from 109 in FY 2014–2015. The country accounts for around 30 percent (by volume) and about 10 percent (value) in the US$ 70 to

80 billion US generics market. India's biotechnology industry comprising bio-pharmaceuticals, bio-services, bio-agriculture, bio-industry, and bioinformatics is expected to grow at an average growth rate of around 30 percent a year and reach US$100 billion by 2025. Biopharma, comprising vaccines, therapeutics, and diagnostics, is the largest subsector contributing nearly 62 percent of the total revenues at Rs. 12,600 crores (US$1.88 billion) (IBEF 2017).

FDI in the Pharmacy Industry

Up till 2000, 74 percent FDI was permitted in the case of bulk drugs and their intermediaries in the Pharma Industry. Investment beyond the threshold limit was subject to government approval on the case to case basis. In 2001, India opened the Pharma sector to 100 percent FDI, making it an attractive sector for foreign investors. Low cost of production, cheap labor, rising education levels, and health awareness among people led to unprecedented Industry growth.

In 2011, the Pharma sector was placed under Special Focus Sector for National Manufacturing Policy 2011, as it enjoyed the competitive and comparative advantage and was further divided into brownfields and green field. FDI in Brownfield pharma sector has been permitted up to 74 percent under the automatic route, and FDI beyond 74 percent and up to 100 percent is allowed under the Government approval route. The move to permit 74 percent FDI under automatic route in Brownfield pharmaceutical sector is aimed at attracting required capital, international best practices and latest technologies in the sector. Further, 100 percent FDI under automatic route is permitted for Greenfield pharma sector.

About Ranbaxy

Ranbaxy Laboratories was established as a private company in 1961, to produce Pharmaceutical formulations for the domestic Indian market. In 1973, the Company became a Public Limited and set up a multipurpose chemical plant for the manufacture of active pharmaceutical ingredients (APIs). In 1977, the company set up its first joint venture in Nigeria for manufacturing formulations. Over time, it became one of India's largest research-based international pharmaceutical companies, which provided a wide range of high quality and affordable generic medicines, in over 150 countries. The company had operations in over 43 countries and 21 manufacturing facilities spread across eight countries. Ranbaxy achieved several regulatory approvals in both developed and emerging markets through its continuous innovation and research and development (R&D) initiatives.

Since 2001, the company consistently contributed to the R&D expenditure. In 2003, with an R&D expenditure of approximately 5.5 percent of its sales, it became the most significant R&D investor in the Indian pharmaceutical industry. It also recorded a continuous rise in its revenue and bottom line contributions. From 2005 onward Ranbaxy re-oriented their geographic mix of business in favors of emerging markets which contributed 54 percent, that is, more than half of their global revenues compared to 40 percent by developed countries. Their worldwide sales recorded a robust growth of 21 percent and exceeded the US$1.6 billion in 2007. Profit after Tax also registered 67 percent growth touching the US$190 million, on the back of balanced growth, across geographies.[1]

About Daiichi Sankyo

Daiichi Sankyo, a Japanese pharmaceutical company, was founded in 2005 by Dr. Jokichi Takamine through the merger of century-old pharmaceutical companies, Sankyo Company Limited, and Daiichi Pharmaceutical Company Limited. It was primarily a research-based pharmaceutical company with revenues of 880.1 billion yen ($8.8 billion) in 2007–2008.

The company had a clear strategy to expand overseas especially to capture Asia, South, and Central America markets. Daiichi with business operations in 21 countries and was aiming to be a Global Pharma Innovator by 2015 and was in the process of spinning off non-pharmaceutical businesses to concentrate on its core pharmaceutical business. Acquisitions of Ranbaxy Laboratories Limited to the Daiichi Sankyo Group was

---

[1] 2.0 Ranbaxy Laboratories Limited. Available at http://who.int/intellectual-property/events/en/Ranbaxy.pdf

one of the measures to realize its vision for 2015 of becoming a Global Pharma Innovator.

The Deal

On 11th June 2008, Daiichi Sankyo the third largest pharmaceutical company in Japan made an offer to buy 34.8 percent control stake for a value $2.4 billion in Ranbaxy from its promoters, the Singh brothers Malvinder and Shivinder. Ranbaxy was then the largest drug-maker by revenue in India. In November 2008, the acquisition deal worth $4.6 billion was finally completed by acquiring a 63.92 percent stake (including the founders' entire stake) in Ranbaxy.[2]

Ranbaxy by then had a well-diversified market across the globe with emerging markets contributing heavily to its revenues. However, the Japan market, with low generics penetration added just $25 million to the top line. Daiichi Sanyo had just begun to re-orient its strategy in favors of the emerging markets and aimed at building a "hybrid business model" with a mix of patented and generic drugs (Figure 6.1). The deal was financed through the combination of debt and cash resources and also required the one of the founder CEO, Malvinder Singh to stay with the company for five years. The deal gave Daiichi Sanyo access to Ranbaxy's basket of 30 drugs which had US approvals. Among them were 10 drugs whose

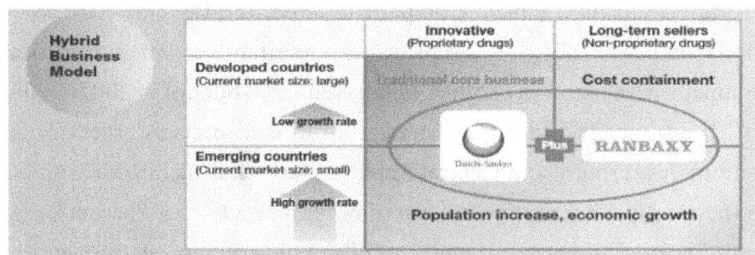

Figure 6.1 Hybrid business model

Source: Daiichi Sankyo Annual Report 2009.

---

[2] https://www.hindustantimes.com/business/japanese-firm-buys-ranbaxy/story-6WiieJNAyrAJMtn9hVfP7H.html

patents were about to expire but Ranbaxy still had exclusive right to sell for six months post the expiry.

Access to New Markets

Daiichi wanted to realize its vision for 2015 of becoming a Global Pharma Innovator. To achieve sustained economic growth, they aimed at tapping business opportunities for its prescription drug business in both advanced and emerging economies. Daichii planned to double its global reach from 21 to 56 countries using Ranbaxy's network. They wanted a strong foothold in emerging economies like India, China, Brazil, South Korea, Taiwan, Thailand, and Russia.

How the Deal Went South

During 2004–2005, Dinesh Thakur and Rajinder Kumar, two Indian employees of Ranbaxy, blew the whistle on Ranbaxy's fabrication of drug test reports. Thakur left India for the United States and contacted the Food and Drug Administration (FDA), which started investigating his claims. As a consequence, on September 16, 2008, the USFDA issued two warning letters to Ranbaxy Laboratories Ltd. and raised an import alert for generic drugs produced by two manufacturing plants in India.[3]

In the past, Ranbaxy tweaked the organizational structure by combining its analytical research and quality assurance (QA) departments to conceal the problem within the company; however, these two departments always have firewalls between them. Daiichi should have assessed not only the standard pharmaceutical organizational structure but also estimated the legal risk arising out of the USFDA letters well before the acquisition of Ranbaxy Apparently, Daiichi Sanyo was keen to tackle the issue as and when occurred instead of spending time evaluating the risk. They should have also inquired about the plant inspections conducted in 2006 along with the report submitted by Ranbaxy in defense.

---

[3] https://www.business-standard.com/article/companies/ranbaxy-daiichi-affair-how-why-the-deal-went-south-116081100270_1.html

Problems emerged soon after the acquisition when Ranbaxy's plants came under scrutiny by the USFDA. In September 2008, the FDA issued warning letters to Ranbaxy regarding the violations of good manufacturing practice at two of its plants Paonta Sahib and Dewas.[4] Restrictions were imposed on the import of drugs manufactured at these plants banning almost 30 Ranbaxy products in the United States. In February 2009, the FDA also invoked its application integrity policy (AIP) against the Paonta Sahib facility for which the inquiry was initiated long back in 2006. According to the FDA report, Ranbaxy's quality control scientists took shortcuts on the stability tests for at least two significant drugs. Claims were also raised against Ranbaxy submitting manipulated data to seek approval for marketing new generic drugs in the United States.[5]

In May 2009, Malvinder Singh the CEO of the company stepped down from his position in Ranbaxy however; according to the original agreement he was to stay as CEO with Ranbaxy for five years after the acquisition. Daiichi was banking on promoters and their team for successfully running the company in the initial few years after acquisition. Malvinder paid hefty severance charges for leaving Ranbaxy before four years of the contractual date. This also raised doubt among foreign companies who were looking for Indian partnerships.[6]

In 2012, drugs were recalled from the Netherlands and United States due to the presence of impurities.[7] In May 2013, Ranbaxy USA, a subsidiary of the Indian company was pleaded guilty to criminal charges related to manufacturing and distribution of adulterated drugs products at the two Indian plants Dewas and Ponta Sahib. They were charged criminal fine and forfeiture of $150 million along with $350 million to settle civil

---

[4] https://www.livemint.com/Companies/xnG35wiaiSOjeJLKsZqfqL/FDA-issues-warning-letters-to-Ranbaxy.html

[5] https://www.livemint.com/Home-Page/yiQBTDPSRz6ZAlR0s6nbjL/Ranbaxy-plant-a-step-closer-to-rehabilitation-by-US-FDA.html

[6] https://economictimes.indiatimes.com/news/company/corporate-trends/ranbaxy-less-aggressive-more-japanese-and-more-healthy-after-3-years-under-japans-daiichi/articleshow/11027019.cms

[7] https://economictimes.indiatimes.com/industry/healthcare/biotech/pharmaceuticals/major-developments-at-ranbaxy-over-the-past-decade/articleshow/20184699.cms?from=mdr

claims under the False Claims Act. This was the most significant false claims case ever prosecuted in the United States and the largest substantia financial penalty paid by a generics company for Food, Drug and Cosmetic Act violations till then.[8]

Daiichi Sanyo filed the case with Singapore International Arbitration Centre (SIAC) in 2013 after being pleaded guilty of misrepresenting data and fraudulent activities in pursuit of fast drug approvals and paid $500-million to the US Department of Justice (US DoJ) as a settlement.[9] Daiichi accused the Singh brothers of concealment and misrepresentation of facts. Daiichi after sinking in $4.6 billion in a cash deal to buy Ranbaxy realized that the deal was not a prudent decision and refrained itself from committing additional money to redeem or justify the investment. In April 2014, it sold Ranbaxy to Sun Pharma for $4 billion, including a debt of $800 million. As a part of the deal, Daiichi got 8.9 percent stake in the new Sun Pharma which it eventually sold off for $3.6 billion in 2015 and retreated from the Indian market.[10] The combination of Sun Pharma and Ranbaxy created the fifth-largest specialty generics company in the world and the largest pharmaceutical company in India. The acquisition made Sun Pharmaceuticals number one in the generic dermatology space. Ranbaxy had a significant presence in the Indian market (21 percent sales) and the United States (29 percent sales), offering a broad portfolio of abbreviated new drug applications (ANDAs) and first-to-file opportunities. In high growth emerging markets (50 percent of Ranbaxy's sales), provided a platform complementing Sun Pharma's strengths. Sun Pharma, on the other hand, has a strong presence in the United States (60 percent of sales) and India (23 percent), while the rest of the world accounted for 17 percent sales. Post this; the combined entity will be more diversified with the United States, the rest of the world

[8] https://in.reuters.com/article/ranbaxy-settlement-felony-usa-idINDEE94C0DA20130513

[9] https://www.vccircle.com/former-ranbaxy-owners-fined-385m-hiding-facts-daiichi-deal/

[10] https://www.thehindubusinessline.com/companies/sun-blazes-with-4-billion-ranbaxy-buy/article20749557.ece1

and India contributing 47 percent, 31 percent, and 22 percent of sales, respectively.[11]

In 2016, SIAC's order revealed that Singh brothers had followed the path of deception through data falsification to obtain approvals for over 200 drugs. The top brass at Ranbaxy willfully hid the information from Daiichi when the Japanese company acquired it and had Daiichi known the details they would not have inked the deal. However, Singh brothers challenged the petition under India's arbitration law to make the award unenforceable.[12] Quite recently in February 2018, the Delhi High Court has allowed Daiichi Sankyo to enforce an international arbitration award and recover $525 million (approximately) from former Ranbaxy promoters Malvinder Singh and Shivinder Singh, marking a victory for the Japanese company.[13]

Timeline: Chronology of Events

- June 2006: USFDA issues a warning letter to Ranbaxy's Paonta Sahib factory.
- June 2007: A whistleblower's lawsuit alleges Ranbaxy defrauded Federal programs.
- June 2008: Daiichi Sankyo acquires a 34.8 percent stake in Ranbaxy for a value $2.4 billion.
- November 2008: Daiichi Sankyo completes the takeover of the company from the founding Singh family in a deal worth $4.6 billion by acquiring a 63.92 percent stake in Ranbaxy. It is the biggest acquisition of a listed Indian company.
- Early 2009: USFDA bans an array of Ranbaxy drugs from the United States owing to manufacturing deficiencies discovered

---

[11] Oberoi, R. 2014. "Bigger and Better, Business Today." Available at https://businesstoday.in/moneytoday/stocks/ranbaxy-acquisition-good-for-sun-pharma-shareholders-experts/story/205526.html (accessed July 14, 2018).

[12] https://www.livemint.com/Companies/D21WaP0ZtLJRJk5moFFtGM/Former-Ranbaxy-owners-fined-Rs2600-crore-by-Singapore-court.html

[13] https://www.businesstoday.in/current/corporate/ranbaxy-singh-brothers-delhi-high-court-upholds-daiichi-rs-3500-crore-arbitral-award/story/269277.html

at several plants in India. Ranbaxy later pays $500 million to USFDA for fraud committed at its facilities.

- April 2014: Daiichi Sankyo sells its India unit of Ranbaxy to Sun Pharmaceutical Industries for $4 billion in an all-share deal.
- May 2016: A Singapore-based arbitration court orders Singh brothers to pay $525 million to Daiichi Sankyo.
- January 31, 2018: Delhi High Court Justice Jayant Nath rejects all objections raised by Singh brothers and orders that the arbitration awarded by announced by the Singapore tribunal was in sync with Indian laws and policy.

Lessons from the Case

What does one infer when a successful global corporation like Ranbaxy willfully defaults on disclosures and reporting of its R&D results to the US Regulators for approval of generic formulation? Prima facie this case relates to the lack of compliance not only with legal rules but also ethical standards for a global corporation. Further, this is a case of a family firm who besides being a thriving domestic competitor in its own right in the pharmaceutical sector in India had successfully established several research and marketing centers all over the world. Non-disclosures or manipulation of R&D data for obtaining approvals from the US regulators is unprecedented considering that the US regulators have high standards of approval. However, in this case, some earlier instances indicate that the United States regulators cleared the results of R&D and this perhaps motivated the company management to take further risks in data presentation.

When the matter was brought to the top management and board's attention by one of the senior Directors of the company supported by other senior colleagues, the board and top management did not take any corrective action and ignored the matters. This would then imply the violation of legal rules of disclosures and reporting. The role of top management and the board of directors are crucial. Further, this also raises specific corporate governance issues.

The whistleblower when ignored by top management and the board resigned from the company and settled in the United States to start a consulting firm on the business practices of pharmaceutical companies. He volunteered to assist the US regulators in the conduct of investigations into the irregularities of business conduct by the Ranbaxy Corporation. In this instance, the whistleblower continued his struggle unabated, certain to render service to the stakeholders and setting an example for pharmaceutical companies to follow international rules and regulations. Eventually, after two inspection visits, the US regulators could detect a lack of compliance by the company in respect of R&D results and a case was filed in the Singapore Arbitration Council.

In the meanwhile Daiichi Sankyo, a Japanese global corporation offered to purchase Ranbaxy (even with the pending legal cases). The Japanese company was confident that they would be able to deal with legal complexities of the case and hence they invested in this brownfield project. This case is a lesson for an acquiring company to analyze properly factors like top-management retention rates, organizational structure, internal firewalls and proper use of financial instruments to hedge risks before executing the deal.

In 2016, the Singapore Arbitration Council (SIAC) ordered Ranbaxy promoters to pay $525 million (Rs. 35,000 crores) to Daiichi Sanyo as damages. However, promoters refused to pay $525 million and instead filed court cases in India but so did the Japanese firm. The Japanese firm was concerned that Ranbaxy would sell off company assets to honor the penalty payments. Within less than two years the Japanese firm felt it had underestimated the enormity of the legal liability and sold Ranbaxy to India's leading pharmacy company Sun Pharma. Further, the whistleblower filed a case in the Supreme Court of India, but the Court did not find any evidence against the applicant and dismissed the petition; at the same time ironically enough the US regulators and Courts awarded $48.6 million to the whistleblower for his assistance in the investigations and successfully concluding the case.

This case illustrates how Japanese outbound investment in Ranbaxy backfired perhaps due to the lack of due diligence and asymmetric information and also shows how the whistleblowers are rewarded and protected by the US regulators.

Pohang Steel Company

Pohang steel company (POSCO), a multinational steel-making company, was established in 1965 in Pohang, South Korea and ever since it had been an inseparable part of the country's economic history. In 1988, it became the world's leading company based on crude steel production. In 2010, it was the world's largest steel manufacturing company by market value and in 2015 became the fourth-largest steel producer. The company has a presence in Africa, Europe, America, and Oceania.[14]

POSCO was keen to invest in India; however, the proposed $12 billion POSCO project, one of the biggest foreign direct investments (FDIs) of its time, ran into trouble ever since POSCO signed a memorandum of understanding (MoU) with the State of Odisha[15] in June 2005. The company planned to construct an integrated steel plant with a total capacity of 12 million tons per annum in Jagatsinghpur district of Odisha.[16] The proposed project faced protests from the local community opposing land acquisition and displacement or on the grounds of environment protection.

The POSCO case raises some fundamental questions from the angle of public policy, regulatory and institutional framework. It questions the clarity in the public policy framework of Indian government regarding FDI in the steel industry in the mid-90s. It also questions the ability of institutional apparatus to monitor such a large FDI. Both the center and state governments seemed not to be sufficiently prepared to identify and manage the veto players. They also lacked foresight hence failed to prepare a conflict resolution strategy and mechanism well in advance.

During the earlier times, the extraction industry in the developing nations failed to scale their production due to lack of domestic

---

[14] www.Posco.com (accessed August 31,2016).

[15] Orissa has been changed to Odisha in 2011 in the constitution, hence we refer it as Odisha.

[16] http://odisha.gov.in/Posco/POSCO-MoU.htm (accessed September 1, 2016).

technological investment additionally; the state policies in respect of investment regimes were also relatively slow to emerge. International experiences in this context indicate that several governments including African, Latin American, and South Asian invited FDI in extractive industries (natural resource sector). This part of contemporary economic history also deals with examples of US and UK investments into mining during the 1950s and 1970s. The literature on resource abundance and economic growth also suggests that point resources such as oil and minerals attracted FDI in the developing nations for a number of reasons as compared to diffuse resources like agriculture products (Rosser 2006).

It was empirically established that usually, democracies attracted more FDI than authoritarian regimes (Jensen 2008). While the countries mentioned previously opened up for FDI much earlier, India decided to open up FDI rules only during the last three decades; as India was already an exporter of minerals. Prior to the Korean steel project, the Indian government had already allowed other investors and joint ventures on the case to case basis in the mineral belt of the country, including domestic investors like BALCO[17] and NALCO[18] and others.

POSCO Project

In June 2005, the South Korean steel manufacturing company, Pohang Iron and Steel Company (POSCO) and the State of Odisha signed a MOU for setting up an integrated steel plant with a total capacity of 12 million tons per annum in Jagatsinghpur district of Odisha.[19] The steel plant initially targeted to produce 4 MT of steel per year which would subsequently rise to 12 MT in phases. POSCO project with an estimated $12 billion worth of investment was one of the biggest FDI in India. Odisha government attracted POSCO to their state by promising

---

[17] BALCO India, http://balcoindia.com/about-us/profile.aspx (accessed August 30, 2016).

[18] NALCO, A Navratna Company, https://nalcoindia.com/Company-Profile.aspx (accessed August 30, 2016).

[19] MOU between Govt. of Odisha and POSCO, http://odisha.gov.in/Posco/POSCO-MoU.htm (accessed August 31, 2016).

generous operational environment. The project amassed considerable support from the majority of government in Odisha, India, and Korea however, their generous behavior was widely criticized by the Indian steel companies, who were not treated alike (Viswanathand Catching 2008) and also by the civil society who believed that the government was favoring POSCO at the cost of common Odisha people (Mukhopadhyay 2006). The MOU signed between the Odisha government and POSCO provided access to large quantities of cheap, high-quality iron ore which was not available in Korea but was crucial to company's commercial success and industrial growth of South Korea (Panda, Park, and Kong 2008).

The proposed site for an integrated steel plant was Kujang Tehsil of Jagatsinghpur district, Odisha, which was 12 kilometers away from Paradeep port. According to the MOU, POSCO was responsible for managing mining facilities, building a railway line connecting mining belt to the Paradeep port and a township with proper infrastructure for supplying water. The state-level institutions had an overall responsibility to monitor various aspects of the project. During the same period, a committee headed by Mr. N.C. Saxena was examining the Forest Rights Act and several other issues related to the proposed bauxite mine lease, related to Vedanta Alumina Ltd., (VAL) in the Niyamgiri hills of Kalahandi district of Odisha. In the Vedanta case, the committee identified the negligence on the part of execution of the Scheduled Tribe and other Traditional Forest Dwellers Act which had adversely affected the tribal's belonging to the Primitive Tribal Groups (PTGs) besides gravely violating the Environment Protection Act and the Forest Conservation Act.

Based on the report, the Ministry of Environment and Forests (MoEF) declined Odisha Mining Corporation's application for forest clearance to start bauxite mining in the Niyamgiri hills. Since both POSCO and Vedanta were mineral-based projects positioned in Odisha occupying major forest area; hence it was a clear indication that POSCO might also receive similar treatment by the Committee and MoEF (Gupta 2010). However, it is worth acknowledging that POSCO and Vedanta was not similar in all aspects as they both operated in diverse environment and conditions. Vedanta's alumina plant was located in the less developed scheduled area in the western part of Odisha which was home to two PTGs. These tribal's being forest dwellers were culturally dependent on dense forests for their livelihood and displacing them would have irreversible consequences. The Indian constitution protects the rights of these tribal groups. POSCO's plant, in contrast was supposed to be positioned in a coastal district which was comparatively developed eastern part of Odisha. The project was supposed to displace eight villages which were virtually not inhabited by any of the scheduled tribes or forest dwellers rather the people there were engaged in agriculture or fishery for their livelihood.

Since the location of POSCO was in an area consisting of sandy and wasteland, it was not a major issue in terms of forest clearance procedure. The Vedanta project was almost nearing completion, though the environment clearance was still pending for certain areas under construction whereas the POSCO project was yet to begin construction as the state government had so far not even handed over the land to the company.

The committee headed by Mr. N.C. Saxena investigating Vedanta case based on the consensus suggested re-assessment of the process to identify forest rights of the villagers however few committee members objected the course of action and others even recommended an alternative compensation arrangement. Few committee members suggested a comprehensive Environmental Impact Assessment (EIA) for both steel plant and port by the MoEF[20] in consultation with the Expert Appraisal Committee (EAC). They recommended proper scrutiny to impose required auxiliary conditions, well before the commencement of construction work of the project. Few committee members also demanded cancellation of environment clearance granted to the steel plant and captive port on account of several shortcomings and flaws (Gupta 2010).

The proposed POSCO project required approximately 6.26 square miles of land which comprised of approximately 10 percent of private land, that is, 0.69 square miles and 5.57 square miles of government land (which included 4.62 square miles of forest land and 0.94 square miles non-forest government land), which would result in displacing approximately471 families (Nayak 2015). Khandhar in Sundergarh district

---

[20] The Ministry of Environment and Forests (MoEF), http://moef.gov.in/ (accessed June 02, 2015).

was the proposed site for iron ore mining, and the state government has already granted a prospecting license to POSCO-India. Nonetheless, the High Court of Odisha in July 2010 instructed the Odisha Government to hear all the applications for mines once again and decide within four months which was instead declined and challenged by the state in the Supreme Court.

The Resistance Movement

In the beginning, all the eight villages were against the POSCO project but eventually knowing that only two villages would be entirely displaced, many villagers changed their opinion. Current livelihood versus promised livelihood was the primary concern of difference in opinions of the villagers. Villagers expected fair compensation with future job security for their family. Along with the villagers, an association known as POSCO Protirodh Sangram Samiti also protested against the project though the political consensus was altogether missing on this subject (D'Costa 2015). The protest focused on diversion of forest land issue as it was used by many villagers to cultivate paan or betel vine and was the primary source of livelihood. The particular exclusive variety was paan (betel) was grown on this forest land.[21]

Reactions and Assessments of Analysts

In mid-July 2007, the then Chief Minister of Odisha along with the representatives of POSCO Pratorodh Sangram Samiti (PPSS) decided to commence land survey in five villages without the consensus among stakeholders. The analyst raised objections regarding the aptness of decisions supporting FDI without any initial assessment of the human and environmental impact of the proposed POSCO plant in the state. There were several deficiencies in the National Mineral Policy and the institutions which were entrusted with the task of mineral exploration

---

[21] Understanding the Impact of the Proposed POSCO Project, Mining Zone Peoples' Solidarity Group, http://miningzone.org/wp-content/uploads/2011/04/POSCO_Backgrounder.pdf (accessed June 15, 2016).

such as Ecological Survey of India, Indian Bureau of Mine and National Mineral Development Corporation too were losing their importance as more players from the public and private sector were allowed in the sector (Mukhopadhyay 2006). POSCO declared financial compensation for 200 families in Jagatsinghpur but the families were much more in number. Many people were losing compensation and rehabilitation benefits due to lack of records.

Das (2005) suggested that the Government should have a monopoly and control over the supply of minerals to plants at the market price and regulate Indian exports. He also suggested setting floor level for concessions. In 2007, P.K. Dang committee not only recommended a restriction on mineral exports foreseeing increased domestic demand but also prohibited any foreign partnership in iron ore if it was located in the scheduled area (Asher 2006). The POSCO deal prompted mass protests that lead to arrests of the activist and even a few people losing their lives. Such a situation prompted social movements across the globe, especially in developing countries. The adverse environmental impact of the project consecutively raised the concern of social equity and justice (Khoday, Kishan, and Natarajan 2012).

POSCO Project Clearance

MoEF assigned the EAC a task to appraise POSCO project by considering EIA reports and public hearing proceedings. Based on the recommended clearance by the committee, the MoEF gave environment clearance for the captive port on May 15, 2007 and the steel plant on July 19, 2007. Based on the recommendations of the Forest Advisory Committee (FAC), forest clearance was also granted on September 19, 2008, post the inquiry by the Central Empowered Committee (CEC) and approval by the Supreme Court. The project was given final clearance on December 29, 2009.

A Letter by Kapavriksh[22] to the MoEF Committee of 2010 indicated that almost 22,000 odd families would be rendered homeless along with

---

[22] Environment and Forest Clearance Related Issues of the Posco Project in Jagatsinghpur. http://kalpavriksh.org/images/EnvironmentandDevelopment/

substantial livelihood income loss with POSCOPOSCO getting the clearance. The proposed port at the mouth of Jatadhari creek will damage the ecosystem irrevocably, and the Kandahar hills, the proposed site for POSCO's mining operations being covered with flora and fauna will also be ruined. Allegations were raised on the process of granting clearances. Khandhar in Sundergarh district was the proposed site for iron, and the state government has already granted a prospecting license to POSCO-India. Nonetheless, the High Court of Odisha in July 2010 instructed the Odisha Government to hear all the applications for mines once again and decide within four months which was rather declined and challenged by the state in the Supreme Court. Amid these persisting hassles, the MOU signed between POSCO and State of Odisha expired on June 22, 2010, without any commissioning of the plant which blocked the road for any future scope of an extension of the MOU.

However, later in 2010, MoEF demanded the consent of forest dwellers before granting any forest clearance, and on August 5, 2010, it issued a letter directing the Government of Odisha to refrain from handling over any forest land to the third party (Gupta 2010). Despite the objections from the Ministry of Shipping, the Odisha state government approved a port site 12 kilometers away from the Paradeep port for the proposed POSCO plant in 2013.

Avenues of Resistance and Remedy

As per the OECD contact point assessments, domestic legal and regulatory process reviewed the project situations regularly. There was a significant political mobilization, and in terms of transnational civil society movements, European, Korean and the US civil society organizations campaigned against the project (Chrimes 2015).

International Human Rights Clinic (IHRC) recommended suspending POSCO's operations in India owing to non-compliance with international human rights standards. They emphasized on inclusive execution of

OpenLetters/POSCOpercentage20committeepercentage20submission,percentage20environmentpercentage20andpercentage20forestpercentage20clearances, percentage20FINAL,percentage209.9.2010.pdf (accessed April 15, 2017).

the Forest Rights Act provisions. Land clearance, diversion or acquisition of forest land needs to be executed in coordination to the rights of the forest dwelling communities. Police officials were instructed to act according to the international standards avoiding capricious arrest and detentions. The communities affected by the project should be granted protection against violence by the private sectors apart from adequate access to food, healthcare, education, and work. Apart from this, ESCR-Net and IHRC recommended that foreign institutional investors of POSCO should take suitable measures to ensure POSCO's respects for human rights.[23]

The MOU between POSCO and Government of Odisha was signed on June 22, 2005, but even until June 2012, final clearance was not given to POSCO. Based on the recommendations of NHRC Report, the state government initiated returning of the acquired land (for the proposed POSCO plant) back to the private parties in July 2012. In August 2012, a study was conducted by MoEF's expert team to investigate the impact of forest diversion on the local environment.[24] In June 2014, the Odisha government requested the new government at the center to fasten the approvals for granting mining licenses to POSCO, however, India's new tribal affairs minister, Jual Oram did not allow it. By March 2015, the news of POSCO exiting India started making rounds when six of its 13 top employees quitted the project.

Ruined Economy, Damaged Ecology

More than 12 years and after several twists and turns owing to the large public resistance to the project as well as regulatory hurdles, the South

---

[23] International Human Rights Clinic, ESCR-Net. 2013. *The Price of Steel: Human Rights and Forced Evictions in the Posco-India Project*. New York, NY: NYU School of Law. https://escr-net.org/sites/default/files/11271400/Theperce ntage20Pricepercentage20Ofpercentage20Steelpercentage20-percentage20Fullp ercentage20(English).pdf) (accessed July 15, 2016).

[24] Jyotiraj Patra Coasts, Ports, and Communities: The Emerging Dynamics of Investment-Risk Interactions in Odisha, 2013 UNISDR, and GAR India, www. preventionweb.net/english/hyogo/gar/2013/en/bgdocs/Patra,percentage202012. pdf (accessed July 17, 2016).

Korean steel major finally officially withdrew from the project. In March 2017 POSCO offered to surrender the land it had acquired because of its inability to start work on the project. Though it is the end of the road for POSCO but the damage that has been done to the area seems irreparable. Millions of stumps of cashew nut and other fruit-bearing trees are tell-tale signs of livelihoods lost and ecology devastated. Today, Nuagaon, the village that backed POSCO, is a picture of despair; its residents have exhausted their compensation amounts and are left with no other means to sustain themselves. More than half of the village is unemployed, and others are making their living as daily-wage laborers. Nuagaon also suffers from a shortage of firewood as its forest cover is all but depleted, another remnant of the project.

Timeline: Chronology of Events

- June 2005: MOU was signed between POSCO and Government of Odisha.
- August 2005: Formation of POSCO Pratirodh Sangram Samiti to oppose the project.
- May 2007: Based on EAC recommendations MoEF gave environment clearance for the captive port.
- July 2007: Based on EAC recommendations MoEF gave environment clearance to the steel plant.
- August 2008: Supreme Court endorsed "in principle" clearance for the use of forest land but informed the MoEF to advance per the law.
- December 2009: The Environment Ministry approved final clearance for diversion of forest land.
- March 2012: The National Green Tribunal adjourned the environment clearance.
- July 2012: Based on the recommendations of NHRC Report, the state government initiated returning of the acquired land (for the proposed POSCO plant) back to the private parties.
- July 2012: POSCO-India approached the state government with a revised proposal seeking transfer of 4.23 mi2 land to set up an 8 MTPA steel plant.

- August 2012: A study was conducted by MOEF's expert team to investigate the impact of forest diversion on the local environment.
- May 2013: India's top court strikes down the Odisha high court order. It asks the central government to decide on granting the mine to POSCO.
- July 2013: Odisha completes acquisition of 2,700 acres of land for the project.
- June 2014: The Odisha government requested the new government at the center to fasten the approvals for granting mining licenses to POSCO. March 2015: News agency Bloomberg reported that the company might finally walk away from the project in India as six of its 13 top employees have already quit the project.
- March 2017: POSCO closed the last chapter in Odisha project.

Lessons from the Case

The complexity of POSCO case was represented by a multiplicity of primary and secondary stakeholders, with a significant range of divergent opinions, views, perceptions, demands and mixed expectations on the likely outcomes of this project. The case has opened up a number of issues such as a legal and regulatory framework for FDI; public policy of steel and mineral and other related infrastructure industries; human rights violations, rising poverty levels; environmental degradation and sustainable development. It also raises questions toward business ethics; CSR; the role of the civil societies and NGOs (as also other activists), the role of the police, state-level bureaucracy and district administration; and a host of public and private institutions associated with or affected by the trends and developments of the project. The case opens up the proverbial debate of the last 60 years of the FDI literature "whether FDI promotes economic growth and development." The case also has major implications on the trade-off between foreign investment and the environmental impact. Also, the case leads to a re-examination of India's trade policy in terms of exports of iron ore which is the most crucial raw material for the steel industry despite an ever increasing demand for this raw material from the domestic investors.

The widely held opinion among the economists of 1950s is that resource abundance enables developing economies to make a transition to the next level of development as it occurred in some Western economies—UK, Australia, and the United States. However, this view was challenged in the 1980s, and it was argued that the nature of commodities placed the developing countries at a disadvantage. Further, economies with resource abundance would experience adverse growth outcomes implying poor economic performance. Such economies perform poorly in agriculture, economic growth and export diversification as compared with non-mineral economies. These issues can be addressed by good economic governance and realistic and dynamic public policies.

The theory of resource curse applies to the mineral-rich Odisha government because the availability of the natural resources by itself cannot automatically ensure growth; technical and managerial skill, technology for the projects, R&D capabilities of promoters, training, and development of labor force, and so on, are very relevant. A country like India has to learn how to realize the benefits of resource abundance. Many countries like Indonesia, Botswana, Norway, Chile, and Malaysia have avoided the resource curse; so have in the 19th-century countries like Australia, Canada, the United States, and the UK. Unless a nation can develop the other sectors of the economy and deal with chronic issues such as poverty (India) the resource curse issue will persist.[25]

In terms of the political economy implications, any FDI project in a developing economy primarily is an outcome of the given political system and its decision on foreign investment. For instance, Indian economy was a closed economy until the 1980s, and therefore a small group of foreign investors who were there in the 1970s like Coca Cola and IBM was driven out when the there was regime change. A vague sense of economic nationalism has prevented many past Indian governments in liberalizing foreign

[25] Stevens, P., G. Lahn, and J. Kooroshy. August 2015. "Energy, Environment and Resources." *The Resource Curse*, https://chathamhouse.org/sites/files/chathamhouse/field/field_document/20150804ResourceCurseRevisitedStevensLahnKooroshy_0.pdf (accessed February 03, 2017).

investment regime which eventually got liberalized toward the end of the previous century. In a decentralized economy like India, the powers of the state and the Centre have been laid down by the Indian Constitution. For the first time, the 13th Finance Commission explicitly built a criterion of environmental performance for the states.

Apart from this arrangement, several Articles of the Constitution provide for the protection of tribal rights (human rights) which the FDI projects and the state governments have to comply with. However, the political economy bias is activated when the state government in a hurry to industrialize, agree to the demands of the FDI project completely ignoring the local conditions. After all before POSCO and Vedanta Alumina projects several large corporations from India have participated in power, steel, minerals sectors and they have also gone through similar experiences of delays and political economy fall out effects.

When the conflicts of claims and counterclaims between the Odisha government and the central government became intense the matter reached the High Court and Supreme Court. Thus when the political executive in a weak democracy cannot decide on essential parameters of project implementation, then the Courts have to take an active role.

In March 2017 POSCO finally closed the chapter of Odisha project, but the damage that has been done to the area seems irreparable.

Vedanta Alumina Limited

The debate on the potential and actual adverse effects of industrialization on the eco-system (water, air, rivers, mountains, and wildlife) continues unabated in the developed and developing economies. Rapid industrialization violates human rights, displaces indigenous people, destroys the sources of livelihood; and creates intra- and inter-generational social equity issues. The host country bears huge FDI seeking cost as they need to provide concessions and guarantees, land, infrastructure, and other suitable incentives straining their budgets. In many large FDI projects, the social and environmental aspects are not adequately taken care of despite the availability of international experiences, guidelines, codes and standards, expertise within the governments and necessary legislative framework of the host countries. In such a context it is the governments and communities who have to bear the direct and indirect costs. The corporations hardly bear the costs barring non-compliance related penalties. At times the corporations are more powerful than some governments and can build a sustained defense of their practices. It is inevitably left to the activists, NGOs and courts to point out the lapses by the foreign investors on the social and environmental front. In the natural resource sector, the respective state governments want to promote competition and generate revenue without upgrading their institutional and public policy environments. Both the primary and secondary stakeholders are adversely affected by these issues. Resource curse is evident in regions of an economy which have a poor track record of economic, social and political governance.

Globally, three distinctive trends paved the way for globalization wave in 1990s namely, increasing democratization of several poor and developing economies, public policy reforms by way of privatization and deregulation in the 1980s, Reaganomics (United States) and Thatcherism (UK)[26]

---

[26] Privatization and Deregulation: A Push Too Far? available at http://worldbank. org/prem/lessons1990s/chaps/06-Ch06_kl.pdf

and macroeconomic reforms induced by the "Washington Consensus[27]" leading to large scale reforms in the legal, institutional and regulatory regimes of the developing and transitional economies. The East Asian Miracle further augmented these trends in the mid 1990s through the export-led growth model practiced by newly industrializing economies (Page 1994). These developments were further armored by technology breakthrough and rapid expansion of cross-border trade and services. Such tends also stimulated unparalleled growth of MNEs through international joint ventures and setting up of wholly owned subsidiaries worldwide. However, developing nations started competing for inward FDI, and it became an urgent agenda among rapidly liberalizing developing nations (Olivera 2010). The proposed projects of Vedanta Resources, a global player in the mineral market, are one of the consequences of the process and content of globalization. India a resource-rich economy in the post-reform era intended to invite FDI projects in select sectors, especially in the minerals sector, given the constraints of investible funds and technical expertise. In the 1990s, Orissa State devised ways and means to attract large FDI projects and managed to negotiate two FDI projects, that is, Posco Steel and Vedanta Resources.

One of the criticisms of the "Washington Consensus" was that many countries that introduced macro-economic reforms based on this Consensus were quite unprepared in terms of the institutional environment, public policy choices and legal framework to anticipate and deal with the consequences for their economies, let alone society and the environments. In other words, globalization based on such a premise and "one size fits all" agenda across the developing world created certain irreversible consequences for sustainable development.

About Vedanta Alumina Limited

Vedanta Resources Plc. was one of the leading diversified global natural resource company, with operations spanning across the vast value

---

[27] By Naim, M. 1999. "Fads and Fashion in Economic Reforms: Washington Consensus or Washington Confusion?" *Foreign Policy Magazine* October 26, 1999. https://imf.org/external/pubs/ft/seminar/1999/reforms/Naim.HTM

chain of exploration, asset development, extraction, and processing and value addition. Geographically, the operations were centered in India, Sri Lanka, Zambia, Namibia, South Africa, Liberia, Ireland, and Australia with over 28,000 employees. The group had undertaken several Green-field and brown-field expansion projects throughout the world; and completed capital expansions, involving complex project technologies and large investments, in record time and at significantly lower costs.

VAL a subsidiary of Vedanta UK proposed the development of the aluminum refinery and bauxite mining in the Niyamgiri Hills of Orissa state in India. In April 1997 Sterlite Industries India Ltd., (SIIL) agreed with Government of Orissa to set up an Alumina Refinery in Lanjigarh with rights to Niyamgiri bauxite granted to Orissa Mining Corporation Limited (OMC), a company owned by the State of Orissa. It was an FTSE 100 listed company. Vedanta, UK had a direct controlling stake of 59.9 percent in Mumbai based SIIL and 70.5 percent in Vedanta Aluminum Limited located in Lanjigarh Orissa.

Orissa state encouraged steel, aluminum and power companies to set up factories and promised them mines to extract iron ore, bauxite and coal like its mineral-rich neighbors Jharkhand and Chhattisgarh but unfortunately, like its neighbors, the state too witnessed people's resistance toward these projects. Besides Vedanta, a number of companies including South Korean steelmaker Posco also faced problems in getting mining leases, environment and forest clearances, and in acquiring land. On July 17, 2013, global steel giant Arcelor Mittal scrapped its Rs. 50,000 crore project in Orissa on account of failed attempts to acquire land and iron-ore mining blocks for the 12-million-ton project. They signed a pact with the state government long back in December 2006 but failed because State allegedly made promises without considering the interest of locals.[28]

---

[28] Tribals in Orissa's Niyamgiri hills reject Vedanta's bauxite mining project in a landmark referendum, September 15, 2013, available at http://businesstoday. in/magazine/features/orissa-niyamgiri-rejects-vedanta-entry-impact-reasons/ story/197972.html (accessed August 12, 2016).

Regulatory and Legal Issues Related to the Case

The economics of alumina production suggests that due to government regulation and power intensity of such projects almost 2 to 3 tons of bauxite was used to produce 1 ton of alumina, due to this fact production in the West had suffered but in India which had one-fifth of the world's bauxite resources the situation was different. India supported the lower cost of capital with weak environments compliances. In March 2002, SIIL submitted a proposal to the Government for alumina refinery project with the captive power plant at Lanjigarh.

In June 2002, villagers received noticed from Gram Sabha about land acquisition for the proposed alumina refinery project, SIIL in Lanjigarh, who had an old MOU with the state government in 1997. As per the notice by the district authorities, 12 villages would be demolished, 60 families would be displaced, and 302 families would lose their farmland, which in turn led to a wide-spread local protest in Orissa.[29]

On March 19, 2003 with the intention to open the refinery, SIIL applied for environment clearance to the MoEF. The application stated that the project was not using any forest area as there wasn't any forest area in the 10 kilometers radius of the refinery. Based on this report MoEF granted them environment clearance unaware of the fact that their application for forest clearance with MoEF was still pending. In June 2003, the state signed afresh MOU with SIIL for 3 million tons of bauxite mine, 1 million ton alumina plant, 75 MW power plant and a 50,000 TPA smelter project. Earlier on December 16, 2002, the Supreme Court passed the order stating that mining may be permitted in forest areas where specific prior approval under Section 2 of the Forest Conservation (FC) Act 1980 has been accorded by the MoEF, Government of India. Earlier in February 2000, the Court had also passed an order banning mining activity in areas notified as Sanctuary or national Park under Wild Life Protection Act 1972 even if prior approval has been obtained from the MoEF under the F.C. Act. The Supreme Court's historical judgment on April 18, 2003, also empowers Gram Sabhas to process all claims

---

[29] www.downtoearth.org.in (accessed August 6, 2016).

on forest rights, in particular, religious rights under the supervision of a District Judge and send the report to MoEF.

In 2004, the state forest department issued a notice to VAL for encroachment of village forest land to the extent of 4.21 hectares and informed the MoEF accordingly. Two activists and a professional also filed a petition before the CEC of the Supreme Court that the VAL had violated the Schedule V of the Indian Constitution resulting into land alienation and destruction of local cultural heritage. In March 2005, the Supreme Court of India objected the legitimacy of environment clearance granted by MoEF and requested the Ministry to hold back the forest clearance until CEC examined the project.[30]

In September 2005, the CEC in their report to the Supreme Court recommended that the clearances should be revoked and mining operations be discontinued. According to the CEC, the MoEF acted in haste in granting clearances to the project. As per the CEC report, 58.943 hectares of forest land was needed for the refinery which consists of 29 hectares of village forest land and 30 hectares of the reserve forest. However, the company neither disclosed the forest land diversion possibility for executing the project nor the likely effects of mining operations on the environment and society; on the contrary, the company claimed that there was no forest land within 10 kilometers radius of the plant.

On the advice of Supreme Court in February 2006, the FAC prepared a report within three months recommending clearances to forest land for the project. However, there was another matter in which the clearance granted by the FAC in 2006 was under review by the Court hence the Supreme Court asked the CEC and the VAL to propose alternate sites for mining. Power plant commenced in February 2007 and trial run at the refinery started in March 2007. The Company stated that it was obtaining bauxite from Gujarat and Chattisgargh amid pending clearances from the Court. On August 8, 2008, the Indian Supreme Court authorized SIIL to divert 660.749 hectares of forest land for undertaking bauxite mining on the Niyamgiri hills in Lanjigarh subject to final

---

[30] http://envfor.nic.in/sites/default/files/Vedanta-24082010.pd

approval by the Indian MoEF.[31] The company began commissioning the Greenfield aluminum refinery project and associated power plant at Lanjigarh Orissa. Consequently, the company also proposed a Greenfield project of 0.5 mta aluminum smelter and a 1,215 MW captive power plant at Jharsaguda. The first phase of the aluminum smelter project was commissioned in 2008.

The Supreme Court granted clearance for forest land diversion in April 2009 which resulted in mass protests from the tribal people[32] with substantial outside support. Other projects in the mineral sector have also faced local protests earlier (like steel, power including the public sector projects); but controversies continued unabated despite all these developments (Mishra 2010).

On August 2010, the state government applied for the final environment clearance to the MoEF, but the FAC recommended that the clearance would be granted only after determining the community rights on forest land under the Forest Rights Act 2006. The FAC provided valuable information stating that the project had violated the Forest Rights Act 2006, Forest conservation Act and Environment Protection Act of 1986. The Committee also noted that the bauxite reserves of 72 million tons would last only for few years, so the proposed expansion form 1 mtpa to 6mtpa was hardly relevant and neither the company proposed any alternate supply of ores.[33]

The rapid environmental impact assessment (REIA) report for SIIL prepared by Tata AIG Risk Management Services Ltd., Mumbai (TARMS) also highlighted that the bauxite reserves in the lease area were approximately 73 million tons which would last only for another 23 years. The proposed mining site was located on the top of Niyamgiri hills.

---

[31] The Vedanta Case in India , EJOLT Fact sheet 046 (2015) available at http://ejolt.org/wordpress/wp-content/uploads/2015/08/FS-46.pdf

[32] A brief report on Ecological and Biodiversity Importance of Niyamgiri Hill and Implications of Bauxite Mining. http://cseindia.org/userfiles/Reportpercentage20onpercentage20Niyamgiri.pdf (accessed April 22, 2017).

[33] Recommendations of the Forest Advisory Committee. August 2010. http://moef.gov.in/sites/default/files/Agendapercentage20Item24082010.pdf (accessed September 21, 2017).

Role of Local and National Bodies

Gram Sabha

In 2010, the MoEF rejected clearance to the project on the grounds that the company violated the FRA, EPA, and the Forest Conservation Act. The state challenged this in the Supreme Court. In July 2013, Supreme Court invited views of the locals on the project at Nyamgiri Hills. Locals believed that the project would destroy God and source of sustenance. There was also disagreement among the company and voluntary organizations on the number of villages to be affected by the project, according to latter at least 122 villages would be affected. According to the Supreme Court's verdict Gram Sabhas were empowered to consider claims under FRA and decide if the project infringes on the "religious and cultural rights" of the local people.[34] The Indian Constitution mandates to protect the identity and rights of the Scheduled Tribes through several of its provisions in various articles.

Legislation vests Gram Sabha's with several powers related to the ownership of minor forest produce, approval of development plans and selection of beneficiaries under various programs. Gram Sabhas were supposed to be consulted well in advance in the matters of land acquisition and also provide a prior recommendation for granting license or mining lease for minor minerals. They were responsible for managing village markets, controlling money lending to STs and prevention of alienation of land. They also had control right on institutions and functionaries in all social sectors besides giving utilization certificate of funds used for the projects and programs of social and economic development, and so on, to the village panchayats.[35]

Various developmental projects displaced the forest dwellers many times rendering them in apprehension. They were worried about losing the benefit of the Act in the absence of their ability to prove residency

---

[34] www.downtoearth.org (accessed August 17, 2017).
[35] Dr. Mahi Pal Gram Sabha in Fifth Scheduled Areas Precept and Practice Kurukshetra May 2013 http://yojana.gov.in/cms/(S(ywrwttrosl2azkr5iwou0j55))/pdf/Kurukshetrapercentage5CEnglishpercentage5C2013/Kurukshetrapercentage20Maypercentage202013.pdf (accessed January 22, 2017).

for three generations in the present village. They were worried about the non-functional Gram Sabhas and ignorance of panchayat functionaries about the law which might undermine their benefits. The predominance of Government officers in both the appellate committees (sub-divisional level committee and district level committee) could also deprive them of justice. They were not able to collect caste certificates as the issuing authority was not confirmed.[36]

Amnesty International Reports

The salient conclusions of Amnesty International report 2010 and 2011 concluded that the project involves a diversion of 660 hectares of protected forest land inhabited by approximately 8,500 strong Dongria Kondh, a protected Adivasi (indigenous) community and a few other marginalized communities threatening the very survival of the community. The project has undermined human rights, including the right to health and a healthy environment, an adequate standard of living, water, work, and food. The report critics the weakness of Indian official bodies to respect and protect the communities' human rights as required under international human rights law.

Recommendations from Amnesty International include provisions for the community to access adequate information, comprehensive human rights and EIA of the mine plans and any implementation should be undertaken in genuine and open consultation with the local stakeholders. It ordered the suspension of all mine and refinery expansion plans until the human rights issues are adequately addressed.[37]

N C Saxena Committee Report

According to the Saxena committee report (2010), ecological costs of mining operations of the intensity proposed in the project spreading over

---

[36] Land Rights and Ownership in Orissa August 2008 Status Report. http://undp.org/content/dam/india/docs/land_rights_ownership_in_orissa.pdf (last accessed June 14, 2017).

[37] Vedanta's Perspective Uncovered Briefing" Amnesty International: Policies Cannot Mask Practices in Orissa 2012. http://indiaenvironmentportal.org.in/files/file/vedanta.pdf (accessed March 20, 2017).

more than 7 square kilometers would severely disturb the important wild-life habitat especially elephants. The Forest Rights Act could be modified only for the conservation of critical wildlife habitats. Section 5 of the Act vests the Gram Sabhas and the forest dwellers with statutory rights to conserve, protect and manage forests, biodiversity, wildlife, water catch-ment areas, and their cultural and natural heritage.[38]

Observations by OECD Contact Point for Multinational Enterprises

The UK National Contact Point (NCP), denied Vedanta from engaging Dongria Kondh, an indigenous community in Niyamgiri hills as the min-ing effects would be detrimental for their health and safety. They further emphasized that Vedanta did not respect the rights of the Dongria Kondh as per India's commitments under the UN International Covenant on Civil and Political Rights, the UN Convention on the Elimination of All Forms of Racial Discrimination, the Convention on Biological Diversity and the UN Declaration on the Rights of Indigenous People.[39] The Indian Centre for Science and Environment stated that Orissa had claimed a maximum amount of forest land for mining operations. Mining of major minerals generated a waste of 1.8 billion tons in 2006 which still lacks a proper disposal system. The report not only suggested future policy changes and condemned any mining operation without the consent of the local people.[40]

In 2014, Vedanta finally lost a battle to mine bauxite in the Niyamgiri hills in Odisha. The rejection forced the firm to import expensive bauxite for an aluminum plant and delay its expansion. The Odisha Mining Corporation, to undermine the rights of the Adivasi communities residing

---

[38] http://indiaenvironmentportal.org.in/files/file/Saxena_Vedanta.pdf (accessed October 03, 2017).

[39] Final Statement by the UK National Contact Point for the OECD Guidelines for Multinational Enterprises Complaint from Survival International against Vedanta, available at www.downtoearth.org.in/blog/do-we-really-the bauxite-from-niyamgiri-42005 (accessed October 21, 2017).

[40] http://mines.nic.in/writereaddata/UploadFile/Sustainable_Development_Framework.pdf

in Niyamgiri, once again, filed a petition challenging the 2013 resolutions of the Gram Sabhas however; the Supreme Court scrapped the petition on May 6, 2016. The people of Niyamgiri won again, and they continue to inspire thousands of such struggles across the country for the assertion of people's rights over their resources. Hopefully, this will be a lesson well learned by corporate and entities that look at ways to undermine people's rights in their lust for profit.[41]

Ongoing Vedanta Trouble in Tamil Nadu

In the wake of massive protests in May 2018, the Tamil Nadu government issued a government order closing another Vedanta subsidary. Sterlite copper smelter in Tuticorin, locally known as Thoothukudi smelter, has been battling local protests on the grounds of its adverse environmental implications. The Supreme Court has directed the National Green Tribunal to reconsider Tamil Nadu Government's petition challenging maintainability and merit of Vedanta Ltd's case filed with the NGT challenging the state government's order of permanently closing the factory in Thoothukudi, Tamil Nadu.[42]

Timeline: Chronology of Events

- April 1997: Sterlite enters into an agreement with Government of Orissa to set up an Alumina Refinery in Lanjigarh and rights to Niyamgiri bauxite granted to OMC.
- March 2002: Sterlite submitted a proposal for Alumina Refinery with the captive power plant at Lanjigarh to the Government.
- August 2002: Sterlite Industries commissions EIAs report.

---

[41] Final Statement by the UK National Contact Point for the OECD Guidelines for Multinational Enterprises Complaint from Survival International against Vedanta, available at www.downtoearth.org.in/blog/do-we-really-the bauxite-from-niyamgiri-42005(last accesses August 17 2017).

[42] https://indiatoday.in/business/story/tuticorin-s-wrath-not-a-first-for-vedanta-the-firm-s-controversial-history-in-5-points-1245998-2018-05-30

- March 2003 First round of Public Hearings conducted in Lanjigarh and Muniguda for both proposed refinery and mine.
- March 2003: Sterlite applies the MoEF seeking environmental clearance for the Lanjigarh refinery.
- June 2003: Sterlite enters into a fresh agreement with the Government of Orissa to set up the 1 Mt per annum Alumina Refinery and 3 Mt per annum bauxite mining facilities.
- April 2004 All the permissions belonging to Sterlite Industries (India) Ltd., were transferred to Vedanta Aluminium Ltd., and an agreement is signed between OMC and VAL.
- September 2004: MoEF approved the setting up of the 1 Mt per annum Alumina Refinery project at Lanjigarh with 75 MW power plant capacity subject to the conditions stipulated.
- November 2004: The Supreme Court, on the basis of the CEC report, commenced hearings of petitions against mining at Niyamgiri.
- December 2004: The Supreme Court initiated an inquiry into allegations of environmental malpractice through CEC.
- March 2005: The Supreme Court of India objected the legitimacy of environment clearance granted by MoEF and requested the Ministry to hold back the forest clearance till CEC examined the project.
- September 2005: The CEC in their report to the Supreme Court denied clearances to the project.
- February 2006: Supreme Court requested the FAC to prepare a report in three months where the FAC recommended clearances to forest land for the project.
- Feb 2007: The Power plant commenced a trial run at the refinery.
- March 2007: The plant started, company stated that it was obtaining bauxite from Gujarat and Chattisgarh amid pending clearance from the Court.

- October 2007: VAL submits an application to MoEF for the expansion of the project within the same footprint.
- November 2007: The Supreme Court of India, as a result of findings of CEC investigation, puts a halt to mining project and proposed the formation of a special purpose vehicle (SPV) to develop rehabilitation package for Niyamgiri mine project.
- March 2008: MoEF issues the Terms of Reference for the preparation of the Environment Impact Assessment Report of the proposed expansion.
- August 2008: VAL and OMC accept the Supreme Court proposal of SPV and were subsequently granted clearance for mining project infrastructure development.
- March 2009: Amnesty International sends a mission to Niyamgiri hills to meet with local communities.
- April 2009: MoEF: grants clearance for mine project after approval from Supreme Court.
- May 2009: Local communities file petition against MoEF decision to approve mine to the National Environment Appellate Authority.
- October 2010: MoEF rejected the clearance to the project on the grounds that the company violated the FRA, EPA, and the Forest Conservation Act.
- November 2010: VAL asks the MoEF to consider the expansion again and issue the Environmental Clearance, but the Ministry responds with a request for a fresh proposal to obtain consent.
- May 2011: Amnesty International report undermined human rights, including the right to health and a healthy environment, an adequate standard of living, water, work, and food. The report criticized the weakness of India's official bodies to respect and protect the communities' human rights as required under international human rights law.
- July 2013: Supreme Court asked locals to give their views on the project at the Nyamgiri Hills.

- August 2013: Gram Sabha voted against mining and OMC filed a petition challenging the 2013 resolutions of the Gram Sabhas.
- January 2014: The environment ministry issued a ban on mining in Niyamgiri and Vedanta lost a battle to mine bauxite in the Niyamgiri hills in Odisha.
- May 2016: The Supreme Court scrapped the petition of OMC.

Lessons from the Case

The case highlights the journey of this controversial Vedanta alumina project in India. The case illustrates the dilemmas of developing economies like India where having invited a massive FDI project; they find it challenging to process various demands of the diverse range of stakeholders. The case also highlights delays in decision making, as various state and central level agencies were involved and eventually further compounded by protracted litigation implications.

The international reactions initially came from the investors and financial institutions who pulled out their investments from the Vedanta companies.[43] International civil society groups and other voluntary organizations besides prominent activist and environmental groups also supported the battle of the tribal people against the various adverse effects of the VAL operations in the two districts of Orissa. The Church of England decided to disinvest from the company in February 2010 on ethical grounds. The British government also had publicly criticized the company for disrespecting human rights.[44] The Joseph Rowntree Charitable Trust and the Dutch PGGM an asset management firm also disinvested from the company. These developments did not augur well for corporate reputation and brand equity of the group companies in India.

---

[43] The Council on Ethics for the Norway Government pension Fund 2007 and the Scottish Investment group Martin Currie 2008. http://banktrack.org/manage/ems_files/download/briefing_on_vedanta_and_the_niyamgiri_hills/vedanta.pdf (accessed August 12, 2017).

[44] http://survivalinternational.org/news/5518 (accessed August 11, 2016).

The UK NCP in point 67 of its final statement highlighted that none of the instruments of international law such as The United Nations International Covenant on Civil and Political Rights (1966), The United Nations Convention on the Elimination of all forms of Racial Discrimination (1965), The Convention on Biological Diversity (1992) and The United Nations Declaration on the Rights of Indigenous People (2007) were applied in the Vedanta Case. Being already the part of the Indian legal framework, some would have rendered appropriate to reduce the adverse implications of the project.[45]

The resource extraction projects in the developing countries have become very complicated due to several legal, regulatory, institutional and governance limitations. Also, the public policy in respect of mining takes a long time to emerge; meanwhile the damage is done to the society and environments. These countries take relatively a long time to develop an absorptive capacity to realize the gains from FDI. Particularly in the context of India, there is no dearth of experience in the mining minerals, but unfortunately, the institutions are not able to derive any worthwhile benefits from the past experiences of local or foreign investors. Also, the delays and litigations at the state and national levels give a mixed message to foreign investors. FDI usually flows to the countries with relatively stable and predictable legal and institutional regimes; (though often FDI is also attracted by the lax environment enforcement in the host countries). In the anxiety to develop their state, Orissa government invited the foreign investors as also domestic investors, but due to the limits of the state public policy and implementation, there were inordinate, delays, litigation, and protests. Some of the power and steel projects of domestic investors have taken decades to fructify. The FDI project would meet a similar fate was a foregone conclusion, but the state authorities got into enormous complexities due to the projects-Posco and Vedanta. On the one hand, the center and state were short of resources and technology to explore the minerals in a mineral-rich state like Orissa while on the other being institutionally unprepared while allowing FDI they could

---

[45] Cirone, M. (CEDAT, Universitat Rovira i Virgili). 2012. "The Vedanta Case in India." *EJOLT Factsheet*, no. 46, p. 8. http://ejolt.org/wordpress/wp-content/uploads/2015/08/FS-46.pd (accessed August 12, 2016).

not achieve the promised FDI objectives. This case study illustrates the hypothesis that generally democracy attracts FDI; however, there is a caveat: a democracy is as good as its institutions and therefore, where the institutional environments are weak, and complex FDI may be difficult to sustain.

This case calls for a review of the institutional environments for decision making on FDI projects in extractive industries. The VAL was allowed, and later expansion was not permitted which has implications for future investors in the state in particular and Indian in general.

Kia Motors India

South Korea's second largest car manufacturer Kia Motors signed an MoU with the Andhra Pradesh (AP) government during April 2017 to build a manufacturing facility along with an ecosystem for ancillaries with a $2-billion investment. With an initial investment if $1.1 billion, the production from India plant will begin from mid of 2019. It is the single largest FDI in the Indian automotive sector. Its parent company, Hyundai, has been in the country since the late 1990s. India being Asia's third-largest car market is the prominent choice for markets seeking foreign investors. The company has chosen Penukonda in Anantapur district in southern AP (state) as its investment destination. Anantapur is close to the automobile ecosystem of Tamil Nadu and near Hyundai's India manufacturing facility at Sriperumbudur, on the outskirts of Chennai. The site is also close to Bangalore, Karnataka's automotive belt.

The company has already started the process of buying land for the factory. Kia's choice of AP—amid intensifying interstate rivalry to draw investments as part of the Make-in-India initiative—has helped the government of the state to showcase their business-friendly credentials.[46]

Competitive Dynamics in the Indian Car Industry

Quite recently in May 2017, General Motors gave up on the Indian consumers by exiting the Indian market. It will not sell cars in India instead will only export cars from India. Out of the major 17 car manufacturers, top 4 captures over 75 percent of the market share. Maruti Suzuki, the domestic player with 47 percent share, dominates the market followed by Hyundai, together making it over 65 percent. Volkswagen, Skoda, Fiat, Nissan, and Ford together capture only 3 to 5 percent market share indicating more exits to be in the offing (Goyal, 2017). Is it challenging

---

[46] https://economictimes.indiatimes.com/industry/andhra-pradesh-likely-to-bag-rs-10000-crore-kia-project/articleshow/58213306.cms

for foreign MNEs to face the competitive dynamics in the Indian car industry?

Advantages Offered by India

The Government of India encourages 100 percent FDI in the automobile sector under the automatic route. Aiming to develop India as global manufacturing and R&D hub the government also provides a wide array of policy support in the form of sops, taxes and FDI encouragement.[47] The rising income, growing middle-class population, more than 50 percent of the young population ready to join the workforce and larger availability of credit and financing options are the major growth drivers propelling India's demand for automobiles. The Indian Automobile market is expected to grow from USD 74 billion in 2015 to USD 260 to 300 billion by 2026; however, there is a crucial need to understand consumers' needs and desires (IBEF, 2017) because this is where General Motors failed and had a fatal end.

Geo-Political Issues

Kia Motors also resorted to the Indian market as they suffered huge sales loss in China due to Seoul's decision to deploy a USA anti-missile system, which disappointed China. According to Han Chun-soo, Kia's chief financial officer, the plunge in consumer sentiment in China stemmed from a political issue, a situation which was beyond the control of an individual firm and was difficult to be resolved within the short term (Jin and Yang 2017). However, they did not enter the Indian market without a prior market and consumer survey, they seem to have made a final entry and gave an affirmative indication to other potential MNEs who are also eying Indian markets. Foreign automobile firms were reluctant to bet on the small car

---

[47] Agence France-Presse. 2017. "South Korea's Kia Motors to invest $1.1 billion in India to Build a Factory by 2019." available at: www.hindustantimes.com/autos/south-korea-s-kia-motors-to-invest-1-1-billion-inindia-to-build-factory-by-2019/story-W4cvQyYehlWAJ1c50To1bJ.html (accessed April 17, 2017).

due to low margins, but management at Kia Motors believed that success in any market was a function of understanding customers requirement to design the right product line up beside reaching the customers through proper channels and create a consistent aspirational brand.[48]

India Operations

The South Korean firm during its first phase of investment in 2017 invested Rs. 6,000 crore in building a car manufacturing facility in AP with an installed capacity to produce 3 lakh units a year. Kia's decision to invest in India has come amid India's growing stature as a manufacturing hub, with several overseas companies responding to the federal government's Make-in-India initiative.

The Industries and Commerce department of AP on April 13, 2017, issued the government order for the acquisition of nearly 600 acres of land by paying Rs. 10.5 lakh an acre "as a special case." The government has accorded permission to the Anantapur district collector to procure land required for the project under the AP Land Acquisition rules 2014.[49]

Kia Motors entered into an MoU with the AP government on April 20, 2017, to produce 3 lakh vehicles annually, with an investment of Rs. 13,000 crore to provide employment opportunities to 11,000 persons, including 4,000 direct jobs. In partnership with the Andhra Pradesh State Skill Development Corporation (APSSDC), Kia Motors has selected 2,000 candidates for the skill training workshop. After completion of training, candidates will be shortlisted in 1:3 ratio for jobs in Kia Motors. The primary objective behind this basic technical skill development course is to enhance the skills of diploma holders to make them job ready in the automobile industry.[50]

---

[48] "Why world's biggest automobile players have failed to win the attention of Indian Buyers." Available at http://economictimes.indiatimes.com/why-worlds-biggest-automobile-players-havefailed-to-win-the-attention-of-indian-buyers/articleshow/52158687.cms, (accessed June 4, 2017).

[49] https://economictimes.indiatimes.com/industry/andhra-pradesh-likely-to-bag-rs-10000-crore-kia-project/articleshow/58213306.cms

[50] https://ncbn.in/kia_motors

Quite recently in March 2018, almost 16 companies signed MoU with the AP government for setting up auto ancillary units to cater to Korean automaker Kia car's manufacturing facility coming up in Anantapuramu district. These companies are expected to invest 737 million USD (Rs. 4,790 crore) and provide 6,583 jobs.

The state government is developing a Korean City in the region to promote various industrial units that will cater to the facility. Kia expects to roll out its first India-specific car from the Anantapuramu plant by mid-2019. Since the Kia factory will be located close to Hyundai's factory, Kia is considering utilizing Hyundai Motor India's paint shop and body shop and many aggregates to keep costs under check, and bring in the economies of scale. Hyundai Motor India, which is utilizing about 90 percent of its capacity, may look at harnessing the Kia facility to ensure quicker return on investments, said an executive aware of the Kia Motors plans.[51]

According to Han-Woo Park, CEO, Kia Motors, the company along with social and economic development plans to invest about $2 billion by 2021 and create over 10,000 jobs for manufacturing different brands. The Anantapur plant is the 15th global manufacturing facility and is expected to become the largest facility for Kia Motors over a period of time. The company globally operates in five countries with 14 manufacturing units producing over 2.7 million Kia vehicles. Indian facility would cater majorly for the domestic market close to 90 percent and export the rest.[52]

Lessons from the Case

Kia Motors Indian venture is the classic case of a market-seeking FDI. Kia motors after facing challenges in China, one of its biggest markets, targeted India for internationalization. The motive behind market seeking

---

[51] https://economictimes.indiatimes.com/industry/auto/auto-components/16-korean-companies-sign-mou-with-andhra-government-to-set-up-ancillary-units/articleshow/63368982.cms

[52] https://financialexpress.com/industry/kia-motors-to-roll-out-first-made-in-india-car-from-andhra-pradesh-by-mid-2019/1076280/

MNEs investment in a foreign country is to exploit the possibilities granted by markets of greater dimensions. These MNEs adapt their goods to local needs or tastes and save the cost of serving a market from a distance. In recent times, the need is felt to have a physical presence on the market to discourage potential competitors from occupying that market.

Kia Motors is currently building a production facility on a Greenfield land in Anantapur district, AP to cater to the Indian growing middle class their preferred small segment SUVs and cars. Market-seeking FDI occurs when companies internationalize to benefit from the production economies of scale that requires a sizable population and the ability of the market to support the expected demand on which the investment is based. As stated by Dunning market-seeking FDI is based on a single central location (L) advantage. Locational advantage offer potential foreign investors significant opportunities to achieve scope and production economies of scale as well as a chance to grow (Franco et al. 2008).

The state government as usual tries to attract foreign investments to promote the development and growth of both state and people. Chief Minister N. Chandrababu Naidu of AP has been giving priority to industrialization with a campaign of "people first and industry first" and "one entrepreneur should be developed in every house in the state."

The state government wants to develop Anantapur district as a major automobile hub by attracting more industries now that Kia motors is already operating there. The state claims to attract a number of industries due to its transparent approval process, which is a significant taking from past failures of foreign investments. The state claims to have signed 628 MoUs in the food processing sector with 7 upcoming mega food parks. The state also claims to have signed another 104 MoUs in the textile sector, 30 MoUs in IT and E-commerce sector. Prima facie the industrial-friendly policies of state government seem to have attracted foreign investments.

The government is also keen to create employment opportunities through these investments and is working in this direction by promoting maximum localization by these MNEs. In partnership with the APSSDC, Kia Motors is conducting technical skill development workshops for the youth, which will make them job ready in the automobile industry. Kia itself will absorb a few of candidates.

Biocon Limited

The Indian pharmaceutical industry traces its roots to the 1901 formation of Bengal Chemical and Pharmaceutical Works in Kolkata by Professor Prafulla Chandra Ray. During the first half of the 20th century India was mostly dependent on the UK, France, and Germany for medicines however; during the second half of the century, the Indian government took first concrete steps toward self-reliance in pharmaceuticals through the establishment of Hindustan Antibiotics Ltd., (HAL) in 1954 and Indian Drugs and Pharmaceuticals Ltd., (IDPL) in 1961. The industry grew at a rapid pace, and by 1965 it collectively had Rs. 168 crore of output, inclusive of bulk drug and formulations.

The 1970 Patent Act permitted patents on processes but not on products, which facilitated local firms to produce compounds that were patented abroad legally. Consequently, Indian pharmaceutical companies gained from reverse-engineering of drugs and selling them at lower prices. Although numerous western observers criticized the 1970 Patent Act, it cannot be denied that such a liberal patent environment benefited both the Indian pharma firms and the pharmaceutical industry as a whole. Over the next three decades, the industry grew from a handful of MNE players to more than 16,000 licensed pharmaceutical companies. The Indian Patent Act 2005 permitted product patent for medicine, drug, chemical processes, and food. The Act is in full conformity with the intellectual property system in all respects and extends full Trade-Related Aspects of Intellectual Property Rights (TRIPS) coverage to food, drugs, and medicines.

About Biocon

Biocon India was established in November 1978 as a joint venture between Biocon Biochemicals of Ireland and Dr. Kiran Mazumdar-Shaw, an Indian entrepreneur to manufacture bulk enzymes. In 1979, Biocon became the first Indian company to manufacture and export enzymes for the food processing industry located both in the United States and Europe. In 1989, Unilever acquired Biocon Ireland, and the company started producing enzymes for Unilever's food business. From 1978 to 1997, Biocon was primarily an enzyme manufacturing company with expertise in various fermentation processes.

Biocon, an innovation-led organization, is Asia's premier biopharmaceutical company committed to ensuring a global right to healthcare by addressing the worldwide need for safe, effective and affordable biotherapeutics. The company is a pioneer in providing high quality, affordable, novel biologics and biosimilars to patients in India and other emerging markets. The company has leveraged its inherent strengths in advanced science to develop, manufacture and deliver a rich portfolio of small molecules APIs and formulations and complex biologics—both Novels and biosimilars—including monoclonal antibodies (MAbs), RH-insulin and insulin analogs.

In 1994, the ability of Biocon's scientist led to the formation of a subsidiary company Syngene that was India's first custom research organization (CRO) to receive special export status from the Government of India. Syngene offered high-value R&D in early-stage drug discovery and development for diverse global clients. It provides customized R&D services to pharmaceutical and biotechnology companies on a secure platform of confidentiality and intellectual property protection.[53]

Clinigene, a wholly owned subsidiary of Biocon, since its inception in 2000 has been helping parent Biocon in clinical research and development. Over the years the company has been positioned as a third party clinical research organization (CRO) offering a range of services encompassing bioequivalence, bioavailability studies as well as undertaking phase I to phase IV clinical trials.[54] Over the years, Biocon and its two subsidiary companies, Syngene International Ltd., and Clinigene International Ltd., have formed a fully integrated biotechnology enterprise, specializing

---

[53] Available at https://biospectrumindia.com/news/73/6771/preferred-cro-partner.html?pollQuestionId=16.

[54] Anil Urs. 2013. "Clinigene to be Third Party CRO." *Business Standard*, https://business-standard.com/article/companies/clinigene-to-be-third-party-cro-105070701110_1.html

in biopharmaceuticals, custom research, clinical research, and enzymes. With successful initiatives in clinical development, and global marketing, Biocon delivers several USFDA and EMEA approved products and solutions to partners and customers across the globe.[55]

Motivation and Rationale for OFDI

Kiran Mazumdar, a pioneer of the biotechnology industry in India, founded the country's leading biotechnology enterprise, Biocon in 1978 at the age of 25. The company had ownership advantage concerning entrepreneurship. Kiran Mazumdar is named among TIME magazine's 100 most influential people in the world and is recognized as a thought leader who has made her country proud by building a globally recognized biopharmaceutical enterprise that is committed to innovation and affordability in delivering best-in-class therapeutics to patients across the globe. She is ranked among "World's 25 Most Influential People in Biopharma" by Fierce Biotech, "100 Most Powerful Women" by Forbes magazine's and Top 25 Most Powerful Women in Asia-Pacific by Fortune.[56] Driven by the vision of "affordable healthcare" at "affordable innovation" Biocon ventured out with the primary motivation of seeking market and technology.

The company had a fully integrated business model with two subsidiaries, Syngene, and Clinigene for preclinical and clinical research respectively. Syngene International Limited is India's largest Contract Research Organization (CRO). It started as India's first CRO and over the years has built a reputation as end-to-end drug discovery and development services provider for novel molecular entities to the global life sciences sector. Clinigene International Limited, a CRO, provides clinical development solutions to pharma and biotech companies. Biologics and

---

[55] Paula Sengupta and GayatriAppaya. 2007. "Biocon's Syngene Enters into Research Partnership with Bristol-Myers Squibb." Available at http://syngeneintl. com/Media/Default/pdf/news_events/Bioconpercentage20Syngenepercentage20 enterspercentage20intopercentage20researchpercentage20partnershippercentage-20withpercentage20Bristol-Myerspercentage20Squibb.pdf

[56] https://biocon.com/

research services are the main drivers of growth for the firm.[57] It has a robust regulatory and quality systems to develop and deliver complex therapeutics.[58] The company ventured out both in developed countries, like the United States and Germany and developing countries, like Malaysia, Cuba, and UAE.

The mission of "affordable healthcare" aligns well to the population residing in developing nations besides market seeking motive. Affordable innovation aligns well with the motive of seeking technology. According to Dunning, strategic asset seeking motive is an important strategy to undertake FDI project. It aims at augmenting the capabilities of the investing firm rather than exploiting the existing ones, which may relate to technological, innovational or managerial skills (Meyer 2015). Biocon's internationalization strategy is based mainly on research partnerships and joint ventures. The company believes in organic growth model to expand overseas.

Biocon Overseas Investments

The vision of "affordable healthcare" pushed Biocon to venture out globally and acquire or build "affordable innovation." According to Kiran Mazumdar-Shaw, CMD of Biocon, the company intended to focus on overseas acquisitions purely for strategic reasons in either intellectual property assets or for marketing and distribution.[59] Biocon realized the benefits of strategic partnerships very early in its evolution and thus pursued global alliances to strengthen its footprints globally.[60]

---

[57] The Hindu. 2018. "Biologics, Research Services to be Main Drivers of Growth in FY19: Biocon." Available at https://thehindu.com/todays-paper/tp-business/biologics-research-services-to-be-main-drivers-of-growth-in-fy19-biocon/article23734126.ece (accessed July 6, 2018).

[58] Annual Report. 2018. "Enduring Edge." https://biocon.com/docs/Biocon_Annual_Report_2018_PO.pdf

[59] Gupta, M. 2006. "Biocon's Shaw Looks at Acquisitions in IPs." *The Economic Times*, Available at https://economictimes.indiatimes.com/industry/healthcare/biotech/biocons-shaw-looks-at-acquisitions-in-ips/articleshow/634625.cms

[60] Biocon Annual Report. 2012. Available at https://biocon.com/docs/Biocon_AnnualReport_2012.pdf

Biocon acquired intellectual property assets of its bankrupt US research partner Nobex Corporation in 2006 for $5 million.[61] According to Kiran Mazumdar, it was indeed a strategic acquisition which provided them with an immensely valuable IP platform. It also gave the company ownership of their ongoing oral insulin, and oral BNP programs to the company proposed to leverage these proprietary assets through a combination of licensing and co-development partnerships.[62]

In 2003, Biocon Biopharmaceuticals Private Limited (BBPL) was incorporated to manufacture and market a select range of biotechnology-based life-saving drugs as a 51:49 joint venture with CIMAB (Cuban Centre of Molecular Immunology) and Biocon. However after seven years, in 2010, Biocon acquired the stake of its Cuban partner CIMB in Biocon Biopharmaceuticals Pvt. Ltd.[63]

In 2007, Biocon and Abu Dhabi based pharmaceutical company Neopharma that had a world-class manufacturing facility for finished formulations[64] signed an MoU to establish a 50:50 JV to manufacture and market a range of biopharmaceuticals for the Gulf Cooperation Council (GCC) countries.

In 2008, Biocon acquired a 78 percent stake in German pharmaceutical company, AxiCorp GmbH for consideration of €30 Million. AxiCorp was a major marketing and distribution player in the Insulin segment in Europe. According to Mazumdar, AxiCorp was an important strategic investment to build a strong marketing and distribution capabilities for biosimilars like Insulin in Europe. Affordable healthcare being the shared

---

[61] Business Standard. 2006. "Biocon buys Nobex for $5 Million." Available at https://business-standard.com/article/companies/biocon-buys-nobex-for-5-million-106032901137_1.html

[62] Biocon's Shaw looks at acquisitions in IPs. 2006. Available at https://economictimes.indiatimes.com/industry/healthcare/biotech/biocons-shaw-looks-at-acquisitions-in-ips/articleshow/634625.cms

[63] https://biocon.com/biocon_invrelation_com_history.aspc

[64] Hindustan Times. 2007. "Biocon in 50:50 JV with Gulf Firm." Available at https://hindustantimes.com/india/biocon-in-50-50-jv-with-gulf-firm/story-queYAWdXpfd0N4gmDPvpjP.html

vision of both the companies was well delivered through a combination of Biocon's low-cost manufacturing and AxiCorp's low-cost distribution.[65]

In 2009, Biocon partnered with Mylan Inc. to develop five complex biosimilar products in the areas of cancer and pain segment however in 2013, Biocon enhanced partnership with Mylan through Strategic collaboration for Insulin Products.[66]

In 2010, Biocon announced a strategic FDI in Malaysia to establish the facility in Bio-XCell with the Malaysian Biotechnology Corporation Sdn Bhd (BiotechCorp). The investment initiative was driven by Malaysia's strategic location, the country's growing role as a rapidly developing global biotech hub, and the enabling Bio-XCell ecosystem capable of offering inclusive support through high-end infrastructure, human resource, and related services.[67]

In 2010, Biocon and Pfizer Inc. the world's leading biopharmaceutical company entered into a strategic global agreement for the worldwide commercialization of Biocon's biosimilar versions of insulin and Insulin analog products. Pfizer was brand strength with vast global marketing network.[68] Biocon was responsible for the clinical development, manufacture, and supply of biosimilar insulin products besides regulatory activities to secure approval for these products in different countries. They both together aimed to build a formidable global footprint in diabetes care through their combined efforts in marketing, manufacturing and research excellence. However, in 2012 Pfizer terminated its licensing deal with Biocon as the latter failed to meet one of the milestones built into

---

[65] Economic Times. 2008. "Biocon Buys 70 pc of Germany's AxiCorp." Available at https://economictimes.indiatimes.com/industry/healthcare/biotech/biocon-buys-70-pc-of-germanys-axicorp/articleshow/2772581.cms

[66] Divya, R. 2012. "Biocon-Mylan Partnership has a Potential of $33 Billion from Biosimilar Drugs." *The Economic Times*. Available at https://economictimes.indiatimes.com/industry/healthcare/biotech/pharmaceuticals/biocon-mylan-Biocon-Mylan partnership has a potential of $33 billion from biosimilar drugs

[67] Biocell, B. 2011. Available at https://biocon.com/docs/PR_Biocon_Malaysia_10092011.pdf

[68] Biocon and Pfizer. 2010. "Enter into Global Commercialization Agreement." Available at http://press.pfizer.com/press-release/biocon-and-pfizer-enter-global-commercialization-agreement

the licensing agreement. Pfizer also cited other priorities in its biosimilar program for the split.[69]

In 2013, Biocon and Quark Pharmaceuticals from Israel collaborated to develop Novel siRNA based therapeutics. Quark Pharmaceuticals, Inc. was the world leader in the discovery and development of siRNA-based therapeutics. This collaboration enabled Biocon to co-develop, manufacture and commercialize a novel siRNA drug candidate for ophthalmic conditions, for India and other key markets.[70]

In 2016, Biocon entered co-development and commercialization agreement with Lab PiSA for RH-Insulin in the United States. This collaboration was a part of Biocon's strategy to cater to the large demand for generic RH-insulin in the United States, which accounts for over 40 percent of the global sales of US $5 billion.[71]

In 2018, Biocon pronounced exclusive global collaboration with Sandoz on next-generation biosimilars. This collaboration would leverage the combined strengths of development, manufacturing, and commercialization of biosimilars. This partnership will be an important part of Biocon and Sandoz' strategy to address the next wave of biosimilars opportunities globally.[72]

Biocon's internationalization strategy is based on organic growth through partnerships (Wilkinson et al. 2016). Its foray in the global market has mainly been through strategic partnerships and joint ventures with the vision to provide affordable healthcare at affordable innovation. Its strategic partnerships aided robust marketing and distribution arrangements in Latin America, Mexico, Middle East, Eastern Europe, and South East Asian countries. Most of the alliances and joint ventures were successful; however, the one with Pfizer broke off within two

---

[69] Kulkarni K., and H. Foy. 2012. "Reuters." Available at https://reuters.com/article/us-pfizer-biocon/pfizer-scraps-insulin-deal-with-indias-biocon-idUSBRE82C05920120313

[70] Biocon Press release. 2013. Available at https://biocon.com/biocon_press_releases_181213.asp

[71] Biocon Press release. 2016. Available at https://biocon.com/biocon_press_releases_170316.asp

[72] Biocon Press release. 2018. Available at https://biocon.com/biocon_press_releases_180118.asp

years. It seems that the company has the right vision and with calculated risk-taking initiatives it is determined to progress and succeed in the coming years leaving more and more global footprints.

Lessons from the Case

From the viewpoint of a new venture that dates back to late 1970s, Biocon adopted specific strategies to enter the mainstream biotechnology; though the real breakthrough on multiple fronts got realized only after a decade and a half. During those days there were several issues related to public policy, institutional environment and international trading environment. Biocon is a story about the determination of the founder who did not wait for ideal conditions in the industry to emerge before starting a venture instead proceeded regardless of being resource constraint. The founder, Kiran Mazumdar with good qualifications but from another discipline decided to enter the emerging field of biotechnology with modest funds and without any specific infrastructure.

This case also illustrates the episode of successful woman entrepreneurship in India at a time when women were not venturing into setting up projects in highly specialized or even a general category of industries. Further, this case points to the sequence and actuals of the process by which the founder and top management teams in Biocon achieved competitive advantage in the global environment which was significantly dominated by the MNEs. The case also is also an ideal example of the concept of dynamic capability in the field of strategy; such capabilities denote a higher order capability to go beyond a given organizational routine; Biocon at several stages showed how higher order capability of problem-solving could be achieved through the lens of corporate and growth strategies. The ability of the founder to carve out an independent niche shows her leadership ability without which the company could not have expanded internationally. The promoter also demonstrated the utility of knowledge creation and networking process which signals the practical framework of strategic alliance and global partnering. The case illustrates how the concept of corporate entrepreneurship can be conceived and implemented as new ventures expand, replicate and scale up the activities and thus reach newer milestones.

The company's business model sought to generate value through the value chain; Biocon shaped its business into four key growth verticals-Biologics (Biosimilars) and novel molecules; branded formulations; small molecules and research services, with the aim to deliver sustainable long term value for patients, partners, healthcare systems across the globe.

References

2.0 Ranbaxy Laboratories Limited. Available at http://who.int/intellectual-property/events/en/Ranbaxy.pdf

Annual Report. 2018. "Enduring Edge." Available at https://biocon.com/docs/Biocon_Annual_Report_2018_PO.pdf

Asher, M. February 18–24, 2005. "Steel Not Enough?" *Economic and Political Weekly* 41, no. 7, pp. 555–56.

Biocon, Profile Kiran Mazumdar- Shaw available at https://biocon.com/docs/KMS_Profile_2016.pdf

D'costa, A.P. 2015. *After-Development Dynamics: South Korea's Contemporary Engagement with Asia.* Oxford University Press, USA.

Daiichi Sankyo Press Release available at https://daiichisankyo.com/media_investors/media_relations/press_releases/detail/005512.html

Daiichi Sankyo. "Annual Report 2009." Available at https://daiichisankyo.com/media_investors/investor_relations/annual_reports/pdf/ar2009_10_01_45_01.pdf

Das, A. 2005. "POSCO Deal: Natural Resource Implications." *Economic and Political Weekly*, pp. 4678–80.

Debrajan. January 12–18, 2008. "Is Struggle for Survival a Criminal Offense?" *Economic and Political Weekly* 43, no. 2.

Don't Need to Sell Assets, can Pay Fine: Ranbaxy Brothers. Available at http://rediff.com/money/report/dont-need-to-sell-assets-can-pay-fine-ranbaxy-brothers/20160525.htm (accessed August 13, 2016).

Financial Express. 2015. "Biocon is the Only Asian Company to be Ranked in Top 20 Global Biotech Employers for 2015." Available at https://financialexpress.com/industry/biocon-is-the-only-asian-company-to-be-ranked-in-top-20-global-biotech-employers-for-2015/160602/

Franco, C., F. Rentocchini, and G.V. Marzetti. 2008. "Motives Underlying Foreign Direct Investments: A Primer." In *Proceedings of the 5th International Conference on Innovation and Management*, (Vols I and II, pp. 2329–45). Wuhan University Technology Press.

Gupta, M., U. Pingle, D. Pandey, V. Suresh. 2010. Majority Report of the Committee Constituted to Investigate into the Proposal Submitted by

POSCO India Pvt, Limited for the Establishment of an Integrated Steel Plant and Captive Port in Jagatsinghpur District, Odisha. Jensen, N.M. 2008. *Nation-States and the Multinational Corporation: A Political Economy of Foreign Direct Investment.* Princeton University Press. Khoday, K., and U. Natarajan. 2012. "Fairness and International Environmental Law from Below: Social Movements and Legal Transformation in India." *Leiden Journal of International Law* 25, no. 2, pp. 415–41.

Gupta, S., and N. Das. 2008. *Biocon: Launching a New Cancer Drug in India.* Harvard Buisness School.

Hohnen, P. 2009. "Annual Report on the OECD Guidelines for Multinational Enterprises 2008 Employment and Industrial Relations." Available at http://vedantaresources.com/investor-relations.aspx (accessed August 1, 2016).

IBEF. "Pharmaceuticals Report." https://ibef.org/industry/pharmaceutical-india/showcase/ranbaxy

Indian Pharmaceutical Industry. 2017. Available at https://ibef.org/archives/detail/b3ZlcnZpZZXcmMzcxMDYmOTA (accessed July 15, 2018)

Mani, V., and Bloomberg. 2018. "Delhi High Court asks Singh Brothers to Pay up Rs. 35 Billion to Daiichi." Available at https://business-standard.com/article/companies/delhi-hight-court-asks-singh-brothers-to-pay-up-rs-35-bn-to-daiichi-118013101542_1.html (accessed July 18, 2018).

Mazumdar-Shaw, K. 2018. "Leveraging Affordable Innovation to Tackle India's Healthcare Challenge." *IIMB Management Review* 30, no. 1, pp. 37–50.

Meyer, K.E. 2015. "What is "Strategic Asset Seeking FDI"?" *The Multinational Business Review* 23, no. 1, pp. 57–66.

Mishra, B. 2010. "Agriculture, Industry, and Mining in Orissa in the Post-liberalization Era: An Inter-District and Inter-state Panel Analysis." *Economic and Political Weekly*, pp. 49–68.

Mukhopadhyay, A.D. 2006. "The POSCO Deal: Boon or Disaster?" *Social Scientist*, pp. 43–54.

Nayak, S. 2015. "Industrial Development vs Resistance-A Study of Posco Project in Odisha." *International Letters of Social and Humanistic Sciences* 50, pp. 55–67.

Oberoi, R. 2014. "Bigger and Better, Business Today." Available at https://businesstoday.in/moneytoday/stocks/ranbaxy-acquisition-good-for-sun-pharma-shareholders-experts/story/205526.html (accessed July 14, 2018).

Oliveira, L.H. 2001. "Foreign Direct Investment and Export-Led Growth: A Challenge to Brazil." Working paper. School of Business and Public Management.

Page, J. 1994. "The East Asian miracle: Four Lessons for Development Policy." *NBER Macroeconomics Annual* 9, pp. 219–69.

Panda, H., J. Park, and D.A. Kong. 2008. "Industrialization through FDI, Displacement and Development: POSCO-India Project in Odisha." *International Area Studies Review* 11, no. 2, pp. 287–307.

Ranbaxy. 2007. "Annual Report." Available at http://sunpharma.com/investors/archives/ranbaxy-archives/annual-reports

Ranbaxy-Daiichi. 2016. "Affair: How and Why the Deal Went South." Available at https://business-standard.com/article/companies/ranbaxy-daiichi-affair-how-why-the-deal-went-south-116081100270_1.html (accessed April 12, 2018).

Rosser, A. 2006. *The Political Economy of the Resource Curse: A Literature Survey.*

Smith, S.E. 2000. "Opening up to the world: India's Pharmaceutical Companies Prepare for 2005." *Occasional Papers*, Asia/Pacific Research Center, Institute for International Studies, Stanford University.

Viswanath, A., and R. Catching. 2008. "Odisha Steel Project Tests India's Mettle." *Far Eastern Economic Review* 171, no. 9, pp. 30–34.

Wilkinson, A., P. Budhwar, and J.A. Mathews. 2016. "Internationalization of Emerging Indian Multinationals: Linkage, Leverage and Learning (LLL) Perspective." *International Business Review*, available at http://iranarze.ir/wp-content/uploads/2017/06/E3904-IranArze.pdf

CHAPTER 7

Conclusions

In the preceding text, an attempt is made to analyze the concept and practice of FDI especially in the context of the developing nations like India. The primary objectives of technology acquisition and obtaining managerial know-how via the FDI route has been well researched in the past; however, these depend upon the relative ability of the host country public policy, regulations, and institutional environments. The countries with the "resource curse" had a comparative disadvantage of not having a coherent macroeconomic policy and institutions which could support FDI policy. It is because of this fact that their natural resources got exploited in the formative years of their economic growth. Their relative political and economic bargaining power was weak, and therefore the process of globalization did little to ameliorate their poor economic conditions for a long time. In the Indian case, post-independence the government had introduced a series of public policy measures but given the complex nature of economic and social structure and the fact that regulations and institutions did take a longer time to evolve delayed any significant policy on FDI inflows. However, outward FDI was not restricted, and in fact, before the 1991 economic reforms many older industry houses set up joint ventures and collaborative projects (primarily because of the restrictions on expansions in the domestic outputs). Also in the formative few decades, there was import substitution policy and inward-looking stance of public policy makers which explains the slow growth and pace of economic reforms until the early 1990s. Historically the British Empire introduced FDI for colonization by way of trade and commerce overseas, so FDI is neither a new phenomenon nor an innovation of the modern day public policy. The first ever FDI was mooted in India in 1608 with the advent of the East India company. This mode of 'international trade' was operative in other monarchies such as the Greeks and Spain in Europe much before the theories of international trade were evolved. In this sense globalization is also not a new practice it has been occurring since the last several hundred years in one format or the other. What is new, however, is the nature of the evolving nations, significant changes in geopolitics and theoretical lens explaining the nature of FDI which is necessarily a technocratic view giving much emphasis on the need for modern technology acquisitions and acquiring managerial know how.

We have stressed in this volume a fundamental aspect of modern day economic policies; i.e., the globalization which is no longer an option and that every nation regardless of the status of economic growth at any given point of time should prepare its institutional order and public policies to be able to participate in the world trade. This is necessary especially for the developing nations who are at various stages of internationalizing their trade and country openness index to develop a capability to benefit from FDI; for the intended and actual benefits of FDI are not automatic. Further, in this book all along we have stressed the fact that the process and content of globalization are relatively more complicated due to the magnitude of variegated demands from multifarious stakeholders for sustainable development. Sustainable development issues arise because during the initial decades of economic development most developing nations focused on GDP growth without including the challenges of sustainability adequately.

We also note that the developing nations are increasingly facing problems in addressing a tradeoff between FDI and ecosystems; the cumulative evidence of the MNEs performance in various developing countries is a living testimony to their operations inflicting irreversible damage to the natural and physical environmental ecosystems in the host economies. Not only in India but even in other resource-rich developing nations of the world there has been enough evidence of such extensive damage to the environment because of the ever-expanding activities of the MNEs besides large domestic national enterprises. Against the above backdrop we may now turn to the specific conclusions of this volume:

- Public Policy: The international debate about government policy on FDI is invariably based on the premise that incremental growth in FDI is feasible since many developing nations have democratized and opened up their respective

economies though quite late in the 1960s, however India in
1990s. This view points to the inherent difficulties in policy
formulation and exercise of policy choices by the developing
nations in their formative stages of economic growth. Political
stability is one of the crucial factors in deciding public policy
both for internal markets and international trade and commerce. Incremental public policy is the preferred option for
many developing nations since the evolution of public policy
and regulations is a time-consuming process. For the initial
few debates there was binary view; state versus the market;
this 'an either/or situation' resulted in inward-looking and
import substitution policy with the increasing presence of the
public enterprises in countries like India. Towards the end of
the 1980s, with the UK and USA focusing on the policy for
privatization and deregulation even the developed economies
felt the need for a fundamental shift in policy making from
state versus market towards the state and market approach,
which was eventually thought slowly followed up by many
developing nations. The Washington Consensus in the 1990s
contained a prescription for the developing world to privatize
and deregulate the industry, and foster private investment
which leads to an international debate on the retreat of the
state. However, not all developing nations were prepared for
such a transition for they did not have enough experience
of deregulation, privatization and supervision of the market
forces as also trade openness. As already delineated in the
preceding text the Indian economy had four distinct phases
of FDI policy evolution. Each phase indicated a guarded
response to the worldwide focus on international trade and
commerce; guarded because India economy was yet to be
deregulated until the late 1990s. Even after liberalization in
1991 deregulation selectively posed a newer set of problems;
i.e., it required a different model of supervision and creation
of the necessary institutional framework. This is one of the
complex challenges resulting from trade openness and overall
economic deregulation including allowing selective FDI

inflows into key segments. Such a problem arises naturally in the context of the developing economies as the process of public policy is non-linear; also, the complexity of policy dynamics get compounded by the interplay of the multilateral institutions which devise asset of standards, codes, practices manual and benchmarks for economic and social growth including sustainable development. To accelerate the process of globalization, the multilateral institutions exert a certain pressure on the formulation of public policies and prescriptions of the developing nations besides invariably supporting their needs through aid packages and assistance in whatever forms the developing nations seeks.

One of the difficulties in the formulation of consistent public policy for foreign trade liberalization is the relative inability of governments to coordinate and synchronize such policy with other sectoral and macroeconomic policies. For instance, the government in India from time to time had many problems in reforming the financial sector, and the labor market. Several other policy subsets include patents, forest rights, and land rights, technology imports, competition policy, regulatory reforms and social sector policies among others. There are also the political economy issues involved in labor market reforms and social sector reforms. Another example in India is the agriculture policy; the case of Monsanto India in the state of Maharashtra illustrates how vividly the state and central level policy coordination became a complex issue.

- Competition policy issues: A critical area of international debate pertains to the effects of FDI on the process of the competition of industries in the host countries. The Indian government has set up a Competition Commission to examine the impact of corporate restructuring, mergers, amalgamations and so on. The moot question to be assessed is how far and whether FDI projects in India adversely affect the scenario of competition for the large and medium-size industries. FDI policy stimulates competition, but there is some anxiety about the potentially unfavorable effects on competition framework. The critiques believe that there may be market distortions because of FDI projects and it may also crowd out private domestic investment. Part of this debate arises from opposing political ideology, and in part, there are also concerns that institutional environments and legal frameworks are still not equipped to sort out the possible market distortions and adverse effects on competition among and between large projects. This is a complex issue and not all FDI projects can have identical results; the point is how far the domestic industry can meet competition in the liberalized policy regime and whether the local industry is geared to meet such competitive scenario. Some concerns call for analyzing whether any additional incentives are required for the domestic industries to face stiff international competition.

- Regulations: Once the liberalization process has started, it becomes quite challenging for any developing economy to strengthen its regulations. Also, most of the newer regulations require Parliamentary approval. It is quite possible that the due effects of competition might only surface in the long run; however, the policy formulation needs immediate assessment of the exact incidence of the considerable adverse impact of FDI. As far as the crowding out of private investments is concerned, it depends upon the size of further investment and the particular segment in which a project is being located; for it is very natural for some traditional industries to perceive threats of competition because the FDI brings in newer technology and skillset of a different order. In a recent interview published in the Indian press, the chief of the American technology giant IBM said that are plenty of jobs available for the young Indian workforce however they lack the required skill sets especially related to technical operations in many core areas, which directly or indirectly speaks volume about the Indian higher education institutions.[1]

---

[1] https://economictimes.indiatimes.com/jobs/skill-gaps-impeding-indians-prospects-in-tech-jobs-ibm-chief/articleshow/68390869.cmschief/article-show/68390869.cms

- Legal framework: The passage of the evolution of a legal framework in global context poses formidable challenges for the Indian lawmakers as so in other nations worldwide. For instance, the newer challenges arise in respect of taxation of foreign projects and the Indian courts in the recent past are no exception to witness much litigation on this issue. There are also several litigations regarding the adverse environmental impact of FDI highlighting the reprehensible adherence of the existing regulations by many FDI projects, especially in extractive and chemical sectors. Further, there have been several litigations on the issue of land acquisition wherein the indigenous tribes have challenged takeover of land for FDI projects. All these litigations delay the startup phases as also later production phases of FDI projects. Besides these, there have been contentious issues in the Courts on intellectual property rights and labor market issues. Therefore, the impact of FDI on a particular sector of the economy needs examination from the perspective of legal jurisprudence context. The issues of corporate governance, business ethics, benchmarks and disclosures, and so on related to foreign investment in a particular sector adversely affects the overall industry structure and competitive scenario in the country. Also, there are adverse litigations when the MNEs do not entirely comply with the local laws and violate or seek extraordinary exemptions from tax liabilities. Both in respect of OFDI and FDI inflows this has happened, and protracted litigation only compounded the costs of FDI for the host economy.

As per a Survey[2] by the PWC 2015, nearly 60 percent of CEOs agree that that transfer pricing (TP) is a crucial issue in the boardroom and is of strategic importance to the companies. Transfer pricing is a critical aspect of managing reputation risk. A significant majority of companies surveyed had to handle transfer pricing adjustments leading to a variety

---

[2] https://www.pwc.in/assets/pdfs/publications/2015/transfer-pricing-in-india-you-said-it.pdf

of litigations besides undergoing TP audit. As per the Survey
TP planning and policy framework emanates from the global
or the regional levels and is implemented within the groups
operating in India. There are challenges of proper regulations
as also documentation, among others. There are also issues
related to the labor market reforms leading to a severe critique
of MNE policies; for instance, MNEs usually look for skillsets
which are located in the organized sector but employ many
people on contracts for project construction and implementation stages which come from the unorganized or informal
sector. This, in turn, leads to industrial relations issues and
labor strikes among others. More automation also means
fewer jobs and hence further implications for the employment
of people from the informal sector. Labor market flexibility
is an essential institutional determinant of FDI from the cost
angle to the firm. In general, FDI positively affects the average
wages in the local firms; which could also be the outcome of
productivity enhancement moreover at the same time MNEs
faces stiff competition with domestic firms for local labors.
Prima-facie, the host country is the beneficiary of inward
FDI though the benefits are not evenly spread out over its
entire population.[3] However; on the other side, competition
or attracting FDI may also have adverse effects on labor
and environmental standards which get compounded by
less stringent regulations of foreign investment by the host
economy. Under strict supervision, FDI can provide higher
returns. Narula[4] suggests the concept of sustainable investing
at the very first stage of investment; focus on environmental,
social and governance factors and adoption of sustainable and
responsible investing practices, among others. The author
recommends the establishment of sustainability indices and

---

[3] https://www.oecd.org/els/emp/The-Social-Impact-of-foreign-direct-invest-
ment.pdf

[4] Narula, K. 2012. "Sustainable Investing'via the FDI Route for Sustainable
Development." *Procedia-Social and Behavioral Sciences* 37, pp. 15–30.

rating, government participation in emerging voluntary international agreements and inclusion of local communities and
NGOs, among others.

- Financing SDGs: FDI is considered an integral source
  of external funding. According to the UNCTAD 2014
  report, the first level financial estimates indicate a shortfall
  of approximately USD 8.5 trillion to achieve 17 SDGs in
  estimated 15 years, though these are only the minimalistic
  approximation[5]. Thenceforth, India indeed a requires huge
  investment both from the public and private sources to at
  least manage a certain level of progress in achieving these
  sustainable goals. Besides India, almost all the developing nations need to promote both their public and private
  investment in SDG-relevant sectors, to collectively overcome
  an estimated annual gap of USD 2.5 trillion to achieve in
  sustainable goals.

- Stakeholder Engagement Issues: Invariably not only in India
  but also in other developing economies, FDI projects have
  either ignored stakeholder interests or partially addressed
  them. While the stakeholders are defined as those who are
  impacted by the operations of the corporations and who in
  turn, can influence the achievement of corporate objectives
  but the reality, however, is not the same. In most of the
  cases stakeholders are not powerful enough both in terms of
  resources and status, to exert any meaningful influence on
  how corporations achieve their objectives. Only in a few cases,
  civil society activism had been effective in exercising some
  check on corporate power abuse. This is because regulations
  and legal framework for moderating corporate actions are not
  stringent enough to check deviant behavior. There has been
  a cumulative incidence of land alienation among the local
  populace; violation of the human rights; displacement of the

---

[5] Achieving the Sustainable Development Goals in India A Study of Financial
Requirements and Gaps, available at https://www.devalt.org/images/L3_Project
Pdfs/AchievingSDGsinIndia_DA_21Sept.pdf

indigenous people; and deprivation of economic rights among others which show that neither the stakeholders can defend their interests, nor the state is effective in doing so, and the market forces keep abusing their interests and rights. For a long time the conventional view that only the shareholders' matter for the corporation prevailed until the appearance of stakeholder theories in the early 1990s; but even afterward till the present time, the issues of protection and service of stakeholder interests have not been resolved in most developing countries. The world's worst industrial disaster (the Bhopal tragedy 1984) and the problems of stakeholders in the ship-breaking industry at Alang in North Gujarat in the late 1990s vividly illustrate how weak are the institutional environments in protecting the stakeholder interests in the Indian economy. There have been numerous other instances of violation of the Environment Policy of India, especially in the mining and mineral sector besides chemical and pharmaceutical segment where FDI projects have been involved.

Both FDI and large domestic counterparts need to adopt the OECD principles of good corporate governance which stress upon, rights of shareholders and their protection; equitable treatment of all types of stakeholders; the role of employees and other stakeholders; timely disclosures and transparency of corporate structures and operations; and responsibilities of the board towards the company, shareowners and other stakeholders.[6]

- FDI and Business Ethics: Several case studies in the last few decades have illustrated different episodes of lack of business ethics by the MNEs both in the developed as also developing economies. These range from weak or poor corporate governance practices, lack of compliance with the regulator in the host economies; violations of international and

---

[6] Focus-Stakeholder Engagement and the Board: Integrating Best Governance Practices, 2009. Available at https://www.ifc.org/wps/wcm/connect/19017b804 8a7e667a667e76060ad5911/FINAL%2BFocus8_5.pdf?MOD=AJPERES

multilateral trade agreement clauses; human rights abuses; inadequate or willful defaults in disclosures, documentation, and reporting; violation of environmental laws and abuse of the a labor markets, among others. Large enterprises have the market and political power, and they often abuse the same to seek supernormal profits which in turn lead to ignoring the principles of business ethics. In the above, we have referred to the OECD principles one of which states that all stakeholders should be treated equitably nonetheless this does not happen in reality as the corporations attend only to minimal groups of stakeholders who demonstrate power, urgency, and legitimacy[7]. The political economy aspects and implications of FDI projects often are implicit in the relative lack of business ethics practices. One of the main reasons for corporate deviant behavior is corporate greed; several corporations in the developed and developing nations are guilty of misconduct and deliberate violation of sound economic, social and governance practices, norms, and benchmarks. This, in turn, places corporate reputation at stake. Well, besides blaming the large enterprises all related and associated stakeholders like the regulators (in some cases), auditors, supply chain partners, collaborators and so on are also guilty of conspiracy compounding to business ethics issues. There are more than 300 guidelines, codes, benchmarks and standards of business ethics; however, their compliance and enforcement become a major problem in different countries.

In the last two decades, many nations have strengthened their legal framework and adopted stringent enforcement of laws; however, there are mixed experiences in making corporations adhere to ethical standards. Moreover, these types of problems are not only confined to FDI in the manufacturing sector but are also evident in the services and agri-

---

[7] Mitchell, R.K., B.R. Agle, and D.J. Wood. 1997. "Toward a Theory of Stakeholder Identification and Salience: Defining the Principle of Who and What Really Counts." *Academy of Management Review*, 22(4), pp. 853–886.

culture sectors. It is not only the FDI projects which lack ethical practices that adversely affect the stakeholders, but the problems get compounded when some other core stakeholders become partners in ignoring ethical standards (related party transactions, transfer pricing and so on).

• FDI and Economic Growth: Besides being an external source of capital, FDI is highly appreciated for its valuable technology and know-how contributions and fostering linkages with local firms hence being a critical driver of economic growth. However; there is mixed evidence about the positive spillover effects of FDI on economic growth of the host economies but past research points to the evidence that not all sectors show positive spillover effects; for instance, they are relatively weak in agriculture (primary sector) as compared to the manufacturing sector; hence such results vary across sectors. FDI effects are generally favorable for those countries that adopt outward-looking economic policies as compared the nations who adopt inward-looking Based on this ideology several emerging and developing countries have offered attractive incentives to encourage foreign direct investments in their economies.

The Indian government's favorable policy regime and robust business environment also aims to attract foreign investment inflows. The government has taken a couple of initiatives in recent years such as relaxing FDI norms across sectors such as defense, PSU oil refineries, telecom, power exchanges, and stock exchanges, among others. India aims to promote its manufacturing sector and increase its GDP contribution besides generating employment. According to the Department for Promotion of Industry and Internal Trade (DPIIT), the total FDI investments in India of the first three quarters of 2018 stood at USD 33.49 billion, indicating that the government's efforts to improve ease of doing business and relaxation in FDI norms is yielding results. We are hopeful of attracting further investments for the manufacturing sector and maximizing the positive spillover effects.

About the Author

Leena Ajit Kaushal is faculty of economics at Management Development Institute (MDI) Gurgaon, India. She earned her PhD in economics and master's in business economics (MBE) from Devi Ahilya University, India. She received a postgraduate certificate in academic practice from Centre for the Enhancement of Learning and Teaching (CELT), Lancaster University, UK and held a status of associate of the United Kingdom Higher Education Academy. Her affiliation with Lancaster University, UK has equipped her with the skills especially needed to respond to the growing demand for meaningful and relevant teaching and evolve professionally over a lifetime.

Her research interest lies in the field of Development Economics, Macroeconomic issues and policies, International Trade, Foreign Direct Investment and Sharing Economy.

She has significantly worked in the field of International Trade and Foreign Direct Investment. The subject matter of her study mainly focuses on issues pertaining to foreign investments. She is currently engaged in exploring how responsible and productive MNEs in India are in attaining UN defined sustainable goals and recommend policy initiatives to enhance the positive contribution of MNEs further and overcome the shortcoming. She believes that finding an answer to these questions is crucial for Governments and MNEs to establish strong links between growth and sustainable development.

She is also engaged in exploring the sustainability connotation of sharing economy which is largely based on the simple philosophy of "owning less and sharing more."

She has co-authored a book on managerial economics by Cengage Publishing. She has also co-edited the book, *Global Entrepreneurship and New Venture Creation in the Sharing Economy*, published by IGI Global. She is associated as visiting faculty with various IIMs and is credited with research publications and case studies in various refereed national and international journals.

Index

OTHER TITLES FROM THE ECONOMICS AND PUBLIC POLICY COLLECTION

Philip Romero, The University of Oregon and
Jeffrey Edwards, North Carolina A&T State University, Editors

- *The Commonwealth of Independent States Economies: Perspectives and Challenges* by Marcus Goncalves and Erika Cornelius Smith
- *Econometrics for Daily Lives, Volume I* by Tam Bang Vu
- *Econometrics for Daily Lives, Volume II* by Tam Bang Vu
- *The Basics of Foreign Exchange Markets: A Monetary Systems Approach, Second Edition* by William D. Gerdes
- *Universal Basic Income and the Threat to Democracy as We Know It* by Peter Nelson
- *Negotiation Madness* by Peter Nelson
- *Economic Renaissance in the Age of Artificial Intelligence* by Apek Mulay
- *Disaster Risk Management: Case Studies in South Asian Countries* by Huong Ha, R. Lalitha S. Fernando, and Sanjeev Kumar Mahajan
- *Disaster Risk Management in Agriculture: Case Studies in South Asian Countries* by Huong Ha, R. Lalitha S. Fernando, and Sanjeev Kumar Mahajan

Announcing the Business Expert Press Digital Library

Concise e-books business students need for classroom and research

This book can also be purchased in an e-book collection by your library as

- a one-time purchase,
- that is owned forever,
- allows for simultaneous readers,
- has no restrictions on printing, and
- can be downloaded as PDFs from within the library community.

Our digital library collections are a great solution to beat the rising cost of textbooks. E-books can be loaded into their course management systems or onto students' e-book readers.
The **Business Expert Press** digital libraries are very affordable, with no obligation to buy in future years. For more information, please visit **www.businessexpertpress.com/librarians**. To set up a trial in the United States, please email **sales@businessexpertpress.com**.